Cognitive Technologies

Managing Editors: D. M. Gabbay   J. Siekmann

Editorial Board: A. Bundy   J. G. Carbonell
M. Pinkal   H. Uszkoreit   M. Veloso   W. Wahlster
M. J. Wooldridge

Advisory Board:

Luigia Carlucci Aiello
Franz Baader
Wolfgang Bibel
Leonard Bolc
Craig Boutilier
Ron Brachman
Bruce G. Buchanan
Anthony Cohn
Artur d'Avila Garcez
Luis Fariñas del Cerro
Koichi Furukawa
Georg Gottlob
Patrick J. Hayes
James A. Hendler
Anthony Jameson
Nick Jennings
Aravind K. Joshi
Hans Kamp
Martin Kay
Hiroaki Kitano
Robert Kowalski
Sarit Kraus
Maurizio Lenzerini
Hector Levesque
John Lloyd

Alan Mackworth
Mark Maybury
Tom Mitchell
Johanna D. Moore
Stephen H. Muggleton
Bernhard Nebel
Sharon Oviatt
Luis Pereira
Lu Ruqian
Stuart Russell
Erik Sandewall
Luc Steels
Oliviero Stock
Peter Stone
Gerhard Strube
Katia Sycara
Milind Tambe
Hidehiko Tanaka
Sebastian Thrun
Junichi Tsujii
Kurt VanLehn
Andrei Voronkov
Toby Walsh
Bonnie Webber

For further volumes:
http://www.springer.com/series/5216

Petra Hofstedt

Multiparadigm Constraint Programming Languages

 Springer

Prof. Dr. Petra Hofstedt
Brandenburgische Technische
Universität (btu) Cottbus
Fakultät 1
Lehrstuhl Programmiersprachen
und Compilerbau
Postfach 101344
03013 Cottbus
Germany
petra.hofstedt@informatik.tu-cottbus.de

Managing Editors

Prof. Dov M. Gabbay
Augustus De Morgan Professor of Logic
Department of Computer Science
King's College London
Strand, London WC2R 2LS, UK

Prof. Dr. Jörg Siekmann
Forschungsbereich Deduktions- und
Multiagentensysteme, DFKI
Stuhlsatzenweg 3, Geb. 43
66123 Saarbrücken, Germany

Cognitive Technologies ISSN 1611-2482
ISBN 978-3-642-26870-0   ISBN 978-3-642-17330-1 (eBook)
DOI 10.1007/978-3-642-17330-1
Springer Heidelberg Dordrecht London New York

ACM Codes D.1, D.3, I.2

Cover design: KunkelLopka GmbH, Heidelberg

Printed on acid-free paper

Springer is part of Springer Science+Business Media (www.springer.com)

For Sebastian and Pierre

Foreword

"Modeling" has become one of the primary concerns in modern Software Engineering. The reason is simple: starting development processes from clear and succinct models has proven to foster not only quality but also productivity. With the advance of modeling there also came a desire for automatic code generation from models. This way, the costly and error-prone implementation in terms of low-level languages should be saved. To this end, the models need to be "executable" in the widest sense.

In this general picture the concepts of constraint programming obtain a new and economically important role. Even though they are not in the current mainstream of UML-style graphical languages, they are extremely well suited for describing models. This is evident by considering the very nature of constraints: one formulates the properties that a software system shall fulfill; the implementation is done automatically by the constraint solver. So the time is ripe for constraint-based programming to come out of the more academic world, to which it still is constrained to a large extent, and show its potential for modeling real-world applications.

However, there is no silver bullet. Classical constraint systems in their pure forms are not expressive enough to be used in a large variety of application domains. Therefore they need to be augmented by other styles and concepts for programming and modeling. This leads into the realm of so-called "multi-paradigm languages". There have been all kinds of approaches in Computer Science to address the "no-silver-bullet" issue. Examples range from voluminous languages such as PL/1 or ADA (which failed miserably), huge libraries (which are non-standardized and thus lead to severe problems in the long run), or Microsoft's .NET approach (which solves the problem at least on the low level of machine code). The keyword DSLs (domain-specific languages) can be viewed as the general circumscription for all kinds of attempts to address the multiparadigm idea. By contrast to .NET the emphasis here is on the integration at the level at which the users formulate their intentions.

In this dynamic evolution of ideas, concepts and efforts, the book by Petra Hofstedt provides a valuable snapshot and assessment of the state of the art and the future directions for potential evolutions. The first part of the book gives an overview of paradigms, languages and compilers that are currently available both for academic experiments and for practical applications. Based on a sound description of the mathematical foundations, the general concepts of multiparadigm constraint languages are explained and the technical means for their implementation in the form of efficient solvers are presented. Of particular interest is the classification of the interplay of the different styles of programming, such as constraint logic programming, constraint imperative programming, constraint object programming, et cetera.

The second part of the book complements this overview of languages and concepts by looking at the application domains. However, the word "case studies" does not refer here to a collection of selected examples. Rather it refers to the techniques that are needed to realize some of the multi-paradigmatic compositions. This is done on two orthogonal dimensions: First, one of the most complex combinations of paradigms is presented quite concretely, namely concurrent constraint-functional programming. Second, a generic framework is elaborated, which shall make it relatively easy to compose all kinds of paradigms within new language shells. This is best expressed by the catch-phrase "from solver cooperation to language integration".

The book by Petra Hofstedt comes at a time of highly dynamic evolutions in Software and System Engineering, in particular with respect to modeling, specification and high-level problem description. It provides a valuable insight into one important aspect of this field, namely the activities centered around the declarative description of systems by way of their properties, that is, by way of constraints. It will help the reader to understand the foundations of the approach and to get a better judgement of the future perspectives.

Berlin, December 2010   Peter Pepper

Contents

Chapter 1
Introduction

This book is concerned with the theory and practice of *multiparadigm constraint programming languages*.

Programming languages are often classified according to their programming paradigms, e.g. in imperative, functional, logic, constraint-based, object-oriented, or aspect-oriented languages. A programming paradigm characterises the style, concepts, and methods of the language for describing situations and processes and for solving problems. In this way each paradigm serves best for programming in particular application areas. For example, an object-oriented language aids the programmer to think of a program as a collection of interacting objects, database programming enables one to handle huge data in a structured way, and logic and constraint-based programming allows one to express search problems in a declarative way.

Real-world problems, however, are often best implemented by a combination of concepts from different paradigms, because they comprise aspects from several realms. This combination is more comfortably realised by *multiparadigm programming languages*. These languages establish an area of programming languages research and application which has attracted increased interest and generated promising solutions in recent years. Examples are the multiparadigm language ADA which provides for distributed, concurrent, imperative, and object-oriented programming, COMMON LISP with the COMMON LISP OBJECT SYSTEM for functional, imperative, and object-oriented programming, the many constraint libraries like CHOCO [44] and GECODE [73] which can be integrated into languages of other paradigms, and even the Microsoft software platform .NET as an integrating platform for components written in different languages.

In this book, we consider in particular *constraint-based languages*. The area of constraint programming has been thoroughly developed in recent decades and the application and importance of constraints in practical and scientific applications has grown remarkably.

Constraints are predicate logic formulae used to describe problems by means of properties of objects or relations between them. They are well suited for the convenient description and efficient solution of problems with incomplete knowledge. Constraints already cover many different problem domains and, in combination with other paradigms, allow comfortable and efficient modeling, programming and solving of problems.

Overview of the Book

The intended audience of this book is senior undergraduate and graduate students, and researchers from the programming languages or constraint programming fields. The book serves as an introduction to the area of multiparadigm constraint programming, discusses in detail two concrete examples with different main focus, and gives an overview and many references to classical and recent approaches in this research field.

The first part elaborates on programming paradigms and languages, on constraints, and on the merging of programming concepts which yields multiparadigm (constraint) programming languages. In Chapter 2 we define basic notions from algebra and predicate logic which are used throughout the book. Programming paradigms and programming languages are introduced and discussed in Chapter 3, where we elucidate the ideas, basic elements and concepts of the most common and widespread paradigms. Chapter 4 is dedicated to constraints as language constructs, the handling and solution of constraints, and constraint programming. We present well-established fields and recent approaches to multiparadigm constraint programming in Chapter 5.

In the second part of this book we inspect two concrete examples of multiparadigm constraint programming systems. In Chapter 6 we consider the concurrent constraint functional language CCFL which combines concepts from the functional and the constraint-based paradigms and allows the description of concurrent processes and even of typical parallelization patterns. We present a general framework for multiparadigm constraint programming and its implementation META-S in Chapter 7.

An outlook, references to related literature, and a detailed index conclude the book.

Acknowledgement

I would like to thank all those people who directly or indirectly contributed to the completion of this book.

I would like to express my deep and sincere gratitude to Peter Pepper. His knowledge, experience, and encouragement provided the ideal foundation for my work. I learned a lot from discussions with colleagues and students at Technische Universität Berlin including Michael Cebulla, Stephan Frank, Martin Grabmüller, Matthias Hintzmann, Dirk Kleeblatt, Florian Lorenzen, André Metzner, Sandro Rodriguez Garzon, and Judith Rohloff.

I am indebted to Kazunori Ueda for his generous scientific, organisational, and personal support during my stay at Waseda University in Tokyo. I am grateful to him and his wife, Yoko Ueda, for their warm hospitality and friendship which made the stay of my family in Tokyo a success. I am deeply appreciative of Oskar Bartenstein and his family for their warm welcome and support. They gave us many wonderful and precious memories of Japan. I am also thankful to the staff at Waseda, in particular the International Office, and the students of the Ueda Laboratory. During my work on the CCFL project I received greatly appreciated support through a postdoctoral fellowship (No. PE 07542) from the Japan Society for the Promotion of Science (JSPS).

I would like to thank the editor of this book, Ronan Nugent from Springer, for his continued support and cooperation when preparing the final version. Also, I would like to express my appreciation to the copy editor at Springer who helped improve the manuscript in many ways through numerous detailed comments and suggestions.

Finally, I thank my husband, Stephan Frank, for his love, patience, encouragement, and understanding.

Cottbus, December 2010   Petra Hofstedt

Part I
Paradigms, Constraints, and Multiparadigm Programming

Multiparadigm programming languages combine concepts and features from different programming paradigms. A programming paradigm, like the functional, the object-oriented, or the constraint-based paradigms, supports a certain view of a problem and an adequate programming style and it allows in this way comfortable and efficient programming and problem solving. Since real-world problems comprise aspects from several domains, they are often best represented by a combination of concepts from different language paradigms. This has yielded many interesting developments in the field of *multiparadigm programming languages*. In this book, we focus on paradigm combinations with *constraints* because constraint-based languages have gained increased importance in practice due to their wide and potent application areas.

In the first part of this work we elaborate on programming paradigms and languages and on constraints and we discuss the combination of programming concepts in multiparadigm (constraint) programming languages. It consists of four chapters.

In Chapter 2 we introduce basic notions from algebra and predicate logic. These are used throughout the book for the definition and the description of important concepts of programming languages and constraints. Chapter 3 is concerned with programming languages. We recall essential notions, concepts, and methods of this area and we discuss classical and new programming paradigms. Chapter 4 is dedicated to the area of constraint programming. We discuss the functionality of constraints as language constructs in general and by examples and present an overview of applications of constraints. Multiparadigm programming languages with constraints are the subject of Chapter 5. We investigate the integration of programming paradigms in general and discuss established and new paradigm combinations with constraints.

Chapter 2
Basic Notions

This chapter provides a brief introduction to basic notions and definitions from algebra and predicate logic. For further discussion, examples, and presentation of concepts see e.g. [55, 22, 169, 106].

2.1 Signatures and Σ-structures

A *signature* constitutes the syntax of a language, i.e. the symbols used to compose language expressions like terms and constraints. Their interpretation or semantics is defined by means of an appropriate *structure*.

Definition 1 (signature) A (many-sorted) ***signature*** $\Sigma = (S, F, R)$ is defined by a set S of *sorts*, a set F of *function symbols*, and a set R of *predicate symbols*. The sets S, F, and R are mutually disjoint.

Every function symbol $f \in F$ and every predicate symbol $r \in R$ is associated with a *declaration* $f : s_1 \ldots s_n \to s$ and $r : s_1 \ldots s_m$, $s, s_i \in S$, $n, m \geq 0$, and thus with an arity n or m, resp. A symbol f with $n = 0$ is a *constant symbol*.

Let X^s be a set of variables of sort $s \in S$. A set of Σ-*variables* is a set $X = \bigcup_{s \in S} X^s$, where the sets X^s are non-empty and mutually disjoint. ◁

A Σ-*structure* builds on a signature Σ and defines the semantics of the symbols of Σ.

Definition 2 (Σ-structure) Let $\Sigma = (S, F, R)$ be a signature. A Σ-***structure*** $\mathcal{D} = (\{\mathcal{D}^s \mid s \in S\}, \{f^{\mathcal{D}} \mid f \in F\}, \{r^{\mathcal{D}} \mid r \in R\})$ consists of an S-sorted set of non-empty *carrier sets* $\mathcal{D}^s$ with $s \in S$, a set of *functions* $f^{\mathcal{D}}$ with $f \in F$, and a set of *predicates* $r^{\mathcal{D}}$ with $r \in R$.

For a function symbol $f \in F$ with $f : s_1 \ldots s_n \to s$ let $f^{\mathcal{D}}$ be an n-ary function, such that $f^{\mathcal{D}} : \mathcal{D}^{s_1} \times \ldots \times \mathcal{D}^{s_n} \to \mathcal{D}^s$ holds.

For a predicate symbol $r \in R$ with $r : s_1 \ldots s_m$ let $r^{\mathcal{D}}$ be a m-ary predicate, such that $r^{\mathcal{D}} \subseteq \mathcal{D}^{s_1} \times \ldots \times \mathcal{D}^{s_m}$ holds. ◁

The following example illustrates these definitions and will be used in the subsequent sections.

Example 1 Let $\Sigma_{\mathbb{N}} = (S, F, R)$ be a signature consisting of the set of sorts $S = \{nat\}$, the set $F = \{succ, plus, mul, 0, 1, 2, \ldots\}$ of function and constant symbols and the predicate symbols $R = \{eq, geq\}$ with the following declarations:

$succ : nat \to nat$
$plus, mul : nat\ nat \to nat$
$0, 1, 2, \ldots : nat$
$eq, geq : nat\ nat$

We define a $\Sigma_{\mathbb{N}}$-structure $\mathcal{D}_{\mathbb{N}}$ by $\mathcal{D}_{\mathbb{N}} = (\{\mathbb{N}\}, \{f^{\mathbb{N}} \mid f \in F\}, \{r^{\mathbb{N}} \mid r \in R\})$, where the carrier-set $\mathbb{N}$ is the set of natural numbers on which the functions $f^{\mathbb{N}}$ and predicates $r^{\mathbb{N}}$ apply, e.g.

$succ^{\mathbb{N}} \colon \mathbb{N} \to \mathbb{N}$ and for every $x \in \mathbb{N}$ holds: $succ^{\mathbb{N}}(x) = (x + 1)$,
$plus^{\mathbb{N}} \colon \mathbb{N} \times \mathbb{N} \to \mathbb{N}$, and for every $x, y \in \mathbb{N}$ holds: $plus^{\mathbb{N}}(x, y) = (x + y)$,

. . .

$0^{\mathbb{N}} \colon \mathbb{N}$ with $0^{\mathbb{N}} = 0$,
$1^{\mathbb{N}} \colon \mathbb{N}$ with $1^{\mathbb{N}} = 1$,

. . .

$eq^{\mathbb{N}} \subseteq \mathbb{N} \times \mathbb{N}$,   where for all $x, y \in \mathbb{N}$ holds: $eq^{\mathbb{N}}(x, y)$ iff $x = y$,
$geq^{\mathbb{N}} \subseteq \mathbb{N} \times \mathbb{N}$, where for all $x, y \in \mathbb{N}$ holds: $geq^{\mathbb{N}}(x, y)$ iff $x \geq y$.   ◊

2.2 Terms, formulae, and validity

Based on the notion of a signature, we define terms and formulae. We provide these syntactic elements with a meaning, i.e. a semantics, and determine the validity of formulae with the help of the corresponding Σ-structure.

In the following, let $\Sigma = (S, F, R)$ be a signature, let X be a set of Σ-variables, and let $\mathcal{D}$ be a Σ-structure.

Terms are built from the symbols of Σ. They are defined inductively. Besides variables and constant symbols, there are terms composed of subterms based on the declarations of the involved function symbols.

Definition 3 (term, ground term) The set $\mathcal{T}(F, X)$ of **terms** over Σ and X is defined as follows: $\mathcal{T}(F, X) = \bigcup_{s \in S} \mathcal{T}(F, X)^s$, where for every sort $s \in S$ the set $\mathcal{T}(F, X)^s$ of terms of sort s is the smallest set containing

1. every variable $x \in X^s$ (of sort s),
2. every 0-ary function symbol $f \in F$ with $f : s$, i.e. every constant symbol, and

3. every expression $f(t_1, \ldots, t_n)$, $n \geq 1$, where $f \in F$ is a function symbol with declaration $f : s_1 \ldots s_n \to s$ and every $t_i, i \in \{1, \ldots, n\}$, is a (composite) term of $\mathcal{T}(F, X)^{s_i}$.

Terms without variables are **ground terms**.   ◁

A *position* p in a term t is represented by a sequence of natural numbers. The empty sequence is denoted by ϵ. We recursively define $t|_p$ to denote the *subterm* of t at position p as $t|_\epsilon = t$ and $f(t_1, \ldots, t_n)|_{i.p} = t_i|_p$. By $t[r]_p$ we denote the term which is obtained from t as the result of the *replacement* of the subterm $t|_p$ with the term r.

Example 2 Let $x, y, z \in X$. For our signature $\Sigma_{\mathbb{N}}$ from above, x, 2, $succ(x)$, $plus(2, succ(3))$, and $plus(succ(x), mul(2, succ(y)))$ are terms.

For a term $t = plus(x, mul(2, succ(y)))$ examples of subterms are $t|_\epsilon = t$, $t|_1 = x$, $t|_2 = mul(2, succ(y))$, $t|_{221} = y$, and replacements are given by e.g. $t[mul(2, z)]_2 = plus(x, mul(2, z))$ and $t[1]_{221} = plus(x, mul(2, succ(1)))$.   ◇

Terms represent elements or objects of the corresponding domain. For example, terms over $\Sigma_{\mathbb{N}}$ are arithmetic expressions. Similarly, boolean expressions can be built over an appropriate signature $\Sigma_{\mathbb{B}}$.

To determine the semantics of terms w. r. t. a Σ-structure $\mathcal{D}$ we must assign values to the variables of the terms. This is done by means of a valuation.

Definition 4 (valuation) An S-sorted family of mappings $\varsigma: X \to \mathcal{D} = (\varsigma^s : X^s \to \mathcal{D}^s)^{s \in S}$ which assigns each variable $x \in X^s$ an element of the carrier set $\mathcal{D}^s$, $s \in S$, is a **valuation**.   ◁

Now, we can evaluate terms w. r. t. a structure $\mathcal{D}$ and a valuation ς.

Definition 5 (evaluation of terms) Let $\varsigma: X \to \mathcal{D}$ be a valuation. The **evaluation** $\tilde{\varsigma}: \mathcal{T}(F, X) \to \mathcal{D}$ of a term w.r.t. the structure $\mathcal{D}$ and the valuation ς is a family of mappings $(\tilde{\varsigma}^s: \mathcal{T}(F, X)^s \to \mathcal{D}^s)^{s \in S}$ with:

- $\tilde{\varsigma}^s(x) = \varsigma^s(x)$ for every variable x of sort s,
- $\tilde{\varsigma}^s(f) = f^{\mathcal{D}}$ for every constant symbol $f \in F$ with $f : s$, and
- $\tilde{\varsigma}^s(f(t_1, \ldots, t_n)) = f^{\mathcal{D}}(\tilde{\varsigma}^{s_1}(t_1), \ldots, \tilde{\varsigma}^{s_n}(t_n))$ for every function symbol $f \in F$ with $f : s_1 \ldots s_n \to s$ and every sort $s_1, \ldots, s_n, s \in S$ and all terms $t_i \in \mathcal{T}(F, X)^{s_i}$, $i \in \{1, \ldots, n\}$.   ◁

The evaluation of a variable is just its valuation, the evaluation of a constant symbol is the corresponding constant from the structure. For a composite term we evaluate its subterms and apply the corresponding function from the structure.

The set $Formulae(\Sigma, X)$ of formulae of (first-order) predicate logic determines the *syntax of predicate logic*.

Definition 6 (formulae of predicate logic) The set of **formulae of predicate logic** over a signature Σ and a set of variables X, denoted by $Formulae(\Sigma, X)$, is inductively defined as follows:

1. For all predicate symbols $r : s_1 \ldots s_m$ and all terms $t_i \in \mathcal{T}(F, X)^{s_i}$, $i \in \{1, \ldots, m\}$, the expression $r(t_1, \ldots, t_m)$ is a (atomic) formula.
2. *true* and *false* are (atomic) formulae.
3. For every formula ϕ the expression $\neg\phi$ is a formula.
4. For all formulae ϕ and ψ the following expressions are formulae too: $(\phi \vee \psi)$, $(\phi \wedge \psi)$, $(\phi \longrightarrow \psi)$, and $(\phi \longleftrightarrow \psi)$.
5. If ϕ is a formula and $x \in X$ is a variable, then $(\forall x.\phi)$ and $(\exists x.\phi)$ are formulae.   ◁

We denote the set of variables occurring in a term or formula F, resp., by $var(F)$. The quantifiers $\forall$ and $\exists$ *bind* variables in formulae. We introduce certain notions concerning quantifiers.

Definition 7 (bound and free variable, open and closed formula) An occurrence of a variable x in a formula $\phi \in Formulae(\Sigma, X)$ is called **bound**, if x appears in a subformula of ϕ in the form $\exists x.\psi$ or $\forall x.\psi$. Otherwise x is a **free** variable. A formula ϕ without occurrences of free variables is called a **closed** formula, otherwise ϕ is **open**.   ◁

Definition 8 (universal and existential closure) Let $\{x_1, \ldots, x_n\} \subseteq X$ be the set of free variables of a predicate logic formula $\phi \in Formulae(\Sigma, X)$. The **universal closure** $\forall\phi$ and the **existential closure** $\exists\phi$ of ϕ are defined by

$$\forall\phi = \forall x_1 \ldots \forall x_n. \; \phi \quad \text{and} \quad \exists\phi = \exists x_1 \ldots \exists x_n. \; \phi, \text{ resp.}$$

The expression $\tilde{Y}$ with $Y \subseteq X$ denotes a (arbitrary) sequence of the variables of the set Y. By $\exists\_{\tilde{Y}}\psi$ we denote the existential closure of the formula ψ except for the variables of Y.   ◁

In the following, we write $\forall x, y.\phi$ instead of $\forall x.\forall y.\phi$ and $\exists x, y.\phi$ instead of $\exists x.\exists y.\phi$ as is usually done.

Example 3 Consider the signature $\Sigma_\mathbb{N}$ and the structure $\mathcal{D}_\mathbb{N}$ from Example 1 and the variables $\{x, y, z\} \subset X$.

The following formulae are elements of $Formulae(\Sigma_\mathbb{N}, X)$:
$true, \, false, \, geq(2, x), \, eq(mul(2, 2), 4), \, \neg geq(2, x) \vee \neg geq(x, 2), \, true \longrightarrow false,$
$eq(2, x) \longleftrightarrow eq(succ(2), succ(x)), \, \forall x, y. \, eq(z, plus(x, y)), \, \forall x. \, \exists y. \, eq(x, succ(y)),$
$geq(x, 2) \longrightarrow \exists x. \, eq(x, 2).$

Consider $p = \forall x, y. \, eq(z, plus(x, y))$ and $q = geq(x, 2) \longrightarrow \exists x. \, eq(x, 2)$. The variables x and y are bound in formula p, while the variable z is free. In the formula q the first occurrence of variable x is free, while its second occurrence is bound by the existential quantifier $\exists$.

The formulae $true$, $false$, $eq(mul(2, 2), 4)$, $\forall x. \exists y. \, eq(x, succ(y))$, and $true \longrightarrow false$ are closed, all other formulae given above are open.

Let $Y = \{x, y\} \subseteq \{x, y, z\} \subset X$. The following holds:
$\exists\_{\tilde{Y}} \, eq(z, plus(x, y)) = \exists\_{x,y} \, eq(z, plus(x, y)) = \exists z. \, eq(z, plus(x, y)).$ ◇

The *semantics of predicate logic* is determined by the assignment of a meaning to every formula w.r.t. the associated structure. We define the validity relation between structures and formulae (see e.g. [55]).

Definition 9 (validity, $\models$, model) Let $\phi, \psi \in Formulae(\Sigma, X)$ be formulae of predicate logic. Let $\varsigma : X \to \mathcal{D}$ be a valuation. A valuation which maps the variable $x \in X$ to $a \in \mathcal{D}$ and all other variables y to $\varsigma(y)$ is denoted by $\varsigma[x/a] : X \to \mathcal{D}$, i.e.

$$\varsigma[x/a](y) = \begin{cases} \varsigma(y) & \text{if } y \neq x, \\ a & \text{otherwise.} \end{cases}$$

The relation $\models$ is defined as follows:

$(\mathcal{D}, \varsigma) \models r(t_1, \ldots, t_m)$ iff $(\tilde{\varsigma}(t_1), \ldots, \tilde{\varsigma}(t_m)) \in r^{\mathcal{D}}$,

$(\mathcal{D}, \varsigma) \models true$,

$(\mathcal{D}, \varsigma) \nvDash false$,

$(\mathcal{D}, \varsigma) \models \neg \phi$ iff $(\mathcal{D}, \varsigma) \nvDash \phi$,

$(\mathcal{D}, \varsigma) \models \phi \wedge \psi$ iff $(\mathcal{D}, \varsigma) \models \phi$ and $(\mathcal{D}, \varsigma) \models \psi$,

$(\mathcal{D}, \varsigma) \models \phi \vee \psi$ iff $(\mathcal{D}, \varsigma) \models \phi$ or $(\mathcal{D}, \varsigma) \models \psi$,

$(\mathcal{D}, \varsigma) \models \phi \longrightarrow \psi$ iff $(\mathcal{D}, \varsigma) \nvDash \phi$ or $(\mathcal{D}, \varsigma) \models \psi$,

$(\mathcal{D}, \varsigma) \models \phi \longleftrightarrow \psi$ iff $(\mathcal{D}, \varsigma) \models \phi \longrightarrow \psi$ and $(\mathcal{D}, \varsigma) \models \psi \longrightarrow \phi$,

$(\mathcal{D}, \varsigma) \models \forall x. \phi$ iff $(\mathcal{D}, \varsigma[x/a]) \models \phi$ for every $a \in \mathcal{D}^s, s \in S, x \in X^s$,

$(\mathcal{D}, \varsigma) \models \exists x. \phi$ iff $(\mathcal{D}, \varsigma[x/a]) \models \phi$ for at least one $a \in \mathcal{D}^s, s \in S, x \in X^s$.

A formula ϕ is **valid** in $\mathcal{D}$, i.e. it holds $\mathcal{D} \models \phi$, if for every valuation $\varsigma : X \to \mathcal{D}$ holds: $(\mathcal{D}, \varsigma) \models \phi$. In this case, we call $\mathcal{D}$ a **model** of ϕ. ◁

Example 4 Consider the signature $\Sigma_{\mathbb{N}}$ and the structure $\mathcal{D}_{\mathbb{N}}$ of Example 1. Let ς be a valuation with $\varsigma(x) = 1$, $\varsigma(y) = 2$, and $\varsigma(z) = 3$. We study the validity of various formulae:

$(\mathcal{D}_{\mathbb{N}}, \varsigma) \models true$ and $(\mathcal{D}_{\mathbb{N}}, \varsigma) \nvDash false$.

$(\mathcal{D}_{\mathbb{N}}, \varsigma) \models geq(2, x)$, because $2^{\mathbb{N}} = 2 \geq 1 = 1^{\mathbb{N}}$.

$(\mathcal{D}_{\mathbb{N}}, \varsigma) \models eq(plus(2, 2), 4)$, because $plus^{\mathbb{N}}(2, 2) = 4$.

$(\mathcal{D}_{\mathbb{N}}, \varsigma) \models \neg geq(2, x) \vee \neg geq(x, 2)$,
     because the validity of one subformula ϕ or ψ of a formula $\phi \vee \psi$ is sufficient and $(1, 2) \notin geq^{\mathbb{N}}$ resp. $1 \not\geq 2$.

$(\mathcal{D}_{\mathbb{N}}, \varsigma) \nvDash true \longrightarrow false$
     according to the definition of validity of formulae of the form $\phi \longrightarrow \psi$ (see above).

$(\mathcal{D}_{\mathbb{N}}, \varsigma) \models (eq(2, x) \longleftrightarrow eq(succ(2), succ(x)))$,
     because $(2, 1) \notin eq^{\mathbb{N}}$ resp. $2 \neq 1$ and $(3, 2) \notin eq^{\mathbb{N}}$ resp. $3 \neq 2$.

$(\mathcal{D}_{\mathbb{N}}, \varsigma) \nvDash \forall x, y. eq(z, plus(x, y))$,
     because there are valuations ς' of x and y such that $3 \neq \varsigma'(x) + \varsigma'(y)$.

$(\mathcal{D}_{\mathbb{N}}, \varsigma) \nvDash \forall x. \exists y. eq(x, succ(y))$, because when x has the value 0 there is no value for y such that $x = y + 1$.

$(\mathcal{D}_\mathbb{N}, \varsigma) \models geq(x, 2) \longrightarrow \exists x.\, eq(x, 2)$, because $(1, 2) \notin geq^\mathbb{N}$.

Of the above formulae the following are valid in $\mathcal{D}_\mathbb{N}$, i.e. they hold in $\mathcal{D}_\mathbb{N}$ for every valuation: $true$, $eq(plus(2, 2), 4)$, $eq(2, x) \longleftrightarrow eq(succ(2), succ(x))$, and $geq(x, 2) \longrightarrow \exists x.\, eq(x, 2)$. $\qquad\qquad\qquad\qquad\qquad\qquad\quad\Diamond$

2.3 Substitutions and unifiers

When defining operational principles of programming languages later on in this book, we will need certain notions concerning substitutions.

A *substitution* applied to a term or atomic formula replaces variables by terms.

Definition 10 (substitution) A ***substitution*** σ is a function $\sigma : X \to \mathcal{T}(F, X)$ with $\sigma(x) \in \mathcal{T}(F, X)^s$ for all $x \in X^s$.

We extend the function σ to $\tilde\sigma : \mathcal{T}(F, X) \to \mathcal{T}(F, X)$, i.e. for application on terms by

- $\tilde\sigma(x) = \sigma(x)$ for all variables $x \in X$,
- $\tilde\sigma(f(t_1, \dots, t_n)) = f(\tilde\sigma(t_1), \dots, \tilde\sigma(t_n))$ for all terms $f(t_1, \dots, t_n)$.

Analogously, σ is extended for application on atomic formulae. In the following, we identify a substitution σ with its extension $\tilde\sigma$ and write σ instead of $\tilde\sigma$. ◁

In this book, we deal with *finite* substitutions σ in the sense that for only finitely many variables x holds: $\sigma(x) \neq x$. A substitution σ can, thus, be represented in the form $\sigma = \{x/\sigma(x) \mid \sigma(x) \neq x\}$, where we explicitly enumerate all its elements. We denote the identity substitution by id.

The *composition* of substitutions describes the sequential application of substitutions on a term or formulae.

Definition 11 (composition of substitutions) The ***composition*** of substitutions σ and ϕ is defined by $(\phi \circ \sigma)(e) = \phi(\sigma(e))$ for all terms and atomic formulae e. $\qquad\qquad\qquad\qquad\qquad\qquad\qquad\qquad\qquad\qquad\qquad\quad$ ◁

Example 5 Consider a set X of variables with $\{x, y, z\} \subseteq X$ and the signature $\Sigma_\mathbb{N}$ from Example 1.

Let σ and ϕ be substitutions with $\sigma = \{x/4, y/plus(3, z)\}$ and $\phi = \{z/1\}$. The following holds:

$\sigma(succ(2)) = succ(\sigma(2)) = succ(2)$

$\sigma(succ(x)) = succ(\sigma(x)) = succ(4)$

$\sigma(mul(3, plus(x, succ(y)))) = mul(3, plus(4, succ(plus(3, z))))$

$$(\phi \circ \sigma)(mul(3, plus(x, succ(y)))) = \phi(\sigma(mul(3, plus(x, succ(y)))))$$
$$= \phi(mul(3, plus(4, succ(plus(3, z)))))$$
$$= mul(3, plus(4, succ(plus(3, 1)))) \qquad \diamond$$

Unifiers are substitutions which allow one to identify certain terms or formulae.

Definition 12 (unifier, most general unifier, *mgu*) Let s and t be terms or atoms. A substitution σ with $\sigma(s) = \sigma(t)$ is a **unifier** of s and t. A unifier σ of s and t is a **most general unifier** (we write $\sigma = mgu(s, t)$) if for every unifier ϕ of s and t there exists a substitution ψ such that $\phi = \psi \circ \sigma$ holds.◁

For algorithms to compute most general unifiers we refer to [194, 106]. If two terms or atoms s and t are not unifiable, we write $mgu(s, t) = \emptyset$.[1]

Example 6 Consider the signature $\Sigma_\mathbb{N}$ and the set $\{x, y, z\} \subseteq X$. The terms $s = mul(x, succ(z))$ and $t = mul(2, y)$ are unifiable with substitution $\sigma = \{x/2, y/succ(z)\}$, i.e. σ is a unifier of s and t:

$$\sigma(s) = mul(2, succ(z)) = \sigma(t)$$

The substitution $\phi = \{x/2, y/succ(3), z/3\}$ is a unifier of s and t too:

$$\phi(s) = mul(2, succ(3)) = \phi(t)$$

The substitution σ is a most general unifier of s and t. For σ and ϕ there is a substitution $\psi = \{z/3\}$ such that $\phi = \psi \circ \sigma$ holds. $\qquad \diamond$

Let the *parallel composition* of idempotent substitutions be defined as in [175]. We compute the parallel composition $(\sigma \uparrow \phi)$ of two idempotent substitutions σ and ϕ as follows:

$$(\sigma \uparrow \phi) = mgu(f(x_1, \ldots, x_n, y_1, \ldots, y_m), f(\sigma(x_1), \ldots, \sigma(x_n), \phi(y_1), \ldots, \phi(y_m))),$$
where x_i, $i \in \{1, \ldots, n\}$, and y_j, $j \in \{1, \ldots, m\}$, are the domain variables of σ and ϕ, resp.

Example 7 Given $\Sigma_\mathbb{N}$, a set X of variables with $\{w, x, y, z\} \subseteq X$, and the substitutions $\sigma = \{x/0, y/z\}$, $\phi = \{w/succ(x), y/0\}$, and $\psi = \{y/0, z/succ(0)\}$, we build their parallel compositions:

$$(\sigma \uparrow \phi) = mgu(f(x, y, w, y), f(0, z, succ(x), 0))$$
$$= \{x/0, y/0, z/0, w/succ(0)\}$$
$$(\sigma \uparrow \psi) = mgu(f(x, y, y, z), f(0, z, 0, succ(0))) = \emptyset$$
$$(\phi \uparrow \psi) = mgu(f(w, y, y, z), f(succ(x), 0, 0, succ(0)))$$
$$= \{w/succ(x), y/0, z/succ(0)\} \qquad \diamond$$

---

[1] Note that $\emptyset$ has a completely different meaning than the identity substitution *id*.

Chapter 3
Programming Languages and Paradigms

Before we can discuss the amalgamation of programming paradigms in Chapter 5, we need to become familiar with basic concepts and notions from the programming languages area.

Thus, we recall essential concepts of programming languages and indicate fundamental and advanced literature in Section 3.1. We introduce the notion of a "programming paradigm" and discuss classical and new paradigms and their representatives in Section 3.2.

3.1 Programming languages and compilation

Programming languages are formal languages for the description and control of the behaviour of computers (and other machines). They are used to realize a precise, reliable, and automatic management and manipulation of data and knowledge. There is a broad variety of literature concerning programming languages, their principles, and implementation, for example [201, 48, 2, 224, 146, 230].

Syntax and semantics. A programming language is defined by its *syntax* and *semantics*. The *syntax* of a programming language is a formal language which defines its correct expressions. It is typically formally fixed using syntax diagrams or (E)BNF ((EXTENDED) BACKUS-NAUR FORM). For example, in Section 6.1 we define the syntax of the language CCFL using EBNF. The *semantics* defines the meaning of the language elements, expressions, and programs. It is sometimes formally specified by means of rules but sometimes only given by its implementation, i.e. the realization of the program execution on hardware and software. There are different approaches to the formalization of the semantics of programming languages, mainly the *operational*, the *denotational*, and the *axiomatic* semantics and combinations of these, which differ in their methods and application goals (cf. [11, 231]). For examples see Sections

3.2 and 5.2–5.5 as well as Sections 6.3 and 7.2, where we formally specify the semantics of several paradigm representatives and concrete programming languages, resp.

Compiler and interpretation. A programming language usually comes with a *compiler* which translates programs (of the *source language*) into another programming language (the *target language*). While the source language is typically a high-level programming language (HLL), the target language may be a lower-level language, like assembly language or machine language, or another HLL.

The compilation of a program is performed in a sequence of phases (see Figure 3.1): *Lexical analysis* (or *scanning*) partitions the source program into its elements, such as keywords, variables, operators, numbers etc., i. e. a stream of tokens. *Syntactic analysis* (in a narrower sense) builds from the tokens an *abstract syntax tree* (AST) representing the semantic components of the program, such as assignments, loops, case-decisions, procedures or functions. This is performed by the so-called *parser*. *Semantic analysis* follows, which verifies resp. computes context conditions and type information and augments in this way the AST. Finally, the *coder* generates target code from the annotated AST (possibly via intermediate program representations). Before and after the actual code generation (optional) optimizations can be applied. The syntactic and semantic analyses constitute the so-called *front-end*, code generation and optimizations the *back-end* of the compiler.

Contrary to the presentation in Figure 3.1, the compilation phases interfere with each other, e.g. the scanner is called by the parser when it needs a further token or type checking and intermediate code generation can be done during syntactical analysis.

HLLs are often distinguished into compiled languages and interpreted languages. An *interpreter* usually performs a syntactic and a semantic analysis, too. On top of this it either executes the source code or AST, resp., nearly directly or generates some intermediate code which is immediately executed.

However, often the borders between compilation and interpretation are blurred, because on the one hand the execution of target code of a compiler can be seen as a special kind of interpretation and, on the other hand, techniques like just-in-time compilation and bytecode interpretation lie in-between. For many languages there exist compilers as well as interpreters.

Running a program. Figure 3.2 shows the system architecture during the *evaluation* of a (target) program. On top of the hardware and the operating system resides the language *runtime system*. A runtime system is software which provides language features or program elements for a running program. Depending on the language it may consist of different elements. For example, the standard C library contains functions for I/O handling, mathematical functions, code for memory management and more. The JAVA Runtime Environment (JRE) provides the JAVA class libraries, used e.g. for I/O, and

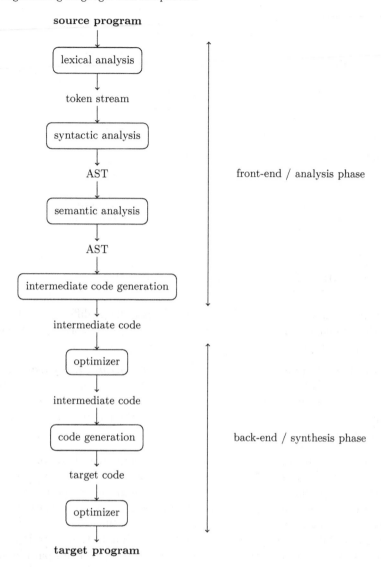

Fig. 3.1 Phases of a compiler

the JAVA Virtual Machine (JVM) for the execution of JAVA bytecode. Garbage collection can also be considered to be part of the runtime system. Languages with constraints evoke the handling and solving of constraints at runtime and, thus, need constraint solvers as part of their runtime system.

Actually, one may loosely consider the runtime system of a language as a collaboration of a number of abstract machines which provide base functions for the compiled program. An *abstract machine* (AM) is, in general, just a

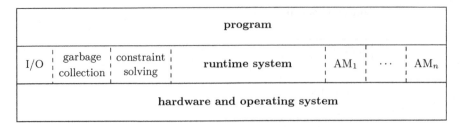

Fig. 3.2 Layer architecture of program evaluation

software implementation of some kind of machine or computer which allows the execution of a program consisting of particular function calls.

3.2 Programming paradigms

Programming languages can be classified into paradigms differentiated by the ways the language constructs support the programmer in solving problems of certain application domains or patterns.

Terminology 1 (programming paradigm) A ***programming paradigm*** is a general approach the programmer can take to describe and solve a problem. This approach is supported by the programming languages of the paradigm which is reflected by the language concepts, i. e. the language constructs and evaluation mechanisms.

For instance, using an object-oriented language, like JAVA or C++, programmers can think of a program as a collection of interacting objects, while in logic programming, using e.g. PROLOG, a program can be thought of a description of a search problem, and a functional program (written in e.g. HASKELL or OPAL) is a collection of mathematical functions.

Programming languages can be classified according to their paradigms. We consider typical classes in the following and we discuss certain paradigms in more detail. This concerns, in particular, paradigms which we will reconsider later in this book in the context of multiparadigm constraint programming languages in Chapter 5 in general and w.r.t. our case studies CCFL and META-S in Chapter 6 and Chapter 7, resp.

3.2.1 Imperative and declarative languages

Imperative programming was probably the earliest programming paradigm. An imperative program consists of a sequence of *statements* or *instructions*

Program 3.2.1 Recursive Fibonacci using C and HASKELL, resp.

```
int fib (int n) {
    if (n < 2)
        return n;
    else
        return fib (n−1) + fib (n−2);
}
```

```
fib n =
    if (n < 2) then n else fib (n−1) + fib (n−2)
```

which change a program state step-by-step over time. This is often called *stateful* or *time-dependent* computation. There is a close connection to the *von Neumann architecture*, since one can consider the imperative paradigm as an abstraction of this model. Typical examples of imperative languages are assembly languages, FORTRAN, ALGOL, PASCAL, and C.

While imperative languages describe *"How"* the computation of the solution for a certain problem takes place, languages of the *declarative paradigm* in contrast describe *"What"* is to be computed. Here, the user provides a declarative description of the problem resp. its solution(s) by means of *functions, relations and/or constraints*, but the actual solution algorithm is left unspecified and realized by the underlying language evaluation.[2] Computations of declarative programs are *stateless* and *time-independent*, i. e. an expression always has the same semantic meaning independent of its context or time. Languages of the declarative paradigm can be classified in general into functional, logic, and constraint-based languages (cf. Sections 3.2.3 – 3.2.5).

Let us illustrate the differences (and similarities) in programming concepts and styles when using an imperative and a functional language, resp.

Program 3.2.1 provides recursive definitions of the Fibonacci function written in C (above) and HASKELL (below). The programs look very similar in structure (as well as in naming). However, the imperative C program describes the computation procedure as "... compute *fib* $(n−1)$ and compute *fib* $(n−2)$, return the sum of both results ...." while the HASKELL version is just a function definition.

The imperative nature of C becomes even more obvious in Program 3.2.2. Here we see explicit variable assignments and reassignments in a loop, where we compute iteratively (a prefix of) the Fibonacci sequence and store it into an array which must also be explicitly described by the programmer.

---

[2] However, many declarative languages, in particular logic and constraint-based instances, allow one to guide the solution algorithm by describing strategies or implementation details (cf. the discussions about extra-logical predicates in PROLOG in Section 3.2.4 and about strategies in META-S in Section 7.3.3).

Program 3.2.2 The Fibonacci sequence, iterative C version

```
int *fibArray (int n) {
    int *fibs = (int*)malloc ((sizeof(int)) * n);
    int a = 0, b = 1, i, sum;
    for (i = 0; i < n; i++) {
        fibs[i] = a;
        sum = a + b;
        a = b;
        b = sum;
    }
    return fibs;
}
```

Program 3.2.3 The Fibonacci sequence using lazy lists in HASKELL

$fibs@(\_:tfibs) = 0 : 1 : \mathbf{zipWith}\ (+)\ fibs\ tfibs$

In functional programming we can compute the Fibonacci sequence in a comparable way (of course without assignments, but by means of definitions). However, in languages with lazy data structures such as HASKELL one will formulate the problem more adequately using infinite lists as given in Program 3.2.3.

The idea here is to define the infinite Fibonacci sequence by itself. This is mathematically possible and in languages like HASKELL also a well-known programming technique: we generate the elements of the list only when we actually need them. Figure 3.3 illustrates the computation. We generate the list *fibs* starting with 0 and 1, where the remaining part of *fibs* is computed by combining *fibs* and its tail using **zipWith** (+). In this way, we compute new list elements step-by-step when they become arguments of the *zipWith* function call. Figure 3.3 shows the first step computing the third list element and a later computation situation.

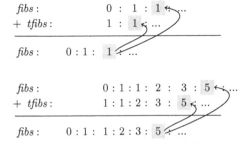

Fig. 3.3 Lazy computation of the infinite Fibonacci sequence

While the computation of the Fibonacci numbers in all the cases presented is based on the same formula, the algorithmic methods may differ considerably depending on the underlying data structures and the concepts of the paradigms and corresponding language features.

3.2.2 Procedural and object-oriented languages

Structured *imperative* programming with subroutines or procedures is called *procedural* programming. Except for assembly languages all imperative languages mentioned in Section 3.2.1 are procedural. The C functions *fib* and *fibArray* in Programs 3.2.1 and 3.2.2 are such subroutines, returning a Fibonacci number and a pointer to an array holding a prefix of the Fibonacci sequence as results resp.

Many popular and widely used programming languages have both procedural and object-oriented programming aspects. *Object-oriented* programming has become very popular recently. Languages of this paradigm use objects encapsulating data and operations and their interactions to describe applications. Armstrong [18] identified a number of fundamental concepts of this paradigm. A "class" defines the characteristics of its elements, the "objects". The objects' abilities are their "methods". "Inheritance" describes a hierarchy of classes and subclasses and the principle of "encapsulation" conceals the functional details of a class. In many cases, object-oriented programming allows an elegant and well structured style close to the real world even for large applications, which in connection with its well-known imperative background has led to its high popularity.

To express simple computations like the Fibonacci function one does not gain from using object-oriented concepts so this is typically realized using an imperative programming style in object-oriented languages, too. However, the object-oriented style of programming and way of thinking supports modeling of complex domains in a convenient way, where the objects directly represent elements of the real world. For example, when programming in a geometrical domain (see Program 3.2.4) it is natural to deal with points, lines, and shapes, their attributes and methods directly, instead of thinking in real and integer variables. The same holds for e.g. domains of animals, production lines, libraries and so on.

Well-known languages of the object-oriented imperative paradigm are JAVA, C#, and C++. However, there are also popular languages which allow the object-oriented programming style in other paradigms, like SCALA [171] combining functional, imperative, and object-oriented programming, COMMON LISP OBJECT SYSTEM CLOS [127, 209] which is part of ANSI COMMON LISP, OBJECTIVE ML [190] integrating object-oriented concepts in the functional language ML, and OZ [165, 212] which supports declarative and object-oriented programming and concurrency.

Program 3.2.4 Java: a geometric domain

```
class Point {
  double x, y;

  void move (double dx, double dy) {
    x = x + dx;
    y = y + dy;
  }

  ...

}

class ColoredPoint extends Point {
  int color;
}

abstract class Shape {
  abstract double area ();
}

class Circle extends Shape {
  Point center  = ...;
  double radius = 0.0;

  void moveTo (Point p) {
    center = p;
  }

  double area () {
    return (3.14 * radius * radius);
  }

  void draw (...) { ... }
}

class Rectangle extends Shape {
  Point anchor  = ...;
  double height = 0.0;
  double width  = 0.0;

  double area () {
    return (height * width);
  }

  ...

}
```

3.2.3 Functional programming languages

Functional languages belong to the *declarative* paradigm. A *Functional* program consists of a set of (data type and) function definitions. It is evaluated by reduction of a functional expression. The typed lambda calculus [24] with constants provides a model for functional programming. Languages which allow a functional programming style (some of them contain features of other paradigms as well) are e.g. HASKELL, ML, and OPAL (see [177, 178, 216, 109, 61, 187]), SCHEME [213], LISP [181], and ERLANG [19].

We briefly sketch the main concepts of the functional programming paradigm, where we consider functional languages from a conceptual point of view. Examples of function definitions using HASKELL are given in Programs 3.2.1 and 3.2.3.

Let $\Sigma = (S, F, R)$ be a signature, consisting of a set S of sorts and a set F of function symbols; let $R = \emptyset$. We distinguish two (disjoint) subsets of the set F of function symbols: the set Δ of *constructors* of the underlying data types and the set Γ of *defined functions*. Let X be a set of variables.

Definition 13 (functional program) A ***functional program*** P over Σ is given by a finite set of rules (called pattern-based definitions) of the form $f(t_1, \ldots, t_n) \to t'$, where $f \in \Gamma$ is a defined function and the parameter terms $t_i \in \mathcal{T}(\Delta, X)$ are linear constructor terms, i.e. they are built up from constructors and variables such that every variable occurs only once. The right-hand side $t' \in \mathcal{T}(F, X')$ is an arbitrary F-term, restricted to those variables $X' \subseteq X$ that actually occur on the left-hand side.   ◁

The evaluation principle of functional languages is *reduction*. A ground term t is stepwise reduced using the rules of a functional program P until a *normal form* is reached, that is no more reduction steps are possible.

Definition 14 (reduction step, reducible expression, redex) Let t be a ground term, let P be a functional program.

If there exist a position p in t, a rule $l \to r$ from P, and a substitution σ such that $t|_p = \sigma(l)$, then

$$t \leadsto_{l \to r} t[\sigma(r)]_p$$

is a ***reduction step***. We write $t \leadsto t[\sigma(r)]_p$ and omit the rule if it is obvious from the context.

The expression $t|_p$ is called a ***reducible expression*** or ***redex***.   ◁

Example 8 Let $x, y \in X$ be variables. We provide rules of a functional program for the addition of natural numbers which are represented by the constructors 0 and s.[3]

1   $add(0, x) \to x$
2   $add(s(x), y) \to s(add(x, y))$

This leads e.g. to the following evaluation sequence, where we underlined the reduced subterms:

$\underline{add(s(0), s(s(0)))} \leadsto_{(2)} s(\underline{add(0, s(s(0)))}) \leadsto_{(1)} s(s(s(0)))$ ◊

---

[3] Note, that for concrete functional languages the syntax will normally differ, e.g. the second *add* rule in HASKELL looks like this: $add\ (s\ x)\ y = s\ (add\ x\ y)$.

In the evaluation of an expression within a functional program, there are two sources of non-determinism: (1) There may be different applicable rules for a chosen subterm caused by overlapping left-hand sides. Thus, the *rule selection strategy* of the language, e.g. first-fit or best-fit, ensures a deterministic rule choice. (2) *Reduction strategies* decide on the redex choice in each step; we distinguish e.g. call-by-value, call-by-name, and call-by-need. These strategies lead to quite different semantics as has been studied extensively in [150]. We refer to [150, 187, 178] for a detailed discussion.

Definition 15 (call-by-value, call-by-name, call-by-need) Using a ***call-by-value*** (or *eager*) strategy all inner (i.e. argument) redexes are evaluated completely before their outer function is called.

A reduction with ***call-by-name*** strategy substitutes function arguments directly (and unevaluatedly) into the function body whose evaluation is preferred.

Call-by-need (or *lazy*) is a variant of the call-by-name strategy using *sharing* to avoid the multiple evaluation of argument expressions (as is possible for the call-by-name strategy).   ◁

The following example underlines the effects of these different reduction strategies.

Example 9 Consider the following tiny functional program:

$$double(x) \; \rightarrow \; x \, + \, x$$
$$addOne(x) \; \rightarrow \; x \, + \, 1$$

Figure 3.4 shows evaluation sequences for the expression $double(addOne(7))$ using the evaluation strategies call-by-value (1), call-by-name (2), and call-by-need (3). The call-by-value strategy chooses the inner redex $addOne(7)$ first, thus it is also called an *innermost strategy*. Call-by-name and call-by-need are *outermost strategies* and reduce (leftmost) outermost expressions first. Thus, if, using an outermost strategy, an argument is not used in the evaluation of the function, it is never evaluated (which may be advantageous in case of non-terminating derivations); if the argument is used several times, it will be re-evaluated each time as we can see for the call-by-name evaluation sequence. This multiple evaluation is avoided with the help of *sharing* of arguments which are evaluated only once in the call-by-need strategy. In Figure 3.4 the shared arguments of the expressions are represented in gray color.   ◊

3.2.4 Logic programming languages

(Definite) clauses and resolution are the main ingredients of *logic* programming (LP) languages. Logic programming languages are based on first-order logic. *Definite clauses* are universally quantified disjunctions of atomic formulae with exactly one positive, i.e. unnegated, atom. They allow one to express

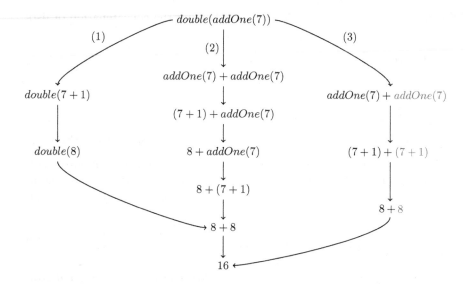

Fig. 3.4 Evaluation of functional programs: reduction strategies

facts and inference rules. Starting from a goal expression, the logic program evaluator searches over the tree of potential proofs using *resolution*. In this way variable bindings or substitutions, resp., are generated and applied to the goal to get valid instances of it.

PROLOG and its dialects, like ECL^{i}PS^e [1, 17] and SICStus [205], and adaptations like MINERVA [157] for intelligent client-server applications on the internet and the parallel system AKL [85] are typical logic languages. For further reading on logic languages we refer to [169, 204, 106].

Let us consider logic programming from a conceptual point of view.

Definition 16 (logic program) A *logic program* P is a sequence of *clauses* of the form Q :- $Q_1, \ldots, Q_n$. where Q and Q_i, $i \in \{1, \ldots, n\}$, are atoms (i.e. atomic formulae). A clause with $n > 0$ is called a *rule*. In case $n = 0$ a clause has the form Q. and is called a *fact*.

The expression Q on the left-hand side of a clause is the *head*, the sequence $Q_1, \ldots, Q_n$ on the right-hand side is the *body* of the clause.

A *goal* for a logic program P has the form ?- $Q_1, \ldots, Q_m$. The expressions Q_i, $i \in \{1, \ldots, m\}$, are atoms, again. ◁

We interpret clauses and goals as predicate logic formulae and assign a *declarative semantics* to a logic program in this way. Therefore, we consider the symbol ":-" as left-oriented implication "⟵" and the commas "," in the rule body and in the goal as conjunctions "∧".

The *empty clause* □ or (? − .) represents the formula *false* ⟵ *true* or *false*.

Example 10 Consider a logic program defining the concatenation of lists (for lists in logic languages see e.g. [106]).

```
1   append([],X,X).
2   append([X|XS],YS,[X|ZS])  :-  append(XS,YS,ZS).
```

This program represents the formula

$$(\forall X. \qquad\qquad append([],X,X))$$
$$\land\ (\forall X,XS,YS,ZS.\ append([X|XS],YS,[X|ZS]) \longleftarrow append(XS,YS,ZS))$$

The first clause describes the fact that an empty list [] combined with another arbitrary list *X* yields again the list *X*. Rule (2) defines the general case: The result of the concatenation of the lists [X|XS] and YS is [X|ZS], if the concatenation of XS and YS yields ZS.   ◇

The *declarative semantics* of a logic program is determined by its *logical consequences*, i.e. implied formulae.

Definition 17 (logical consequence, $\vDash$) A closed formula F is a **logical consequence** of a logic program P, written $P \vDash F$, if F holds in every model of P.   ◁

A correct answer is a substitution which we can apply to a goal G to obtain a logical consequence of a program.

Definition 18 (answer, correct answer) Let P be a logic program, let G be a goal with $G =$?- $Q_1, \ldots, Q_m$. A substitution σ (for the variables of G) is an **answer** for (P, G). An answer σ for (P, G) is **correct** iff the formula

$$\forall\ (\sigma(Q_1) \land \ldots \land \sigma(Q_m))$$

is a logical consequence of P.   ◁

The *operational semantics* describes the evaluation of a logic program with the aim to compute correct answers for goals. Logic programs are evaluated using *SLD-resolution*. In the following, let a *variant* of a clause R denote a clause obtained by the unique replacement of the variables in R by other variables.

Definition 19 (SLD-resolution step) Given a logic program P and a goal $G =$?- $R_1, \ldots, R_m$. with $m \geq 1$. If

- there is a variant $C = (Q$:- $Q_1, \ldots, Q_n.)$, $n \geq 0$, of a clause of P, such that G and C do not have a variable in common and
- there is an $i \in \{1, \ldots, m\}$ such that R_i and Q are unifiable with most general unifier σ, i.e. $\sigma = mgu(R_i, Q)$,

then $G \mapsto_{\sigma,C} G'$ is an **SLD-resolution step** with
$G' =$?- $\sigma(R_1), \ldots, \sigma(R_{i-1}), \sigma(Q_1), \ldots, \sigma(Q_n), \sigma(R_{i+1}), \ldots, \sigma(R_m)$.

We write $G \mapsto_\sigma G'$ if C is clear from the context.   ◁

A sequence of resolution steps builds a derivation.

Definition 20 (SLD-derivation, SLD-refutation) Given a logic program P and a goal G.

An **SLD-derivation** of (P, G) is a (potentially infinite) sequence $G \mapsto_{\sigma_1, C_1} G_1 \mapsto_{\sigma_2, C_2} G_2 \mapsto_{\sigma_3, C_3} G_3 \mapsto \ldots$ of resolution steps.

An **SLD-refutation** of (P, G) is a finite SLD-derivation $G \mapsto_{\sigma_1, C_1} G_1 \mapsto_{\sigma_2, C_2} G_2 \mapsto \ldots \mapsto_{\sigma_n, C_n} G_n$ of (P, G), where $G_n = \square$.   ◁

An SLD-refutation of a goal generates substitutions whose composition is called a *computed answer*.

Definition 21 (computed answer) Let P be a logic program, let G be a goal. Let $G \mapsto_{\sigma_1, C_1} G_1 \mapsto_{\sigma_2, C_2} G_2 \mapsto \ldots \mapsto_{\sigma_n, C_n} \square$ be an SLD-refutation. The substitution $\sigma = \sigma'|_{var(G)}$, where $\sigma' = \sigma_n \circ \sigma_{n-1} \circ \ldots \circ \sigma_1$, is a **computed answer** of (P, G).   ◁

Example 11 Consider the `append` program from Example 10. We show two possible SLD-refutations for the goal $G = $?- `append(A,B,[6,3,2])`.

?- `append(A,B,[6,3,2])`.
$\qquad \mapsto_{\sigma_1} = \{$A/[], B/[6,3,2], X/[6,3,2]$\}$, (1)

$\square$

We obtain the computed answer σ as follows:

$\sigma = \sigma'|_{var(G)} = \{$A/[], B/[6,3,2]$\}$, where $\sigma' = \sigma_1$.

Another derivation of G is the following:

?- `append(A,B,[6,3,2])`.
$\qquad \mapsto_{\delta_1} = \{$A/[6|XS], YS/B, X/6, ZS/[3,2]$\}$, (2)
?- `append(XS,B,[3,2])`.
$\qquad \mapsto_{\delta_2} = \{$XS/[], B/[3,2], X1/[3,2]$\}$, (1)

$\square$

The substitution δ is the computed answer:

$\delta = \delta'|_{var(G)} = \{$A/[6], B/[3,2]$\}$ with
$\delta' = \delta_2 \circ \delta_1$
$\qquad = \{$A/[6], X/6, XS/[], YS/[3,2], ZS/[3,2], B/[3,2], X1/[3,2]$\}$.   ◇

Lemma 1 determines the relation between the *operational semantics* and the *declarative semantics* of logic programs.

Lemma 1 (soundness and completeness of SLD-resolution, cf. [169]) *Let P be a logic program, let G be a goal.*

1. *Every computed answer is a correct answer of (P, G).*

2. *For every correct answer σ of (P, G) there exist a computed answer ϕ and a substitution ψ with $\sigma(x) = (\psi \circ \phi)(x)$ for all $x \in var(G)$.*

While every computed answer is correct, there may be correct answers σ which cannot be computed using SLD-resolution. This is caused by the fact that SLD-resolution computes most general unifiers. Instead, it is possible to compute a more general (correct) answer ϕ, such that $\sigma = \psi \circ \phi$.

Negation can be represented using the *Clark completion*. Since this is also fundamental to the interpretation of *constraint logic programming* later on, we briefly sketch its essential issues.

The main point is a change in the interpretation of clauses. We assume now that all positive knowledge is explicitly contained in or implied by the logic program.

Definition 22 (Clark completion) Let P be a logic program. The **Clark completion** $P^{\leftrightarrow}$ consists of the formulae obtained by the following transformations:

- We replace every m-ary predicate p with clauses of the form

  $p(\tilde{t_1})$:- G_1.
  $\ldots$
  $p(\tilde{t_n})$:- G_n.

  by the formula

  $$\forall \tilde{X}. \, (\, p(\tilde{X}) \longleftrightarrow \exists \tilde{Y_1}.(\tilde{X} = \tilde{t_1} \wedge G_1) \vee \ldots \vee \exists \tilde{Y_n}.(\tilde{X} = \tilde{t_n} \wedge G_n) \,), \text{ where}$$

  $\tilde{t_i}$ are sequences of terms according to the arity of p,
  $\tilde{Y_i}$ are sequences of the variables appearing in G_i and $\tilde{t_i}$, and
  $\tilde{X}$ is a sequence of m different variables which do not occur in G_i or $\tilde{t_i}$, $i \in \{1, \ldots, n\}$.

- We replace every predicate symbol q which only occurs in the body of a rule by the formula
  $$\forall \tilde{X}. \, \neg \, q(\tilde{X})$$

- Finally, we add the following axioms for equality:

$\forall$	$x = x$	(1)
$\forall$	$x = y \longrightarrow y = x$	(2)
$\forall$	$x = y \wedge y = z \longrightarrow x = z$	(3)
$\forall$	$x_1 = y_1 \wedge \ldots \wedge x_n = y_n \longrightarrow f(x_1, \ldots, x_n) = f(y_1, \ldots, y_n)$	(4)
$\forall$	$x_1 = y_1 \wedge \ldots \wedge x_n = y_n \longrightarrow (p(x_1, \ldots, x_n) \longrightarrow p(y_1, \ldots, y_n))$	(5)
$\forall$	$f(x_1, \ldots, x_n) = f(y_1, \ldots, y_n) \longrightarrow x_1 = y_1 \wedge \ldots \wedge x_n = y_n$	(6)
$\forall$	$f(x_1, \ldots, x_m) = g(y_1, \ldots, y_n) \longrightarrow false, \text{ if } f \neq g \text{ or } m \neq n$	(7)
$\forall$	$x = t \longrightarrow false, \text{ if } x \text{ is a variable appearing in } t.$	(8)

The axioms (1) – (3) and (4) – (5) ensure that $=$ is an equivalence relation and congruence relation, resp. The axioms (6) – (8) formalize the properties of unification.   ◁

The Clark completion $P^{\leftrightarrow}$ of a program P does not delete or add positive information, i. e.

$$P \vDash A \iff P^{\leftrightarrow} \vDash A.$$

However, negative literals can be logical consequences of a program P resp. its completion $P^{\leftrightarrow}$, now.

Presuppose a selection strategy for goal literals. An *SLD-tree* (or *search-tree*) [106, 169] represents all possible SLD-derivations for a goal ?- G. If there is a finitely failing tree, i. e. all its branches are finite but unsuccessful (i. e. they terminate with goals $\neq \Box$), then ?- G. is finitely failed and $\neg\, G$ holds.

Lemma 2 (soundness, completeness of negation (as finite failure), cf. [169])
Let P be a logic program, let ?- G be a goal.

1. *If ?- G. has a finitely failing SLD-tree, then $P^{\leftrightarrow} \vDash \forall\, \neg\, G$.*
2. *If $P^{\leftrightarrow} \vDash \forall\, \neg\, G$ holds, then there exists a finitely failing SLD-tree for (P, G).*

For a more detailed discussion we refer to [106, 169, 71, 117].

Prolog and its dialects are implementations of the presented concepts, and thus, in general, adaptations and extensions.

PROLOG's computation method always chooses the first or leftmost, resp., subgoal of a goal for the next resolution step. The clauses of a program are explored according to their order in the program from top to bottom. Since PROLOG traverses the tree of possible derivation sequences, i. e. the *search-tree,* using *depth-first search* and *backtracking,* the completeness of SLD-resolution is lost. That means that the PROLOG evaluation may follow a non-terminating branch, even in the case of existing SLD-refutations.

Furthermore, PROLOG offers the developer extra-logical predicates with the aim to make programming more comfortable and to allow one to restrict the search-tree traversal. This encompasses the *cut* (written as "!") for "cutting away" certain (e.g. failing or redundant) branches of the search-tree, a restricted form of negation (based on the cut), and built-in arithmetic. For details see e.g. [106, 169].

3.2.5 Constraint-based programming languages

Today, most PROLOG systems, like ECL^{i}PS^e [1, 17] or SICStus [205] support *constraint programming* (CP) techniques. And vice versa, most constraint programming languages are logic languages. This is caused by the fact that logic programming can be interpreted as an instance of constraint programming which is, thus, a natural extension of the former. Also historically logic languages were the first to be extended by constraints.

In general, constraint languages allow one to describe problems by means of relations between variables in the form of constraints. *Constraints* are particular first-order predicate logic formulae and are handled by *constraint solvers*. These are specialized optimized algorithms, which are integrated into the corresponding language evaluation mechanisms.

We introduce constraints and related concepts and notions in Chapter 4. We consider constraint-based languages in detail in Chapter 5 as multiparadigm languages, because constraints are typically integrated into languages of other paradigms which provide the environment for structured programming.

3.2.6 Sequential, concurrent, and parallel languages

Programs of a *sequential* programming language are evaluated by a sequence of steps, either originally described by a sequence of instructions as in *imperative* languages or specified by the solution method or the evaluation algorithm in the case of *declarative* languages.

Concurrent systems allow the concurrent performance of causally independent actions, i.e. actions which do not need computation results from each other. Independent actions, which are often also called processes or agents, may be performed either sequentially in arbitrary order on one processor, even interleaved, or in *parallel* on several processors and possibly at the same time.

The sequential, parallel, and concurrent paradigms are *orthogonal* to the classification of languages into imperative and declarative ones. Accordingly, there are several languages which appear in different versions. For instance, besides the originally sequentially evaluated (imperative) language FOR-TRAN, there is the parallel version HIGH PERFORMANCE FORTRAN (HPF) [193]. Similarly, there exist concurrent and parallel versions and extensions of the functional language HASKELL, for instance CONCURRENT HASKELL [179], GLASGOW PARALLEL HASKELL (GPH) [140], GLASGOW DISTRIBUTED HASKELL (GDH) [183], and DATA PARALLEL HASKELL [40]. Furthermore, many languages allow different programming styles with respect to this classification, like ADA, and this is often realized by means of libraries, as in JAVA or OPAL [177].

For further reading on concurrent and parallel languages and programming methods we refer to [95, 135, 13]. We discuss concurrent programming with constraints in Section 5.3 and Chapter 6.

3.2.7 Languages of further paradigms

Further paradigms which are mainly *orthogonal* to the above-mentioned classification include e.g. *aspect-oriented* programming and *literate* programming.

On the other hand there are languages belonging to very specific classes like *visual* languages, *database* languages or so-called *domain-specific* languages (DSL).

Aspect-oriented programming (AOP) [129, 111] is intended to aid programmers in the separation of cross-cutting concerns, that is aspects like logging, synchronization, security or error handling which defy typical encapsulation and "cut" across multiple modules in a (often object-oriented) program.

The concerns (the aspect code) are implemented separately to the actual program code (the business code). This approach simplifies the maintenance of code and allows its expansion and exchange. The aspect code is woven (aspect weaving) into the business code before or after compilation or even at runtime.

Examples of AOP languages are HYPERJ [110] and ASPECTJ [128] for JAVA, ASPECTL [49] for COMMON LISP/CLOS, and ASPECTML [51] for ML.

Literate programming is a methodology combining an actual programming language with a documentation language with the goal to improve its readability by humans. This makes the programs more robust, more portable and more easily maintained. Examples are WEB [130] and its derivatives.

Visual programming languages rely on the idea to specify programs by manipulating program elements graphically instead of textually. The main language concepts are visual expressions and the spatial arrangements of text and graphical symbols. Examples are SIMULINK, the constraint-based language THINGLAB [28], and the MICROSOFT VISUAL PROGRAMMING LANGUAGE (MVPL) for programming robots in the MICROSOFT ROBOTICS STUDIO.

Database or query languages are used to request information from databases and information systems. The STRUCTURED QUERY LANGUAGE (SQL) is the standard interactive and programming language for querying and modifying data and managing databases. Its origin goes back to the nineteen-seventies. Besides, there are many other query languages which differ according to the underlying database model or type, like XQUERY [34] which is used to query collections of XML data, DATALOG [38] which is syntactically a subset of PROLOG but applied to deductive databases, and the object query language OBJECT CONSTRAINT LANGUAGE (OCL) [227, 170] as an ingredient of UML.

Domain specific languages [223] are dedicated to a particular problem domain, problem representation or solution technology, again with the aim to enhance quality, flexibility, and coding performance of software. Well-known examples are the ABSTRACT SYNTAX DESCRIPTION LANGUAGE (ASDL) [45] for the description of tree-like data structures in compilers, the BACKUS-NAUR FORM (BNF) which is a compact meta-syntax used to express context-free grammars, the document markup language LATEX and the typesetting system language TEX itself, the software development tool MAKE for building large applications, and the HYPERTEXT MARKUP LANGUAGE (HTML) for web pages. Many of the languages mentioned in the above sections and paragraphs can be considered as DSLs (and are considered as such, dependent on the context and background of the observer).

Chapter 4
Constraints

This chapter deals with constraints and constraint programming (CP). In Sections 4.1 and 4.2 we introduce fundamental notions of constraint programming and illustrate them by means of examples. We show the appearance and use of constraints in programming languages in Section 4.3 and discuss applications of constraints in Section 4.4.

Based on the concepts introduced here, in Chapters 5 – 7 we discuss the extension of programming languages and paradigms by constraints which yields multiparadigm constraint programming languages.

For further reading we refer to the following books [106, 71, 15, 153, 195] and articles [119, 118]. The presentation of Sections 4.1 and 4.2 partially rely on [106], Chapter 3, which is due to the author of this book.

4.1 Constraints and constraint systems

Constraints are predicate logic formulae used to describe problems by means of properties of objects or relations between them. Constraints are classified into domains by the applicable solution algorithms. A constraint system gives a clear description of a corresponding class.

Definition 23 (constraint, constraint system) Let $\Sigma = (S, F, R)$ be a signature, where the set R contains a predicate symbol $=^s$ for every sort $s \in S$; let X be a set of Σ-variables. Let $\mathcal{D}$ be a Σ-structure with equality, i.e. for every predicate symbol $=^s$ there is an equality predicate which is a congruence relation. Let $\mathcal{T}$ be a Σ-theory.

A **constraint** (over Σ) has the form $r(t_1, \ldots, t_m)$, where $r \in R$ is a predicate symbol and t_i are terms of appropriate sorts. The set $\mathcal{C}$ of constraints (over Σ) additionally contains the constraints *true* and *false* with $\mathcal{D} \models true$ and $\mathcal{D} \not\models false$.

A 5-tuple $\zeta = (\Sigma, \mathcal{D}, \mathcal{T}, X, \mathcal{C}ons)$, where $\{true, false\} \subseteq \mathcal{C}ons \subseteq \mathcal{C}$ is a **constraint system**. ◁

The theory $\mathcal{T}$ is intended to describe important properties of $\mathcal{D}$. Thus, in the following, $\mathcal{T}$ must reflect the structure $\mathcal{D}$ sufficiently, i.e. $\mathcal{D}$ and $\mathcal{T}$ must *correspond*.

Definition 24 (correspondence of $\mathcal{D}$ and $\mathcal{T}$, [119])
Let $\zeta = (\Sigma, \mathcal{D}, \mathcal{T}, X, \mathcal{C}ons)$ be a constraint system. The structure $\mathcal{D}$ and the theory $\mathcal{T}$ **correspond** w.r.t. the constraints of $\mathcal{C}ons$ if

- $\mathcal{D}$ is a model of $\mathcal{T}$ and
- for every constraint $c \in \mathcal{C}ons$ holds: $\mathcal{D} \vDash \exists c$ iff $\mathcal{T} \vDash \exists c$.   ◁

Moreover, we presuppose *satisfaction completeness* of $\mathcal{T}$, i.e. for every constraint $c \in \mathcal{C}ons$ either $\mathcal{T} \vDash \exists c$ or $\mathcal{T} \vDash \neg \exists c$ holds.

Typical examples are finite domain constraint systems, systems defining the linear arithmetic domain, domains with non-linear arithmetic constraints, and Boolean constraints. Even logic programming with the Herbrand-structure based on the Herbrand-universe can be interpreted as constraint programming. Corresponding solving and constraint handling algorithms are based on consistency checking and search (see e.g. [153, 106]) for finite domain constraints, on the simplex method [180, 54, 152] or Gaussian elimination [30] for linear arithmetic constraints, on Buchberger's Gröbner bases algorithm [35, 160], interval arithmetic [15, 96], or a simple delay mechanism [47] for non-linear constraints, on Boolean unification [154], local consistency techniques [155, 46] or an adaptation of Buchberger's Gröbner bases algorithm [3] for Boolean constraints, and on resolution (see Definitions 19 and 20) for the Herbrand-domain. For a collection of (further) references and a presentation of some of these solving algorithms see e.g. [106, 98]).

4.1.1 Linear arithmetic constraints

As a first example we consider linear arithmetic constraints. They allow efficient handling of linear equations, inequalities, and disequations on real numbers. Typical examples come from operations research (see e.g. [54, 106]).

Let $\zeta_{\mathbb{R}_{lin}}$ be a constraint system with

$$\zeta_{\mathbb{R}_{lin}} = (\Sigma_{\mathbb{R}}, \mathcal{D}_{\mathbb{R}}, \mathcal{T}_{\mathbb{R}_{lin}}, X_{\mathbb{R}}, \mathcal{C}ons_{\mathbb{R}_{lin}}).$$

The signature $\Sigma_{\mathbb{R}}$ contains constant symbols for the real numbers, binary function symbols $+$, $-$, $*$, and $/$, and the binary predicate symbols $=$, $>$, $<$, $\leq$, $\geq$, and $\neq$.

$$\Sigma_{\mathbb{R}} = (S_{\mathbb{R}}, F_{\mathbb{R}}, R_{\mathbb{R}}) = (\{real\}, \{0, 1, -1, 2, \ldots, +, -, *, /\}, \{=, >, <, \leq, \geq, \neq\}).$$

The structure $\mathcal{D}_{\mathbb{R}}$ consists of the set of real numbers $\mathbb{R}$, corresponding constants and the functions $+^{\mathbb{R}}$, $-^{\mathbb{R}}$, $*^{\mathbb{R}}$, $/^{\mathbb{R}}$ and predicates $=^{\mathbb{R}}$, $>^{\mathbb{R}}$, $<^{\mathbb{R}}$, $\leq^{\mathbb{R}}$,

$\geq^R$, and $\neq^R$ which are defined as usual.

$$\mathcal{D}_R = (\{\mathbb{R}\}, \{0^R, 1^R, -1^R, 2^R, \ldots, +^R, -^R, *^R, /^R\}, \{=^R, >^R, <^R, \leq^R, \geq^R, \neq^R\}).$$

We restrict $Cons_{\mathbb{R}_{lin}}$ to linear constraints and $\mathcal{T}_{\mathbb{R}_{lin}}$ to linear arithmetic. Thus, the set $Cons_{\mathbb{R}_{lin}}$ of constraints of $\zeta_{\mathbb{R}_{lin}}$ contains besides *true* and *false* constraints of the following form, exclusively:

$$a_1 * x_1 + \ldots + a_n * x_n \odot b,$$

where $x_1, \ldots, x_n \in X_{\mathbb{R}}$ are variables, $a_1, \ldots, a_n, b$ are real numbers, and $\odot \in \{=, >, <, \leq, \geq, \neq\}$ is a predicate symbol.

Expressions like $(2 * x - 1 * z < 1)$ and $(3 * x = 4)$, where $x, z \in X_{\mathbb{R}}$, are linear constraints. However, we will consider also e.g. $((3+2) * (x - y) < z)$ or $(3.2 * x = \pi * y)$ as linear constraints, i.e. expressions which can be transformed into the above form.

The set $Cons_{\mathbb{R}_{lin}}$ is a proper subset of $\mathcal{C}_{\mathbb{R}}$ because non-linear constraints, like $(x * x + y * y = z * z)$ are elements of the set $\mathcal{C}_{\mathbb{R}}$ but not contained in the set $Cons_{\mathbb{R}_{lin}}$. This restriction is required by the simplex method used as a solving algorithm for constraints of this domain. We refer to [106, 54, 176, 152, 114] for further reading.

4.1.2 Finite domain constraints

Another example are *finite domain constraints*. They are characterized by the fact that the domains of the involved variables are a priori finite.

Let $\zeta_{\mathcal{FD}}$ be a constraint system with

$$\zeta_{\mathcal{FD}} = (\Sigma_{\mathcal{FD}}, \mathcal{D}_{\mathcal{FD}}, \mathcal{T}_{\mathcal{FD}}, X_{\mathcal{FD}}, Cons_{\mathcal{FD}}).$$

Constraints of $\zeta_{\mathcal{FD}}$ allow the formulation of arithmetic problems in which variable domains are finite sets.

Let the signature $\Sigma_{\mathcal{FD}}$ contain integer symbols, arithmetic function symbols, unary predicate symbols for determining membership of finite domains and binary predicate symbols to express equality, inequality, and disequations.

$$\Sigma_{\mathcal{FD}} = (\{int\}, \{0, 1, -1, 2, \ldots, +, -, *, /\},$$
$$\{\in \{e_1, \ldots, e_k\} \mid e_i \in \mathbb{Z}\} \cup \{=, \neq, <, > \leq, \geq\}).$$

The structure $\mathcal{D}_{\mathcal{FD}}$ consists of the set of integers $\mathbb{Z}$ and functions and predicates appropriate to the symbols of $\Sigma_{\mathcal{FD}}$ which, however, operate on integers.

The set of constraints $Cons_{\mathcal{FD}}$ contains all constraints of $\mathcal{C}_{\mathcal{FD}}$. Examples of FD-constraints are $x \in \{3, 6, 9, 10\}$, $x \neq 7$ and $x * y \leq 8$.

A finite domain constraint as defined above does not a priori finitely restrict the domain of all involved variables. This property is realized by means of *constraint satisfaction problems* which determine the actual form a problem description must take when solved using a finite domain constraint solver.

Definition 25 (constraint satisfaction problem (CSP)) A ***constraint satisfaction problem (CSP)*** is a conjunction $C = C' \land E_1 \land \ldots \land E_n$ of constraints of $Cons_{\mathcal{FD}}$ over the variables $x_1, \ldots, x_n \in X_{\mathcal{FD}}$ such that

- the constraint conjunction C' does not contain constraints of the form $x \in D$,
- $var(C) \subseteq \{x_1, \ldots, x_n\}$ holds, and
- the constraints E_i have the form $x_i \in \{e_{i,1}, \ldots, e_{i,k_i}\}$. The constraint E_i assigns a finite set of values to the variable x_i. The set $D(x_i) = \{e_{i,1}^{\mathcal{FD}}, \ldots, e_{i,k_i}^{\mathcal{FD}}\}$ is called the *domain* of the variable x_i.

The constraints *true* and *false* are also CSPs.   ◁

Finite domain constraints are solved by domain narrowing using consistency checking algorithms (node consistency, arc consistency, path consistency) nested with search techniques. We refer to [153, 106] for detailed descriptions, references, and applications.

Example 12 A typical example which "has finally reached the masses" [207] is the puzzle sudoku.

A 9×9 grid is partitioned into 3×3 blocks. Every position may take one of the numbers $1, 2, \ldots, 9$, where some assignments are already fixed. The aim is to fill all positions of the 9×9 grid such that each column, each row, and each of the nine 3×3 blocks contains the digits from 1 to 9 only once each.

An example of an initial situation is given in Figure 4.1. The constraint solving process performs a narrowing of possible values comparable to the human deduction process.

Consider e.g. the 3×3 block at the middle position in the lowermost row. For each of the remaining positions the set of potential values is $\{3, 5, 6, 9\}$, which follows from the values already used within this 3×3 block. This is illustrated by Figure 4.2 (a). These sets can be narrowed by means of the known values in the complete rows (Figure 4.2 (b)) of the 9×9 grid and in its columns (Figure 4.2 (c)). Since the bottom left value is finally fixed to 3, this value can be deleted from the domains of the other positions (Figure 4.2 (d)). With a final step we reach the configuration given in Figure 4.2 (e): The middle position is the only one where the value 5 is allowed.

The correct distribution of 6 and 9 at the remaining positions can be found out by search or by further narrowing of other areas of the 9×9 grid, which again restricts the domains of these positions.   ◇

		8				6		
	4	9		2		5		
		6	4	8				
	3	9		2		1	7	
	1						3	
	8	5		1		2	6	
			2	8	7			
	6		1		4		8	
		2				5		

Fig. 4.1 Sudoku

(a)

2	8	7
1	3 5 6 9	4
3 5 6 9	3 5 6 9	3 5 6 9

(b)

2	8	7
1	3 5 9	4
3 6 9	3 6 9	3 6 9

(c)

2	8	7
1	3 5 9	4
3	3 6 9	3 6 9

(d)

2	8	7
1	5 9	4
3	6 9	6 9

(e)

2	8	7
1	5	4
3	6 9	6 9

Fig. 4.2 Stepwise narrowing of the domains

4.2 Constraint solvers

Given a constraint-based problem description the user of a constraint programming system is typically interested in finding out about satisfiability and concrete solutions.

In the following, let $\zeta = (\Sigma, \mathcal{D}, \mathcal{T}, X, Cons)$ be a constraint system.

Definition 26 (satisfiability) A conjunction $C = \bigwedge_{i \in \{1,\ldots,n\}} c_i$ of constraints $c_1, \ldots, c_n \in Cons$ is

> **satisfiable** or **consistent** in $\mathcal{D}$ if $\mathcal{D} \models \exists C$,
> **unsatisfiable** or **inconsistent** in $\mathcal{D}$ if $\mathcal{D} \models \neg \exists C$.   ◁

If a constraint (conjunction) is satisfiable, then there exists at least one solution.

Definition 27 (solution) A valuation $\varsigma : X \to \mathcal{D}$ is a **solution** of a conjunction $C = \bigwedge_{i \in \{1,\ldots,n\}} c_i$ of constraints $c_1, \ldots, c_n \in Cons$ if $(\mathcal{D}, \varsigma) \models C$.   ◁

Example 13 Let the constraint system $\zeta_{\mathbb{R}_{lin}}$ for linear arithmetic be given. The constraint conjunction $x \geq 3 \land y \geq x \land y + x \leq 7$ is satisfiable. A solution (but not the only one) is $x = 3 \land y = 4$. The constraint conjunction $x \geq 3 \land y > x \land y + x = 6$ is unsatisfiable.   ◇

While a solution is, in fact, a mapping from the set of variables into the carrier set, in the following we simplify the presentation.

We assume that a solution ς of a constraint conjunction C can always be represented by means of a conjunction of equality constraints

$$\bigwedge_{x \in var(C)} (x = f_x),$$

where f_x are 0-ary function symbols of the signature Σ and it holds:

$$(\mathcal{D}, \varsigma) \models \bigwedge_{x \in var(C)} (x = f_x).$$

Note, that this is actually not necessarily satisfied for every constraint conjunction of a constraint system, but it is often or mostly so.

A **constraint solver** is a set or a library of tests and operations on constraints of a constraint system. Typically these include a satisfiability test, an entailment test, and a projection function. Further operations are e.g. simplification and determination detection (see [106, 119]). They are realized by means of particular algorithms specialized for particular constraint domains. We mentioned some of these algorithms in the previous section in connection with the corresponding constraint domains.

In the following, let

$$\varDelta \mathcal{C}ons = \{c_1 \land \ldots \land c_m \mid m \in \mathbb{N} \text{ and } c_1, \ldots, c_m \in \mathcal{C}ons\}$$

denote the *set of all constraint conjunctions* of ζ and

$$\nabla\!\varDelta \mathcal{C}ons = \{C_1 \lor \ldots \lor C_l \mid l \in \mathbb{N} \text{ and } C_1, \ldots, C_l \in \varDelta \mathcal{C}ons\}$$

the *set of all disjunctions of constraint conjunctions*.

Let us consider four main constraint solver operations: satisfiability, entailment, projection, and simplification.

Satisfiability is the most important property of constraints checked by constraint solvers. The satisfiability test

$$solve : \varDelta \mathcal{C}ons \rightarrow \{true, false, unknown\}$$

checks whether a constraint conjunction C is satisfiable in structure $\mathcal{D}$. The following must hold:

If $solve(C) = true$, then C is satisfiable in $\mathcal{D}$: $\mathcal{D} \models \exists\, C$ and
if $solve(C) = false$, then C is unsatisfiable in $\mathcal{D}$: $\mathcal{D} \models \neg\,\exists\, C$.

Example 14 A constraint solver for linear arithmetic applied on the constraints of Example 13 yields the following results:

$solve(x \geq 3 \wedge y \geq x \wedge y + x \leq 7) = true$ and
$solve(x \geq 3 \wedge y > x \wedge y + x = 6) = false$.   ◇

Definition 28 ((in)complete satisfiability test) A satisfiability test $solve : \Delta\mathcal{C}ons \rightarrow \{true, false, unknown\}$ is **complete** if it decides the satisfiability in $\mathcal{D}$ for all $C \in \Delta\mathcal{C}ons$, i.e. for every C in $\Delta\mathcal{C}ons$ holds $solve(C) \in \{true, false\}$. Otherwise the test is **incomplete**.   ◁

Example 15 Often linear arithmetic solvers are equipped with a simple delay mechanism to handle non-linear constraints. The delay mechanism suspends non-linear constraints until they become linear because of certain variable bindings.

While a linear solver is not able to handle a constraint $x * y + y * z = z * x$, it may receive bindings for x and y during the solution process and, thus, be able to handle the corresponding constraint conjunction later on:

$solve(x * y + y * z = z * x) = unknown$ and
$solve(x * y + y * z = z * x \wedge x = 4 \wedge y = 3) = true$.   ◇

This completeness property also applies to the corresponding constraint solver.

Definition 29 ((in)complete constraint solver) A constraint solver is **complete** if its satisfiability test is complete. Otherwise the solver is **incomplete**.◁

Entailment is a second important property of constraints checked by constraint solvers. The *entailment test*

$$entail : \Delta\mathcal{C}ons \times \nabla\!\Delta\mathcal{C}ons \rightarrow \{true, false, delay\}$$

checks whether a constraint conjunction C entails a disjunction E of constraint conjunctions. The following must hold:

If $entail(C, E) = true$, then C is satisfiable and E follows from C in $\mathcal{D}$:
$\mathcal{D} \models (\exists\, C) \wedge \forall\, (C \longrightarrow E)$.

If $entail(C, E) = false$, then E is not entailed by C (while C must hold):
$\mathcal{D} \models \neg\,\exists\, (C \wedge (C \longrightarrow E))$.

The result *delay* covers the situation that both of the following hold:
$\mathcal{D} \models \exists\, (C \wedge (C \longrightarrow E))$ and $\mathcal{D} \models \neg\, ((\exists\, C) \wedge \forall\, (C \longrightarrow E))$.

In this case the entailment of E by C cannot be decided yet but is *delayed* (or *suspended*). Adding a new constraint to C may allow one to decide the entailment relation later on.

The result *delay* can be used furthermore to express that a solver is not (yet) able to deal with C or E, i.e. it is not able to find out about the entailment relation.

Example 16 Consider the constraint system $\zeta_{\mathbb{R}_{lin}}$ from Section 4.1.1 and the constraint $C = x \geq 3$. An entailment test may yield the following results:

$entail(C, E) = delay$, where $E = (x \leq 5)$,
because the entailment of E by C cannot be decided yet.

We add further constraints to the store such that the entailment test yields *true* or *false*, resp.

$entail(C_1, E) = true$, where $C_1 = C \wedge (x < 4)$.
$entail(C_2, E) = false$, where $C_2 = C \wedge (x > 5)$.   ◊

Projection extracts knowledge about a certain restricted set of variables from a given constraint conjunction.

$$proj : \Delta Cons \times \mathcal{P}(X) \to \nabla\!\Delta Cons$$

And it holds:

If $proj(C, Y) = C'$, then $\mathcal{D} \models \forall ((\exists_{-\tilde{Y}} C) \longleftrightarrow C')$, where $Y \subseteq var(C)$.

The result of the projection of a constraint conjunction C w.r.t. a subset Y of its variables is a disjunction C' of constraint conjunctions such that C' describes a part of the knowledge of C, actually the relations of the variables of Y. Projection is, thus, also called *variable elimination* because for the result C' all other variables except those of Y are eliminated.

Example 17 Consider again the constraint system $\zeta_{\mathbb{R}_{lin}}$ for linear arithmetic. Let $C = (x \geq y) \wedge (y = 4) \wedge (z = x+y) \wedge (w \leq z - 3 * x)$. We build projections w.r.t. different sets of variables:

$proj(C, \{x\})$ $= (x \geq 4)$,
$proj(C, \{y\})$ $= (y = 4)$,
$proj(C, \{z\})$ $= (z \geq 8)$,
$proj(C, \{x, w\})$ $= (x \geq 4) \wedge (w \leq 4 - 2 * x)$,
$proj(C, \{x, y, z, w\}) = C$.   ◊

Note that projection is a *partial* function because it is not always possible to build a projection. Since, furthermore, the projection operation may become very costly, in practice the condition to build a projection is often softened such that the equivalence relation is replaced by an implication:

If $proj(C, Y) = C'$, then $\mathcal{D} \models \forall ((\exists_{-\tilde{Y}} C) \longrightarrow C')$, where $Y \subseteq var(C)$.

Simplification is a constraint solver operation which "*simplifies*" a conjunction C and builds an equivalent conjunction C' which is "simpler" in a certain sense.

$$simplify : \Delta Cons \rightarrow \Delta Cons$$

And it holds:

If $simplify(C) = C'$, then $\mathcal{D} \vDash \forall (C \longleftrightarrow C')$.

The concrete relation "is simpler than" depends on the particular solver. Often the result of a simplification is some kind of *normal form* subject to the underlying constraint system.

The constraint store

A constraint solver is usually equipped with a *constraint store*. The constraint solver operations given above operate on this store which is taken into account by the first argument of type $\Delta Cons$ in each case. That is, the satisfiability test checks the satisfiability of the constraint store, the entailment test analyses the entailment of constraints by the store, projection projects it and simplification normalizes the store.

4.3 Constraints as language constructs

In this book we consider multiparadigm constraint programming languages. We are, thus, interested in the functionalities in which constraints may act as language elements. We mainly distinguish three categories: (1) *abstraction* over a number of basic language constraints, (2) *stating properties* of objects and (3) *checking or questioning* of conditions. We discuss the three aspects in the following.

4.3.1 Constraint abstractions

A constraint language usually provides the user with a set of basic constraints, e.g. as built-in constraints or by constraint libraries. However, to write compact and readable programs in a convenient way, it is often desirable to summarize or abstract over sets of constraints, just as functions abstract over statements. Such abstractions are called **user-defined constraints** or **constraint abstractions**.

Example 18 In PROLOG the user abstracts over a set of constraints (and/or predicates) by defining a predicate. Program 4.3.1 shows the definition and

Program 4.3.1 A user-defined domain constraint in ECL^{i}PS^e-Prolog

```
:- use_module(library(ic)).
myDom(X,L,R) :- X #>= L, X #=< R.
predicate(...) :- ... myDom(A,0,9), myDom(B,-1,1), ...
```

Program 4.3.2 A user-defined domain constraint in Turtle

```
1   constraint domain (v: !int, min: int, max: int)
2     require v >= min and v <= max;
3   end;
4   ...
5   var a: !int;
6   var b: int := 0;
7   require domain(a,b,9);
```

use of a domain constraint *myDom* for integer variables in ECL^{i}PS^e-Prolog. It restricts the integer variable X to values between L and R, i.e. $L \leq X \leq R$, and uses the finite domain integer constraints (#>=) and (#=<) of the constraint library *ic*.   ◊

Example 19 Turtle [77, 106] (see also Section 5.6) is a multiparadigm language merging concepts from the constraint-based and the imperative paradigms. Program 4.3.2 shows the definition and use of a domain constraint corresponding to Program 4.3.1 using this constraint-imperative language.

In Turtle, variables of type ! *int* are constraint variables which are determined by constraints, while imperative variables (e.g. *b* of type *int*) are set to values by assignment statements.   ◊

The user-defined constraint *alldifferent* as given in Program 4.3.3 using Turtle is another example of a constraint abstraction. This constraint is applied to a list *s* of n variables and restricts these to be pairwise different by means of $\frac{n*(n-1)}{2}$ disequality constraints.

However, unlike in Program 4.3.3, *alldifferent* is typically a global constraint. **Global constraints** [25] are logical combinations of constraints of a constraint system ζ which are provided by constraint libraries and languages. In contrast to a user-defined constraint, a global constraint is not handled and solved like its ingredient constraints but by a dedicated specialized and optimized algorithm. The use of specialized algorithms allows in general a more efficient computation and/or a stronger restriction of the sets of potential solutions. For example, the global *alldifferent* constraint is usually solved by means of graph algorithms [189, 108, 215] or Hall-intervals [145, 185].

Program 4.3.3 A user-defined *alldifferent*-constraint in TURTLE

```
 1   constraint  alldifferent  (s:  list  of  !int)
 2      while  (tl  s  <> null)  do
 3        var  ss:  list  of  !int  :=  tl  s;
 4        while  (ss  <> null)  do
 5          require hd  s  <> hd  ss;
 6          ss  :=  tl  ss;
 7        end;
 8        s  :=  tl  s;
 9      end;
10   end;
```

4.3.2 Tell-constraints for constraint propagation

The most natural and most common application of basic as well as user-defined constraints in a language is their use to state properties of problems or their solutions. These constraints are often called **tell-constraints**. Examples are e.g. the evocation of *myDom(A,0,9)* in Program 4.3.1 or *domain(a,b,9)* using **require** in Program 4.3.2.

Languages with constraints integrate *constraint solvers* into their runtime system which are used to check the satisfiability of constraints and to compute solutions at runtime. They can be interpreted as abstract machines of the runtime system, as shown in Figure 3.2.

A constraint solver is usually equipped with a *constraint store*. During the program evaluation, constraints are stepwise collected and propagated into the constraint store. Adding a new constraint to the store is called *constraint propagation* (or *tell*). Thereby, either the consistency of the store is ensured immediately or after a number of propagations, e.g. by particular statements or commands. Checking the consistency of the store is done using the *satisfiability test* of the constraint solver (cf. Section 4.2).

Constraint solvers mostly work *incrementally*: When constraints are stepwise propagated to the store, it is not solved again and again from scratch. Instead, the store usually contains an intermediate or normal form of the constraints added so far which is enhanced and simplified (using the *simplification* operation of the constraint solver, cf. Section 4.2) with every new constraint propagation. This saves computation steps and makes the solution process more efficient.

4.3.3 Ask-constraints for process coordination

The third functionality of constraints frequently appearing in constraint languages is to check conditions to influence the program evaluation. This

Program 4.3.4 A producer and a consumer communicating over a shared buffer in CCFL

```
fun produce :: a -> [a] -> C
def produce item buf =
        with buf1 :: [a]
        in buf =:= item : buf1 & produce item buf1

fun consume :: [a] -> C
def consume buf =
        buf =:= first : buf1 ->
            consume buf1

fun main :: C
def main =
        with buf :: [a]
        in produce 1 buf & consume buf
```

typically concerns reactive systems, i.e. systems where concurrently working processes cooperate and coordinate their work. So-called **ask-constraints** are used to synchronize processes for the cooperative work on a common task and to decide between alternative computation paths. The cooperative processes work on a shared *constraint store* which is used to collect the common knowledge propagated by *tell-constraints* and to synchronize the processes using *ask-constraints*. Synchronisation using ask-constraints is done by checking their entailment by the constraint store using the *entailment test* of the constraint solver (cf. Section 4.2).

This behaviour can be modeled using the *concurrent constraint programming (CCP)* model of Saraswat [199, 200]. We discuss concurrent constraint programming in general in Section 5.3 and w.r.t. the concurrent constraint functional language CCFL in Chapter 6.

Example 20 Program 4.3.4 shows a producer-consumer setting in the concurrent constraint functional language CCFL.

The producer process *produce* (of result type *C*, i.e. a constraint) generates infinitely many items (here just the number 1) of a buffer *buf* (represented by a list of type [a]). At this, the free variable *buf1* is instantiated by the tell-constraint *produce item buf1* during the computation.

The consumer process works on the same buffer *buf*. A *guard* consisting of the ask-constraint *buf =:= first : buf1* ensures that *consume* can only be processed when the buffer contains at least one element *first*. In this way, the consumer is forced to synchronize with the producer process.   ◊

Example 21 Ask-constraints can also be used by a process to decide between alternative computation paths. Program 4.3.5 shows a *member*-constraint in CCFL which non-deterministically chooses a value from a given list.

Program 4.3.5 Non-deterministic choice of alternative paths in CCFL

```
fun  member  ::  [a]  ->  a  ->  C
def  member  l  x   =
     l  =:=  y  :  ys  ->  x  =:=  y  |
     l  =:=  y  :  ys  ->  case  ys  of  []      ->  x  =:=  y  ;
                                         z  :  zs  ->  member  ys  x
```

The expression *member* [1,2,4] *b* reduces to *Success* and generates *one* of the three possible solutions {*b*/1}, {*b*/2}, or {*b*/4}.

The member-constraint behaves non-deterministically. While classical PRO-LOG uses backtracking and potentially explores the complete search-tree, concurrent declarative languages like CCFL follow exactly one computation path. While the former is called *don't know non-determinism*, for the latter the term *don't care non-determinism* (or *committed choice*) is used.   ◇

4.3.4 Computing solutions

During the computation of a constraint problem, constraints are propagated stepwise to the constraint store, thereby narrowing the set of potential solutions described by the store. Eventually the store contains constraints which describe the set of solutions, that is, in general, more than exactly one valuation. Thus, an interesting aspect for the user of a constraint programming language is the way of computing concrete solutions, i.e. one, n, or all solutions or a global or local optimum, resp.

The computation of solutions strongly depends on the solving mechanism of the constraint solver and, thus, of the concrete constraint domain. For example, for finite domain problems the set of solutions is a priori finite. Thus, finite domain constraint solvers usually offer a constraint *labeling(L)* which instantiates all variables of the list L to values of their remaining domains (consistent with the constraints) and computes in this way a solution (and potentially all solutions by a subsequent search).

Example 22 Program 4.3.6 shows a simple finite domain problem and corresponding system answers using ECL^{i}PS^e-PROLOG.

The goal *?- fdProblem(L).* just initiates a consistency check of its (sub)constraints and narrows the domains of the variables. Using *labeling* we are able to compute the concrete solutions.   ◇

In contrast, consider linear arithmetic constraints over real numbers, where, in general, a constraint problem may have infinitely many solutions. The simplex method as solving mechanism considers the solution set as a polyhedron and initially computes one solution, a so-called basic feasible solution, to

Program 4.3.6 ECL^{i}PS^e-PROLOG: application of the *labeling*-constraint

```
:- use_module(library(fd)).

fdProblem(L) :-
  L = [A,B,D],
  L :: 1..3,
  alldifferent(L),
  A #< B.

fdSolve(L) :-
  fdProblem(L),
  labeling(L).

?- fdProblem(L).
L = [A{[1, 2]}, B{[2, 3]}, D{[1..3]}]
There are 4 delayed goals.
Yes

?- findall(L, fdSolve(L), R).
R = [[1, 2, 3], [1, 3, 2], [2, 3, 1]]
Yes
```

Program 4.3.7 ECL^{i}PS^e-PROLOG: linear optimization

```
:-use_module(library(eplex)).

linProblem(L) :-
  L = [A,B,D],
  L :: 0.0..3.0,
  A $>= B + 1.5,
  B $>= D + 1.0,
  optimize(min(A),V).

?- linProblem(L).
L = [2.5, 1.0, 0.0]
Yes
```

check the satisfiability of the constraint problem. To obtain concrete solutions the problem is optimized with respect to a certain objective function. In this way, the algorithm computes vertices of the solution polyhedron as concrete solutions.

Example 23 Program 4.3.7 is a linear arithmetic problem description in ECL^{i}PS^e-PROLOG, where the domains of the variables A, B, and D are restricted to *real* numbers between 0.0 and 3.0. The goal *optimize(min(A),V)* eventually minimizes the value of the variable A, where V is the value of the computed optimal solution (and just the value of A in this program). In this

example, the linear arithmetic solver *eplex* based on the simplex method is
used.   ◊

4.4 Constraint-based applications

Scientific applications of constraint programming frequently come from the
area of artificial intelligence, like natural language processing, automatic
theorem proving, and spatial and temporal reasoning, and even from the area
of molecular biology. In the *industrial* context, constraints are often used for
planning and scheduling and optimization tasks, such as for stand allocation of
airplanes and ships, for network configuration, and for assembly line scheduling.
Other typical applications are timetabling and crew rotation or personnel
assignment, e.g. for hospitals and flight and railway companies. Besides,
constraints are used for electrical circuit design and verification, graphical
systems and user interfaces. For concrete examples see e.g. [225, 184, 195, 206].

Since we are dealing with constraints in *programming languages*, we briefly
review the application of constraints in this context.

One application area is *static analysis*. The aim of static program analysis
is to find out information about the runtime behaviour of a program at
compiletime. This information can be used to make programs safer (e.g. by type
checking or error correction), faster and shorter (both by optimization). Beside
other approaches, like fixpoint definitions, closure-condition based definitions,
rule-based approaches, and game-theoretics approaches, the constraint-based
paradigm has been applied to program analysis.

Constraint-based program analysis performs in two steps: First, the source
program is investigated and constraints are generated which describe possible
values computed by the program. In the second step, a constraint solver is
applied on the constraints to provide solutions which contain useful static
information about the program. This clear separation of constraint generation
and program analysis by constraint resolution is seen as an advantage of
the constraint-based approach over other approaches. It allows a clear mod-
ularization of analysis systems and supports understanding of the analyses,
reuse and specialization in this way. For example, the toolkit for building
constraint-based analyses BANSHEE [23, 132] and its predecessor, the Berkeley ANalysis Engine BANE [6], use this separation and can, thus, e.g. free the
analysis designer from writing a constraint solver. Besides this, constraints allow a simple but concise description of the program properties. The constraints
are usually local w.r.t. the parts of the analyzed program but contribute all
together to the overall global property to be analyzed.

The most widely used approaches to constraint-based program analysis are
based on set constraints and on equality constraints.

Set constraints [4, 90] describe relations between sets of terms of a free algebra. For a set C of constructors and a set X of variables, set expressions are defined by the following grammar, where $\alpha \in X$ and $c \in C$:

$$E ::= \alpha \mid \emptyset \mid c(E_1, \ldots, E_n) \mid E_1 \cup E_2 \mid E_1 \cap E_2 \mid \neg E_1$$

There are several extensions, like projections and function spaces (primarily used in the analysis of functional programming languages).

Set constraints allow one to describe all kinds of data types commonly used in programming. Aiken [5] illustrates this by expressing some classical program analysis problems, i.e. data flow analysis, type inference, and closure analysis, using set constraints as the common language.

It is decidable whether a conjunction of set constraints is satisfiable, and all solutions can be finitely presented. Respective resolution algorithms can in general be computationally expensive. However, certain restrictions allow one to improve this situation (cf. [4, 174] for further references).

Early applications of set constraints in program analyses were used for the optimization of LISP programs by eliminating runtime type checks [192] and to reduce reference count operations at garbage collection [123]. Examples of the use of set constraints for type inferencing in functional programs are [159, 7, 8, 89, 151]. For logic programs the first set-based analysis was by Mishra [158]. Other set-based approaches to the analysis of logic programs e.g. with respect to types, termination, and partially instantiated structures, are [90, 91, 92, 87]. An example of a set-based analysis of concurrent constraint programs with the aim of a static prediction of the runtime error "deadlock or failure" is [182]. Analysis of imperative or object-oriented program aspects using set constraints are discussed e.g. in [63, 59, 56, 121].

Many other constraint-based analyses rely on *equality constraints*. The Hindley-Milner type inference system [50, 156] is a classical example. Other, more recent examples are [214, 93, 43]. While equality constraints can be solved via unification in nearly linear time and, thus, scale well to large programs, they are often less precise than set constraints, because they cannot model the direction of the value flow in a program. In contrast, methods based on set inclusion constraints are quite precise, but often inefficient in practice. [58] describes a framework for constraint-based program analyses that allows one to embed terms and set expressions within each other and thus to combine set inclusion constraints and equality constraints over terms. The authors discuss the improved efficiency and show applications for ML.

Other constraint domains applied in program analysis include *finite domain*, *Boolean* and *arithmetic constraints*. For example, [168] uses finite domain constraints or Boolean constraints, resp., for the analysis of logic programs w.r.t. non-termination. The mode inference system of MERCURY described in [173] is based on mapping each predicate to a system of Boolean constraints. Set-based analysis can be extended to produce accurate information on numeric ranges [88], e.g. for eliminating array bounds checks and for array data dependence analysis.

Besides optimization and (type) error detection, one application of program analysis which developed into a proper research area is *recovery from and explanation of errors*. In particular, the constraint-based approach supports these applications because of the partitioning of the analysis process into constraint generation and solution. Such approaches may, thus, work on the complete set or on subsets of the generated constraints e.g. to find out about conflicting subsets, and they may influence the order of constraint propagation. We enumerate some work in this area.

The automated error correction system KIMA [10] for concurrent logic programs builds on the mode system [43] of MODED FLAT GHC which uses equality constraints (see above). Another example is the HELIUM system [79, 86] (for a beginner-friendly variant of Haskell) which uses heuristics to determine the propagation order of constraints generated from the type analysis system. It allows one to improve type-error messages and even to suggest corrections in certain cases. *Explanation-based constraint programming* [124, 125] tries to find (minimal) sets of constraints justifying propagation events of the constraint solver, like value removal, bound update, or contradiction. The resulting constraint sets can be used for debugging purposes, automatic constraint relaxation, dynamic problem handling, and even to build new search algorithms.

An area related to program analysis is *test data generation* from program code. There are few constraint-based approaches in this field. The main idea is again to generate constraints from the program code and to solve them in a subsequent step, but now with the aim to obtain test data.

There are early approaches [186, 52] on FORTRAN (subsets) which use equality constraints or even some forms of linear constraints and rather simple constraint solving techniques. Consistency techniques and mixed-integer linear programming, resp., are used in [75] and [136] for test data generation for C programs.

Another promising approach is GLASSTT [163] for JAVA in which constraint generation can be parametrized by a test criterion; its solving mechanism is based on a solver manager which dynamically handles a cooperation of linear and non-linear constraint solvers. This approach has been adopted in [62] for an application to functional logic programs of the language CURRY [82]. The constraint solving for generating test cases was realized here by the narrowing-based execution mechanism of CURRY itself.

Chapter 5
Multiparadigm Constraint Programming Languages

The notion "*multiparadigm programming language*" refers to the integration of concepts and constructs of two or more paradigms such that the programmer can describe problems and their solutions in a mixed style using an appropriate view at any one time. This allows comfortable and efficient modeling, programming and solving of problems. For instance, to integrate a database application into a functional program, the user is best served if the functional language provides established database concepts and terminology. Another example is the description of scheduling tasks within an imperative program which is more appropriately done using e.g. constraint-based expressions rather than a pure imperative description.

Interest in multiparadigm programming languages and systems has grown in recent years (see e.g. [31, 60, 83, 84, 164] or the annual workshops on "Functional and (Constraint) Logic Programming" (WFLP) and on "Multiparadigm Programming with Object-Oriented Languages" (MPOOL)). One can observe approaches of a loose coupling of paradigm concepts on the one hand and languages with a tighter paradigm integration on the other hand. For example, the first class comprises the Microsoft software platform .NET with the standardized intermediate code CIL (Common Intermediate Language) as common base for .NET programming such that components written in different languages may interact. These languages may come from different paradigms, e.g. from imperative and object-oriented programming, like C#, C++, VISUAL BASIC .NET, and J#, from the functional paradigm, e.g. HASKELL.net, OPAL.net, sml.net or DOTLISP, or even from logic programming: PROLOG.NET. The approach described by Zave [232] is based on a similar idea, namely a loose coupling by concurrently, cooperatively working elements of the separate paradigms.

In the context of this book, we are interested in the second class, that is the tight integration of concepts from different paradigms in one language. Popular representatives are e.g. COMMON LISP with the COMMON LISP OBJECT SYSTEM (CLOS) for functional, imperative, and object-oriented programming, ADA for distributed, concurrent, imperative, and object-oriented programming, and AOP languages. While we mentioned the latter as a single paradigm in Section 3.2.7, in fact AOP languages may be considered as multiparadigm languages, because they integrate aspects into the paradigms of their host-languages.

There is a wide variety of multiparadigm programming languages. We will consider in particular *multiparadigm constraint programming languages* because the use of constraints for convenient description and efficient solution of problems has generated a remarkable increase of interest in and application of constraint-based programming in science and practice.

This chapter is structured as follows: In Section 5.1 we discuss paradigm integration by programming languages and libraries, in general. Sections 5.2 to 5.7 provide fundamentals and examples of particular paradigm combinations with constraints.

5.1 Language integration and programming libraries

In the tight integration of concepts from different programming paradigms, one distinguishes two main forms: The *language approach* and the *library approach*. We briefly sketch both and discuss their advantages and disadvantages.

The language approach directly allows a paradigm and language integration by creating a new language or by introducing new facilities and concepts into an existing language on both the syntactic *and* the semantic level.

This method is well suited for the realization of an actual and fine-grain paradigm integration. It is most appropriate for the exploration of new problem classes and new solution ideas. As an example of this, consider the integration of concurrency into (constraint) logic programming languages. While (constraint) logic programs describe search problems and their evaluation is based on a possibly complete exploration of the search-tree (also called *don't know non-determinism*), concurrent (constraint) logic programs describe applications as systems of communicating processes which pass through solely one branch of the search-tree and discard all other alternatives (*don't care non-determinism*). We discuss the underlying principles and ideas in detail in the Sections 5.2 and 5.3.

The drawback of the language approach is that extension of a language semantics is, in general, non-trivial and its development may demand a long period of time. Moreover, the process of acceptance of a new language or even a new paradigm in practice is much more complicated and questionable than that of a new programming library for an established language. Most of the systems discussed in the following sections are examples of the language approach, e.g. ECL^{i}PS^e-Prolog, AKL, Oz, Curry, Toy, CCFL, Kaleidoscope, and Turtle. They all come with a new or extended semantics.

The library approach enables the extension of an existing language based on programming libraries, where the language semantics and evaluation principles are not altered. The library approach allows one to *simulate programming concepts* of one paradigm within a language of another paradigm.

Macros, templates, overloading, and other concepts present in the base language, like classes in object-oriented languages or functions (e.g. in their role of closures) in functional languages, can support a smooth integration or emulation of foreign constructs. However, such an emulation will always lack the convenience and clearness of the original language realisation.

Examples from the constraint programming area are constraint libraries and toolkits for imperative and object-oriented languages (cf. Section 5.6), like the JAVA-library CHOCO or the C++-libraries GECODE, IBM ILOG Solver, and TURTLE++. Such constraint libraries are used to conveniently implement search and optimization problems within e.g. reactive applications, like flight or railway booking systems or even complete airport planning and scheduling systems including the "parking slot" or stand allocation of airplanes, schedules for departures, arrivals, and connecting flights, and airline crew scheduling.

To summarize, language extensions by libraries are suited for problem classes which are widely examined and whose instances can already be expressed in an appropriate way in the language itself. In contrast, the language approach is well suited for the exploration of new problem classes and new solution ideas.

In the following, we focus on particular paradigm integrations and refer to representatives of the language and library approaches, resp.

5.2 Constraint logic programming (CLP)

Constraint logic programming (CLP) augments logic programming by constraints. Although we introduce constraint logic programming *(CLP)* as a multiparadigm approach here, actually this is not completely true. The reason is twofold: First, CLP relies on a relatively simple extension of logic programming, such that logic programming can be considered as constraint programming. Therefore, and secondly, CLP can be considered as and, nowadays, *is* established as a separate paradigm itself.

Many (maybe most) logic programming systems provide constraints, e.g. ECL^{i}PS^e-PROLOG [1, 17], SICStus-PROLOG [205], CHIP [42], and GNU PROLOG [74]. They can be considered as representatives of the language approach.

The presentation of this section is taken from [106], Chap. 6, which is due to the author of this book. We refer to [106, 153, 119, 118] for detailed presentations of this paradigm.

Program 5.2.1 ECL^{i}PS^e-PROLOG: a diet menu

```
1    :- use_module(library(fd)).
2
3    lightmeal(A,M,D) :- 10 #>= I+J+K,
4        appetizer(A,I), main(M,J), dessert(D,K).
5
6    appetizer(pasta,4).
7    appetizer(radishes,1).
8
9    main(pork,11).
10   main(beef,7).
11
12   dessert(fruit,2).
13   dessert(icecream,6).
```

Constraint logic programming extends logic languages to include concepts from constraint programming. In the first place this means that the *syntax* of a logic language is extended by allowing constraints on the right-hand side of rules and in goals. These constraints are tell-constraints. Thus, from a (operationally) *semantical* point of view, the evaluation mechanism resolution is enhanced by collecting constraints in a *constraint store* and checking their satisfiability.

Definition 30 (constraint logic program) Let $\zeta = (\Sigma, \mathcal{D}, \mathcal{T}, X, Cons)$ be a constraint system. A **constraint logic program** P is a sequence of *clauses* of the form

$$Q :- Q_1, \ldots, Q_n.$$

where Q is an atom and Q_i, $i \in \{1, \ldots, n\}$, are atoms or constraints of $Cons$. A clause with $n > 0$ is called a *rule*. In case of $n = 0$ a clause has the form

$$Q.$$

and is called a *fact*.

A **goal** for a constraint logic program P has the form ?- $Q_1, \ldots, Q_m$. The expressions Q_i, $i \in \{1, \ldots, m\}$, are atoms or constraints.   ◁

Example 24 Program 5.2.1 is a simple CLP example taken from [72] and adapted for our presentation. This ECL^{i}PS^e-PROLOG program describes a diet menu consisting of an appetizer, a main meal, and a dessert. Six facts state calorific values for certain dishes. In line 1 it imports the finite domain constraint programming library. The only finite domain constraint of the program is 10 #>= I+J+K. The aim of a goal ?- $lightmeal(X,Y,Z)$. is to find appropriate dishes such that the overall calorific value does not exceed a value of 10.   ◇

Practical CLP systems not only allow one to use built-in constraints in rule bodies to restrict the variables' domains, but they enable the computation of concrete solutions and the optimization of solutions w. r. t. objective functions by specialized methods.

Example 25 Using ECL^{i}PS^e-PROLOG we can specify the sudoku problem of Example 12 as given in Program 5.2.2.

The predicate *sudoku* specifies the 9×9 grid with certain predefined values in the lines 4–14 and calls the predicate *sudokuConstraints* describing the typical constraints of this game. The constraint *Vars* :: 1..9 in line 20 restrict the values of the remaining positions to 1 to 9. The *alldifferent*-constraints in lines 22, 25, and 28 state that the values within each row, each column, and each of the nine 3×3 blocks must be different, where we used a built-in iterator construct *foreach*. Finally, in line 30 the *labeling* method instantiates the problem variables taking the constraints into account and searches for a concrete solution.

The transposition of the 9×9 grid and an appropriate transformation to get a list of lists representing the 3×3 squares are done using the PROLOG predicates *transpose* and *transform* whose definitions are left out in Program 5.2.2 but indicated by "..." in the program's last line.   ◇

In the following, let P be a constraint logic program. We presuppose a *constraint solver* for the constraints of ζ with the operations *solve$_\zeta$* and *simplify$_\zeta$*.

The *operational semantics* of CLP is an extension of the resolution principle of logic programming by constraint handling. Thus, we denote a *system state* by means of a pair $Z = \langle G, C \rangle$ consisting of a goal G (as for logic programming) and a conjunction of constraints $C \in \Delta Cons$, i. e. the constraint store. The constraint store C collects constraints and substitutions σ computed during resolution as equality constraints $\mathcal{E}(\sigma) = \bigwedge_{x/t \in \sigma}(x = t)$. The operational semantics is given by sequences of derivation steps $\mapsto_{c,\zeta,P}$ on system states (actually a *state transition system*).

Definition 31 (CLP-derivation relation $\mapsto_{c,\zeta,P}$)
Let $Z = \langle G, C \rangle = \langle \text{?-} R_1, \ldots, R_m., C \rangle$, $m \geq 1$, be a system state. The derivation relation $\mapsto_{c,\zeta,P}$ is composed of three subrelations:

- *unfold*: Let R_i be an atom. If there is a variant $A = Q :- Q_1, \ldots, Q_n.$, $n \geq 0$, of a clause in P, such that Z and A do not have a variable in common, and there exists a most general unifier σ of R_i and Q, i. e. $\sigma = mgu(R_i, Q)$, then it holds:

$$\langle G, C \rangle \mapsto_{c,unfold,\zeta,P}$$
$$\langle \text{?-} R_1 \wedge \ldots \wedge R_{i-1} \wedge \mathcal{E}(\sigma) \wedge Q_1 \wedge \ldots \wedge Q_n \wedge R_{i+1} \wedge \ldots \wedge R_m., C \rangle$$

Program 5.2.2 ECL^{i}PS^e-PROLOG: sudoku

```
1    :- use_module(library(fd)).
2
3    sudoku :-
4        L = [[_,_,8,   _,_,_,   6,_,_],
5             [_,4,_,    9,_,2,   _,5,_],
6             [_,_,_,    6,4,8,   _,_,_],
7
8             [_,3,9,    _,2,_,   1,7,_],
9             [_,1,_,    _,_,_,   _,3,_],
10            [_,8,5,    _,1,_,   2,6,_],
11
12            [_,_,_,    2,8,7,   _,_,_],
13            [_,6,_,    1,_,4,   _,8,_],
14            [_,_,2,    _,_,_,   5,_,_]],
15
16        sudokuConstraints(L).
17
18   sudokuConstraints(L) :-
19            flatten(L,Vars),
20            Vars :: 1..9,
21            % different row elements
22            ( foreach(List,L) do alldifferent(List) ),
23            transpose(L,TL),
24            % different column elements
25            ( foreach(List,TL) do alldifferent(List) ),
26            transform(L,Squares),
27            % different square elements
28            ( foreach(List,Squares) do alldifferent(List) ),
29            % solve by search
30            labeling(Vars).
31
32   ...
```

- *failure*: Let R_i be an atom. If there is no clause in P, such that an *unfold*-step on R_i is possible, then it holds:

$$\langle G, C \rangle \mapsto_{c,failure,\zeta,P} \langle \Box, false \rangle$$

- *propagate (1)*: Let R_i be a constraint. If $solve_\zeta(R_i \wedge C) \neq false$, then the following holds:

$$\langle G, C \rangle \mapsto_{c,propagate,\zeta,P} \langle ?\text{-}R_1 \wedge \ldots \wedge R_{i-1} \wedge R_{i+1} \wedge R_m \cdot, C' \rangle$$

where $simplify_\zeta(R_i \wedge C) = C'$, i.e. $\mathcal{D} \models \forall (R_i \wedge C \longleftrightarrow C')$.

- *propagate (2)*: Let R_i be a constraint. If R_i cannot be propagated to the store C, i.e. $solve_\zeta(R_i \wedge C) = false$ and $\mathcal{D} \models \neg \exists (R_i \wedge C)$, then

$$\langle G, C \rangle \mapsto_{c,propagate,\varsigma,P} \langle \Box, false \rangle.$$

The CLP-derivation relation $\mapsto_{c,\varsigma,P}$ is defined by

$$\mapsto_{c,\varsigma,P} \; = \; \mapsto_{c,unfold,\varsigma,P} \cup \mapsto_{c,failure,\varsigma,P} \cup \mapsto_{c,propagate,\varsigma,P} .$$

If P and ς are clear from the context, we just write $\mapsto_c$.   ◁

The relation $\mapsto_{c,propagate,\varsigma,P}$ realizes the propagation of constraints to the store using the satisfiability test and the simplification operation of the constraint solver. The relations $\mapsto_{c,unfold,\varsigma,P}$ and $\mapsto_{c,failure,\varsigma,P}$ implement SLD-resolution. Note, however, that unifiers generated during resolution are not immediately added to the store but added to the goal instead for a later propagation by $\mapsto_{c,propagate,\varsigma,P}$. It is possible to emulate SLD-derivations using CLP-derivations in a simple way (cf. [106]).

A CLP-derivation of a goal G starts with an empty constraint store $C = true$, i. e. from the *initial state* $\langle G, true \rangle$, and consists of a sequence of derivation steps. As for logic programming, CLP-derivations can be finite or infinite. We consider the results of *finite* CLP-derivations $\langle G, true \rangle \mapsto_c \langle G_1, C_1 \rangle \mapsto_c \ldots \mapsto_c \langle G_n, C_n \rangle$ such that no more derivation step is possible on $\langle G_n, C_n \rangle$.

There are two possible forms of final states: A state $\langle \Box, C \rangle$ with $C = false$ or with $C \neq false$ is called a *failed final state* and a *successful final state*, resp. Note that even for a successful final state $\langle \Box, C \rangle$ the constraint conjunction C of the store may be unsatisfiable in case of an incomplete solver. Such a solver may propagate a constraint c to its store C_i if the answer of the satisfiability test $solve_\varsigma(C_i, c)$ is *unknown*.

Definition 32 (answer) Let $\langle G_0, true \rangle = \langle G_0, C_0 \rangle \mapsto_c \ldots \mapsto_c \langle G_i, C_i \rangle \mapsto_c \ldots \mapsto_c \langle \Box, C_n \rangle$ be a finite derivation. An **answer** of a goal ?- G_0. is an expression which is equivalent to the formula $\exists_{-\widetilde{var(G_0)}} C_n$.   ◁

Example 26 Recall the diet problem of Program 5.2.1. Let us assume that, in general, $I, J, K \geq 0$ holds.

We consider a CLP-derivation of the goal ?- $lightmeal(X, Y, Z)$. A superscript n on a derivation step $\ldots \mapsto_c^n \ldots$ denotes an n-fold application. Line numbers of the rules from Program 5.2.1 applied in an *unfold*-step are marked as subscript (m), i. e. by $\ldots \mapsto_{c,unfold \ (m)} \cdots$

$\langle$?- $lightmeal(X, Y, Z)$., $true \rangle$

     $\mapsto_{c,unfold \ (3)}$

$\langle$?- $X{=}A, \ Y{=}M, \ Z{=}D,$
     10 #>= $I{+}J{+}K$, $appetizer(A, I)$, $main(M, J)$, $dessert(D, K)$.,

$true \rangle$

     $\mapsto_{c,propagate}^3$

$\langle$?- 10 #>= $I{+}J{+}K$, $appetizer(A, I)$, $main(M, J)$, $dessert(D, K)$.,

$X=A \land Y=M \land Z=D \rangle$

$\longmapsto_{c,propagate}$

$\langle ?- \; appetizer(A,I), \; main(M,J), \; dessert(D,K).,$

$10 \; \#>= \; I+J+K \land X=A \land Y=M \land Z=D \rangle$

$\longmapsto_{c,unfold}$ (7)

$\langle ?- \; A=radishes, \; I=1, \; main(M,J), \; dessert(D,K).,$

$10 \; \#>= \; I+J+K \land X=A \land Y=M \land Z=D \rangle$

$\longmapsto^2_{c,propagate}$

$\langle ?- \; main(M,J), \; dessert(D,K).,$

$9 \; \#>= \; J+K \land X=radishes \land A=radishes \land I=1 \land Y=M \land Z=D \rangle$

$\longmapsto_{c,unfold}$ (10) $\cdots \longmapsto^2_{c,propagate}$

$\langle ?- \; dessert(D,K).,$

$2 \; \#>= \; K \land X=radishes \land A=radishes \land I=1 \land Y=beef \land M=beef \land J=7 \land Z=D \rangle$

$\longmapsto_{c,unfold}$ (12) $\cdots \longmapsto^2_{c,propagate}$

$\langle ?- \; \Box, \; C_{final} \rangle$ with

$C_{final} = (X=radishes \land A=radishes \land I=1 \land Y=beef \land M=beef \land J=7 \land$
$\qquad\qquad Z=fruit \land D=fruit \land K=2)$

The latter state is a successful final state. The constraint conjunction of the store is satisfiable. An answer of the goal $?- lightmeal(X,Y,Z).$ is

$$Answer = (X=radishes) \land (Y=beef) \land (Z=fruit) \text{ with} \qquad \Diamond$$

$\mathcal{D} \vDash \forall \; X,Y,Z. \; (Answer \longleftrightarrow \exists \; A,I,M,J,D,K. \; C_{final}).$

The *declarative semantics* associates answers of CLP-derivations and solutions of goals. We need the following notion: A constraint solver is *theory-complete* [118] if for every constraint $c \in Cons$ holds:

$solve_\varsigma(c) = false$, iff $\mathcal{T} \vDash \neg \exists c$ and
$solve_\varsigma(c) = true$, iff $\mathcal{T} \vDash \exists c$.

A *search-tree* for a CLP goal G representing all possible derivations of G is constructed as for a logic program (see Section 3.2.4 and [106]).

Lemma 3 (soundness and completeness of CLP-derivations, [119, 118]) *Let P be a constraint logic program, let G be a goal.*

1. *If G has a successful derivation (i. e. a derivation with successful final state) with answer c, then $P^{\leftrightarrow}, \mathcal{T} \vDash \forall (c \longrightarrow G)$.*

2. *If G has a finite search-tree with answers $c_1, \ldots, c_n$, then $P^{\leftrightarrow}, \mathcal{T} \vDash \forall (G \longleftrightarrow \bigvee_{i \in \{1,\ldots,n\}} c_i)$.*

3. *Let $c \in \Delta Cons$ be a constraint conjunction. If $P^{\leftrightarrow}, \mathcal{T} \models \forall(c \longrightarrow G)$, then there are derivations of G with answers $c_1, \ldots, c_n$, such that the following holds: $\mathcal{T} \models \forall(c \longrightarrow \bigvee_{i \in \{1, \ldots, n\}} c_i)$.*

4. *If G has a finitely failing search-tree, then $P^{\leftrightarrow}, \mathcal{T} \models \neg \exists G$.*

5. *If $P^{\leftrightarrow}, \mathcal{T} \models \neg \exists G$, then G finitely fails, i. e. we always get a finitely failing search-tree for G, for any fair literal selection rule and a theory-complete constraint solver.*

The soundness statements (1) and (2) correspond to Lemma 1(1) for logic programs. The completeness statement (3) is related to its counterpart Lemma 1(2); propositions (4) and (5) concern finitely failed search-trees and correspond to Lemma 2(1) and Lemma 2(2) for logic programs, resp. For a more detailed discussion and corresponding proofs we refer to [118, 119, 106].

Practical constraint logic programming systems like ECL^{i}PS^e-PROLOG or SICStus-PROLOG use the same goal and rule selection strategies as discussed for logic programming systems in Section 3.2.4. That is, the leftmost subgoal is always chosen for derivation and the clauses are searched from top to bottom in the program. Moreover, the search-tree of a goal is traversed using *depth-first search* and *backtracking*.

5.3 Concurrent constraint logic programming (CCLP)

Concurrent constraint logic programming (CCLP) arose from concurrent logic programming [203]. However, one may consider this paradigm also as an extension of CLP by concurrency. The following presentation partially relies on [106], Chap. 7, which is due to the author of this work. We also refer to [106] for many application examples.

CCLP relies on the *concurrent constraint model* of Saraswat [200, 199]. The main idea is to describe cooperatively working processes or agents, which communicate and synchronise by means of a common *constraint store*. Thus, on the one hand, processes may propagate constraints to the store as in CLP. On the other hand, the processes synchronize by questioning the store about the entailment of constraints. Clauses of a concurrent constraint logic program include a guard which is partitioned into *ask-constraints* for checking their entailment by the store and *tell-constraints* for propagation to the store.

Definition 33 (concurrent constraint logic program) Consider a constraint system $\zeta = (\Sigma, \mathcal{D}, \mathcal{T}, X, Cons)$. A ***concurrent constraint logic program*** P is a sequence of *clauses* of the form

$$\underbrace{Q}_{\text{head}} \; :- \; \underbrace{A_1, \ldots, A_n}_{\text{ask}} : \underbrace{T_1, \ldots, T_m}_{\text{tell}} \mid \underbrace{Q_1, \ldots, Q_p}_{\text{body}}.$$

Program 5.3.1 A producer-consumer setting

```
1    produce(X)  :-  true  :  X=[]     |  .
2    produce(X)  :-  true  :  X=[1|Z]  |  produce(Z).
3    consume(X)  :-  X=[]     :  true  |  .
4    consume(X)  :-  X=[1|Z]  :  true  |  consume(Z).
```

---

where Q and Q_k, $k \in \{1, \dots, p\}$ are atoms, and A_i, $i \in \{1, \dots, n\}$, and T_j, $j \in \{1, \dots, m\}$, are constraints of $\mathcal{C}ons$.

The expression $A_1, \dots, A_n : T_1, \dots, T_m$ is the *guard* of the clause (or rule). It consists of the *ask-constraints* $A_1, \dots, A_n$ and the *tell-constraints* $T_1, \dots, T_m$. The *head* Q of a clause has the form $p(X_1, \dots, X_h)$, where X_i, $i \in \{1, \dots, h\}$, are different variables.

A **goal** has the form

$$?- B_1, \dots, B_r.$$

where the literals B_i, $i \in \{1, \dots, r\}$, are atomic formulae. ◁

Example 27 Program 5.3.1 describes a producer and a consumer of a potentially infinite list of ones. We discuss its reading in Example 28 in connection with the operational semantics of CCLP. ◇

In the following, let P be a concurrent constraint logic program over the constraint system ζ.

We consider the *operational semantics*. The evaluation of a goal comprises a process for each of its subgoals. The processes communicate over a common store. The rule choice for a process is controlled by the guards of all rules with matching rule heads. There is no predefined order for the rule choice. Instead all rules compete and one rule is chosen non-deterministically, if the ask-constraints of its guard are entailed by the store *and* the tell-constraints of its guard are satisfiable in conjunction with the store.

The operational semantics is formally given by means of a derivation relation on system states. As for CLP, a *system state* is represented by means of a pair $Z = \langle G, C \rangle$ consisting of a goal G and the constraint store C. The *initial state* for a goal G is $\langle G, true \rangle$.

Definition 34 (derivation relation $\mapsto_{cc, \zeta, P}$)
Let $Z = \langle G, C \rangle$ with $G = ?- R_1, \dots, R_m.$, $m \geq 1$, be a state, where R_i, $i \in \{1, \dots, m\}$, is an atom. If

1. there is a variant $K = H :- A : T \mid Q.$ of a clause in P, such that Z and K do not have a variable in common and R_i and the clause head H are unifiable with a most general unifier σ,

2. the ask-constraints A of the guard of K are entailed by the store C *(ask)*: $\mathcal{D} \models \forall(C \longrightarrow \exists \tilde{X}(\mathcal{E}(\sigma) \wedge A))$ with $X = var(K)$, and

3. the tell-constraints T of the guard of K are satisfiable in conjunction with C (tell): $\mathcal{D} \models \exists(\mathcal{E}(\sigma) \wedge C \wedge A \wedge T)$,

then there is a derivation step

$$\langle G, C \rangle \mapsto_{cc,\varsigma,P} \langle ?-R_1 \wedge \ldots \wedge R_{i-1} \wedge Q \wedge R_{i+1} \wedge \ldots \wedge R_m., C' \rangle$$

where $\mathcal{D} \models \forall((\mathcal{E}(\sigma) \wedge C \wedge A \wedge T) \longleftrightarrow C')$.

If P and ς are clear from the context, then we write $\mapsto_{cc}$.   ◁

Example 28 Consider Program 5.3.1 and a goal
?- *produce(A)*, *consume(A)*. A derivation sequence might start as follows:

$\langle ?-$ *produce(A)*, *consume(A)*., *true* $\rangle$

    $\mapsto_{cc,(2)} \langle ?-$ *produce(Z)*, *consume(A)*., $A=[1|Z] \wedge \ldots \rangle$

    $\mapsto_{cc,(2)} \langle ?-$ *produce(Z1)*, *consume(A)*., $A=[1,1|Z1] \wedge \ldots \rangle$

    $\mapsto_{cc}$ ...

In the derivation sequence, we underline the goals with applicable rules. In the initial situation, for *produce(A)* either of the rules (lines 1 and 2) could have been applied. The ask-constraints of both clauses are **true** and, thus, always entailed. The tell-constraints are satisfiable with the store because of the unbound variable A. Actually, for an unbound buffer variable, the producer can always produce ones independent from the consumer as can be seen exemplarily by the second step.

In contrast, the ask-constraints of the guard of the consumer rules check for a binding of the buffer variable. To apply a rule, the buffer must either be bound to an empty list "[]" (line 3) or to a list starting with "1" (line 4). Thus, in the initial situation the consumer *suspends* because there is no applicable rule.

The derivation sequence may continue now by a number of consumer and producer steps. Note however, that the consumer suspends if the producer did not provide a value to the buffer. Of course, in contrast to the example derivation sequence given below, the producer-consumer-cooperation may be infinitely prolonged.

    ...

    $\mapsto_{cc,(2)} \langle ?-$ *produce(Z1)*, *consume(A)*., $A=[1,1|Z1] \wedge \ldots \rangle$

    $\mapsto_{cc,(4)} \langle ?-$ *produce(Z1)*, *consume(Z2)*., $Z2=[1|Z1] \wedge \ldots \rangle$

    $\mapsto_{cc,(2)} \langle ?-$ *produce(Z3)*, *consume(Z2)*., $Z2=[1,1|Z3] \wedge \ldots \rangle$

    $\mapsto_{cc,(4)} \langle ?-$ *produce(Z3)*, *consume(Z4)*., $Z4=[1|Z3] \wedge \ldots \rangle$

    $\mapsto_{cc,(4)} \langle ?-$ *produce(Z3)*, *consume(Z5)*., $Z5=Z3 \wedge \ldots \rangle$

    $\mapsto_{cc,(1)} \langle ?-$ *consume(Z5)*., $Z5=[] \wedge \ldots \rangle$

    $\mapsto_{cc,(3)} \langle ?-$ □, $Z5=[] \wedge \ldots \rangle$ ◊

While for the derivation relation $\mapsto_c$ for constraint logic programs (cf. Definition 31) there were three subrelations, actually $\mapsto_{c,unfold}$, $\mapsto_{c,failure}$, and $\mapsto_{c,propagate}$, the relation $\mapsto_{cc}$ for concurrent programs is defined unitarily. Constraint propagation and unfolding of rules are merged; failure is not taken into consideration, so that a derivation sequence may just end with a non-empty goal G.

We distinguish two forms of *final states* $\langle G, C \rangle$, i.e. states for which no derivation step is possible any more: A state $\langle \Box, C \rangle$ is a *successful final state*. All other final states are *deadlocked*. We call a derivation with deadlocked final state a *deadlocked derivation*. Note, that for every final state $\langle \Box, C \rangle$ in CCLP holds $\mathcal{D} \vDash \exists C$. This is caused by the fact that for every constraint c' added to the constraint store C' the satisfiability of $c' \wedge C'$ is ensured (*tell*).[4]

Let the notion *answer* of a CCLP-derivation of a goal be defined analogously to Definition 32, where we just replace $\mapsto_c$ by $\mapsto_{cc}$.

To discuss soundness and completeness results, we interpret concurrent constraint logic programs as follows: The symbols ":", "|", and "," on the right-hand side of rules are considered to be conjunction operators "$\wedge$". In this way, we obtain predicate logic formulae.

Lemma 4 (soundness of CCLP-derivations [149, 119]) *Let P be a concurrent constraint logic program, let G be a goal. If G has a derivation with answer c, then $P^{\leftrightarrow}, \mathcal{T} \vDash \forall(c \longrightarrow G)$.*

This is according to the soundness results for logic and constraint logic programs in Lemma 1(1) and Lemma 3(1), resp.

Concerning completeness, note that in CCLP we consider only *one* derivation sequence, in contrast to the generation of a complete search-tree by backtracking as for (C)LP. Moreover, concurrent processes may intentionally work infinitely long (for reactive systems) and the rule choice is non-deterministic. To allow a completeness statement, we use the notion of a *determinate* program.

Definition 35 (determinate program [149, 119]) *A concurrent constraint logic program P is **determinate** if every reachable state $\langle G, C \rangle$ is determinate. A state is determinate if for every chosen goal there is at most one applicable rule.* ◁

That is, if a program P is determinate, derivations which are not deadlocked differ only in the order of rule applications.

Lemma 5 (completeness of CCLP-derivations [149, 119]) *Let P be a determinate concurrent constraint logic program, let G be a goal with at least one fair derivation. Let $c \in \Delta Cons$ be a constraint conjunction. If $P^{\leftrightarrow}, \mathcal{T} \vDash \forall(c \longrightarrow G)$ and $\mathcal{T} \vDash \exists c$ hold, then every derivation of G is successful and has an answer c' with $\mathcal{T} \vDash \forall(c \longrightarrow \exists c')$.*

---

[4] In Definition 34 we presuppose that entailment and satisfiability can be checked completely (cf. [119]). If this is not the case or the associated solver is incomplete, we just get more deadlocked final states.

This result corresponds to Lemma 1(2) and Lemma 3(3) for logic and constraint logic programs, resp.

In CCLP, one considers only one possible derivation sequence of a search-tree. The rule choice is protected by means of a guard, and once a rule is chosen this choice cannot be undone. This behaviour is called *committed choice* or *don't care non-determinism*, while considering the complete search-tree as in (C)LP is described by the term *don't know non-determinism*.

In our implementation of CCLP by Definition 34 the relation $\mapsto_{cc}$ presupposes the entailment of the ask-constraints by *and* the satisfiability of the tell-constraints in conjunction with the store. This procedure is costly but ensures that the constraint store always remains satisfiable. This form of the propagation operation is also called *atomic tell*. There is an alternative CCLP model, called *eventual tell*, where for the rule choice only the entailment of the ask-constraints by the store is checked. Thus, it may happen that a rule with incompatible tell-constraints is chosen which yields a suspending (or failing) derivation.

Representatives of the CCLP paradigm are e.g. GUARDED HORN CLAUSES (GHC) [218], CONCURRENT PROLOG [202], PARLOG [78], AKL [120], and Oz [212, 165]. Also the constraint-based functional language CCFL (cf. Chapter 6) relies on the concurrent constraint model. All these examples are exemplars of the language approach (cf. Section 5.1). The languages GHC, PARLOG, AKL, Oz, and CCFL (cf. Chapter 6) are based on the *eventual tell*, while CONCURRENT PROLOG relies on the *atomic tell*.

5.4 Functional logic programming (FLP)

Functional logic programming languages amalgamate concepts from the functional and from the logic paradigms. Hanus [80] gives an overview on functional logic programming, from which we extract the following observation: "In comparison with pure functional languages, functional logic languages have more expressive power due to the availability of features like function inversion, partial data structures, and logic variables. In comparison with pure logic languages, functional logic languages have a more efficient operational behaviour since functions allow more deterministic evaluations than predicates."

While syntactically a functional logic program looks like a functional program, the difference lies in the evaluation mechanism. Functional logic programs allow the solution of *equality constraints over functional expressions* (as tell-constraints) using narrowing [80, 14, 81] and residuation [210, 9]. Languages based on the former evaluation principle are e.g. BABEL [162], CURRY [82], BROOKS [104], and FCLL (in the context of META-S, cf. Sections 7.2.2 and 7.3.2), while Oz [165, 211] and ESCHER [138] rely on the latter. They typically follow the language approach and they have an extended semantics w.r.t. functional or logic languages, resp. The language CCFL (cf. Chapter 6) is a constraint-based functional language and uses the evaluation principle residuation for handling free variables in functional expressions, as described in this section.

In the following, we presuppose a signature $\Sigma = (S, F, R)$, where $R = \emptyset$ and F is partitioned into the disjoint subsets Δ of constructors and Γ of defined functions. Let X be a set of variables. Let the syntax of functional logic programs be defined as for functional programs (cf. Definition 13).

At first, we consider the *operational semantics* by *narrowing*.

Definition 36 (narrowing step) Let t be a term in $\mathcal{T}(F, X)$. Let P be a functional logic program.

A **narrowing step** $t \leadsto_{l \to r, p, \sigma} t'$ is defined as follows: a term t is narrowable to a term t' if there is a non-variable position p in t, i.e. $t|_p \notin X$, $l \to r$ is a new variant of a rule from P, $\sigma = mgu(t|_p, l)$, and $t' = \sigma(t[r]_p)$.

We write $t \leadsto_{l \to r, \sigma} t'$ and $t \leadsto_{\sigma} t'$ if p and/or the rule $l \to r$ are obvious from the context.   ◁

A functional logic computation is composed of a sequence of narrowing steps.

Example 29 Consider the program defining the addition of natural numbers in Example 8. In contrast to functional programming, using narrowing it is possible to reduce non-ground terms, i.e. terms containing variables.

Note, that variables in functional logic languages are typically denoted by strings starting with an upper letter (like in logic languages) in contrast to functional languages, where variables start with lower letters.

In order to solve the equality constraint $add(s(A),B) = s(s(0))$ we apply narrowing. This leads e.g. to the following evaluation sequence, where the reduced subterms are underlined:

$\underline{add(s(A),B)} = s(s(0))$

$\leadsto_{(2),\{X1/A,\ Y1/B\}}\ s(\underline{add(A,B)}) = s(s(0))$

$\leadsto_{(1),\{A/0,\ X2/B\}}\ s(\underline{B}) = s(s(0))$

Thus, a solution of the initial equality constraint is given by the substitution $\sigma = \{A/0,\ B/s(0)\}$ which we gain from the composition of the substitutions of the derivation sequence and from the unification of $s(B)$ and $s(s(0))$ after the last narrowing step.   ◇

Confluence of the rewrite system of the functional logic program is essential for completeness. Thus, the rules of functional logic programs must usually satisfy particular conditions, e.g. linearity of the left-hand sides, no free variables on the right-hand sides and (weak) non-ambiguity for lazy languages (cf. [80]). Furthermore, as for functional programming languages, different evaluation strategies are possible which have been discussed in depth in [80, 14, 81].

An alternative evaluation principle is *residuation*. It is based on the idea to delay function calls until a deterministic evaluation is possible. To allow non-deterministic search, however, there are also *generating* rules to be evaluated with resolution or narrowing. Note that residuation is an incomplete evaluation principle.

Example 30 Consider again the addition of natural numbers as given in Example 8. Additionally we presuppose generating rules for natural numbers in a logic programming style:

```
3  nat(0).
4  nat(s(X))  :- nat(X).
```

We want to evaluate the expression $add(A,s(0)) = s(s(0))$ & $nat(A)$ using residuation. The operator "&" stands for the *concurrent* evaluation of the subexpressions.

Initially, the evaluation of $add(A,s(0)) = s(s(0))$ by residuation suspends, because both rules (1) and (2) match. Thus, we continue with the evaluation of the second expression $nat(A)$ using resolution. We underline reduced subterms.

$add(A,s(0)) = s(s(0))$ & $\underline{nat(A)}$
$\rightsquigarrow_{(4),\{A/s(X1)\}} add(s(X1),s(0)) = s(s(0))$ & $nat(X1)$
$\rightsquigarrow \ldots$

Now, for the leftmost subterm a deterministic evaluation using rule (2) is possible:

$\underline{add(s(X1),s(0))} = s(s(0))$ & $nat(X1)$
$\rightsquigarrow_{(2),\{X2/X1,\ Y2/s(0)\}} s(add(X1,s(0))) = s(s(0))$ & $nat(X1)$
$\rightsquigarrow \ldots$

In the next step, again the evaluation control switches to the second expression and returns to the first as soon as a deterministic rule choice is enabled.

$s(add(X1,s(0))) = s(s(0))$ & $\underline{nat(X1)}$
$\rightsquigarrow_{(3),\{X1/0\}} s(\underline{add(0,s(0))}) = s(s(0))$
$\rightsquigarrow_{(1),\{X3/s(0)\}} s(s(0)) = s(s(0))$

A solution of the constraint conjunction $add(A,s(0)) = s(s(0))$ & $nat(A)$ is, thus, $A = s(0)$. ◊

5.5 Constraint functional logic programming (CFLP)

Functional and functional logic languages can be extended further by guarding the rules with sets of constraints. This yields *constraint functional (logic) programming*.

Again, we consider a constraint system $\zeta = (\Sigma, \mathcal{D}, \mathcal{T}, X, \mathcal{C}ons)$ with $\Sigma = (S, F, R)$, where F is partitioned into a set Δ of constructors and a set Γ of defined functions.

Definition 37 (constraint functional logic program)
A **constraint functional logic program** P over Σ is given by a finite set of rules of the form

$$f(t_1, \ldots, t_n) \to t \text{ where } G$$

where $f \in \Gamma$, $t_i \in \mathcal{T}(\Delta, X)$, $t \in \mathcal{T}(F, X)$, and $G \subset \mathcal{C}ons$ denotes a set of basic constraints over Σ and X. $\lhd$

A first step from functional logic programming (cf. Section 5.4) in the direction of *constraint* functional logic programming was the introduction of equality constraints on functional expressions in the part $\ldots$ **where** G of the rule. These constraints were solved recursively by narrowing; the extended operational principle was called *conditional narrowing* (see [80] for a discussion and further references). BABEL [162] is a functional logic language with conditional equations.

An extension of conditional equations by constraints of other constraint domains yielded *constraint functional logic programming languages*. Constraint functional logic programs are evaluated using *constraint narrowing* [144]. A term t is narrowed to a term t' using a rule of a program P while the constraints of the constraint part $\ldots$ **where** G of the rule are collected and checked for satisfiability.

We use this principle for the language FCLL which we integrate into the solver cooperation system META-S as discussed in Sections 7.2.2 and 7.3.2. A *narrowing step with constraints* is applied on a subterm of an equality constraint e and yields an updated equation and a constraint conjunction to be handled by external constraint solvers.

Definition 38 (narrowing step with constraints) Let e be an equation, let P be a constraint functional logic program.
If in e there is a non-variable subterm t at position p, that is, $e|_p = t$ with $t \notin X$, a new variant $(l \to r \text{ where } G)$ of a rule in P, and a substitution σ, such that $\sigma = mgu(t, l)$, then $e \leadsto_{c,\sigma} (\sigma(e[r]_p), \sigma(G))$ is a ***narrowing step with constraints***. It yields the new equation $\sigma(e[r]_p)$ together with the instantiated constraint $\sigma(G)$. $\lhd$

Other approaches using constraint narrowing include the language TOY [57, 217] for which the integration of different arithmetic constraint domains has been examined over the recent years and OPENCFLP [131] which integrates lazy narrowing and collaborative constraint solving over different domains. The integration of linear constraints over real numbers into the functional logic language CURRY is shown in [148].

An integration of functional (logic) programming and constraints can, however, also be realized based on a different (syntax and) semantics as can be seen e.g. by the residuation-based languages Oz [165, 211] and CCFL (cf. Chapter 6) and by the functional constraint library FACILE [32].

5.6 Constraint imperative programming (CIP)

With constraint programming concepts gaining attraction in practice, interest arose in integrating constraints into imperative and object-oriented languages. What is now traditionally called *Constraint imperative programming (CIP)*, actually comprises the combination of concepts from the constraint-based paradigm with procedural languages on the one side and with object-oriented languages, like JAVA or C++, on the other side.

Both the imperative (including object-oriented languages) and the constraint-based paradigms are specific to certain application areas. Imperative languages allow a precise and efficient modeling of the behaviour of real-world processes. They are very popular and widely used in practice. Constraints, in contrast, have a clear mathematical foundation, support elegant modeling and come with efficient solution mechanisms.

The combination of concepts from both paradigms is, however, intricate, because imperative programs depend on a global machine state while constraints as formulae are independent of time and state. As a consequence, *constraint-based* and other *declarative languages* widely separate the declarative problem description in the user program on the one side and the program evaluation or computation of solutions by the language evaluation mechanism on the other side. A declarative paradigm combination can, thus, often be realized on a clear mathematical and operational basis. In contrast, in *imperative languages* the user is responsible for describing both in one program, i. e. the problem and its solution, and these are, moreover, strongly interwoven which makes a combination with declarative constraints challenging.

The notion *constraint imperative programming* was originally coined by Freeman-Benson [70] to cover all languages with concepts from the constraint-based and the imperative and object-oriented programming paradigms. The following example originates from [143].

Example 31 (cf. [102]) Program 5.6.1 uses a pure imperative approach to describe the positioning of a graphical element in a user interaction. The graphic can be dragged with the mouse inside certain borders. By pressing a mouse-button its vertical coordinate y is adapted within a minimum and a maximum range. This description reflects the temporal – i.e. imperative – behaviour but also requires declarative properties, like the range restrictions, to be expressed imperatively. They are ensured by explicit tests which must be performed in each pass within a while-loop as long as the button is pressed.

In contrast, Program 5.6.2 gives an equivalent CIP implementation in the syntax of the CIP library TURTLE++. The initial instantiation of y by a so-called *preferred value* *mouse.y* gives an orientation for the optimization w.r.t.

Program 5.6.1 A user interface example in imperative style

```
1   while (mouse.pressed)
2   {                                    // message  processing  is  left  out
3     int y = mouse.y;
4     if (y > border.max)
5       y = border.max;
6     if (y < border.min)
7       y = border.min;
8     draw_element (fix_x, y, graphic);
9   }
```

Program 5.6.2 The user interface example using the CIP library TURTLE++

```
1   while (mouse.pressed)
2   {
3     constrained<int> y = mouse.y;
4     require (y >= border.min && y <= border.max);
5     draw_element (fix_x, y(), graphic);
6   }
```

---

the required constraints. It will be overwritten by *border.min* or *border.max*, resp., in case the mouse exceeds a border. Program 5.6.2 is not only shorter, but expresses the relationship between the border-object and the y-coordinate in exactly the way a programmer would think about it.   ◇

Languages of the CIP paradigm are the constraint-based object-oriented language KALEIDOSCOPE [142] used to specify constraints between attributes of objects, a language combination LEDA [36] for imperative and relational programming, ALMA-0 [16] which is an extension of MODULA-2 by logic elements and backtracking, and TURTLE [77]. Besides, there are a number of popular CIP representatives following the *library approach*, like the CHOCO constraint solver [44] on finite domain constraints written in JAVA, GECODE [73] for finite domain constraints and finite set constraints implemented in C++ (with bindings to several languages), the C++ library IBM ILOG Solver [112] for different constraint domains, and the C++ library TURTLE++ [102] as has been used in Program 5.6.2.

In the following, we discuss the *Turtle* family as an example of CIP. We sketch popular examples of constraint-based object-oriented programming libraries in Section 5.6.2.

5.6.1 The Turtle family for CIP

TURTLE is a multiparadigm programming language enabling procedural programming enhanced by constraints. The C++ library TURTLE++ inherited the main ideas from the TURTLE language but was extended for smooth integration into C++. While both approaches rely on the same general ideas and concepts for the integration of constraints into the imperative paradigm, they differ in many details and may even support a different programming style for particular applications. We only sketch their common concepts and refer to [102, 76, 77, 106] for details.

In both approaches, four concepts enable constraint programming in an imperative context: *constraint variables*, *constraint statements*, *user-defined constraints*, and *constraint solvers*.

Constraint variables are distinguished from *imperative variables*. While values of normal, imperative variables are given by assignments as usual, constraint variables are determined by constraints.

As an example consider the definition of the Send-More-Money problem in Program 5.6.3. This is a crypto-arithmetic puzzle such that the equation *send + more = money* holds and each letter of *s, e, n, d, m, o, r, y* represents a different digit. The constraint variables *s, e, n, d, m, o, r, y* are introduced by certain data type annotations, e.g. a constraint integer variable is declared with type ! *int* (cf. lines 6–8). An initialization of a constraint variable (not shown in the example) is possible but can be overwritten by following constraints. Apart from that, both constraint and imperative variables are handled throughout the program in the same way.

Constraint statements allow the programmer to place constraints on constraint variables. A constraint statement consists of a constraint conjunction introduced by the keyword **require** and of a sequence of statements, called the body. The constraints in the conjunction are enforced, i.e. they must hold, as long as the body executes. While in the TURTLE language a particular solution is computed immediately when the body of a constraint statement is entered, TURTLE++ delays the computation of particular values for the variables until they are actually needed, e.g. for a function call. There are **require**-statements without a body, such that their constraints hold as long as the constraint variables they constrain exist.

In our example, the **require**-statement establishes constraints on the constraint variables in lines 9–14 and prints a solution of these in its body (lines 16–18).

The third concept of TURTLE is *user-defined constraints* which abstract over constraints to support re-usability of frequently used logical combinations of constraints. User-defined constraints imperatively generate a declarative construct, i.e. a conjunction of constraints.

Specifications of the user-defined constraints *domain* and *alldifferent* as used in Program 5.6.3 were shown in the Programs 4.3.2 and 4.3.3, resp.

Program 5.6.3 TURTLE: the Send-More-Money problem

```
 1   module smm;
 2   import io;
 3    ...
 4
 5   fun main(args: list of string): int
 6     var s: !int;
 7      ...
 8     var y: !int;
 9     require domain(s,0,9) and domain(e,0,9) and ...
10        domain(y,0,9) and
11        alldifferent([s,e,n,d,m,o,r,y]) and
12        (s * 1000 + e * 100 + n * 10 + d) +
13        (m * 1000 + o * 100 + r * 10 + e) =
14        (m * 10000 + o * 1000 + n * 100 + e * 10 + y)
15     in
16        io.put ("s="); io.put (!s); io.nl ();
17         ...
18        io.put ("y="); io.put (!y); io.nl ();
19     end;
20     return 0;
21   end;
```

The parameters of the *domain*-constraint (cf. Program 4.3.2, line 1) are the constraint variable *v* and the imperative variables *min* and *max*, where the latter must be bound to ground values if the *domain*-constraint is called. Similarly, the *alldifferent*-constraint abstraction receives a list of constraint variables and places inequality constraints on each pair of list elements (cf. Program 4.3.3). The require-statements appear without a body in these abstractions, such that their constraints shall hold globally in the subsequent code.

Constraint solvers have been integrated into TURTLE and TURTLE++, resp., to ensure satisfiability or compute solutions of constraints at runtime. The language TURTLE comprises a linear solver based on the indigo algorithm [29] and a finite domain constraint solver, while the TURTLE++ library contains a linear arithmetic solver using the simplex algorithm and a Boolean solver.

Both instances of the *Turtle* family allow the use of *constraint hierarchies* (not shown in the examples). Constraint hierarchies allow one to assign strength to individual constraints which represent their importance. The solver respects these strengths when solving the constraint store and tries to satisfy the most important constraints, even if that means that less important ones (preferential constraints) are left unsatisfied. Especially for over-constrained problems this is very useful.

Program 5.6.4 A magic-square problem using IBM ILOG Solver, cut-out from [113]

```
 1   // create environment
 2   IloEnv env;
 3   // step 3: initiate search
 4   try {
 5     // create model
 6     IloModel model(env);
 7     // step 1: declare variables
 8     ...
 9     IloIntVarArray square(env,n*n,1,n*n);
10     IloInt sum = n*(n*n+1)/2;
11     // step 2: declare constraints
12     model.add(IloAllDiff(env,square));
13     ...
14     // constraints on rows
15     for (i = 0; i < n; i++){
16       IloExpr exp(env);
17       for(j = 0; j < n; j++)
18         exp += square[n*i+j];
19       model.add(exp == sum);
20       exp.end();
21     }
22     ...
```

5.6.2 Constraints as objects

Constraint programming libraries based on object-oriented languages are very successful in practice. They typically model the CP concepts such as constraints, constraint stores, solvers, search spaces, and choice points by objects and define corresponding methods for constraint propagation, satisfiability checking, the generation of choice points, and the activation of search.

Program 5.6.4 shows a cut-out of a magic squares problem using the commercially very successful C++ library IBM ILOG Solver [112]. The program declares the problem constants and variables, i.e. an array *square* of n^2 elements ranging from 1 to n^2 and an integer value *sum* in lines 9–10. The problem constraints are given starting from line 12: First, an alldifferent constraint *IloAllDiff* states that the variables of the array *square* are all different from each other. Lines 15–21 create constraints on the rows of the array which state that the sums of the rows are all equal to the value *sum*. The rest of the program, where similar constraints are stated on the columns and the diagonals of the array and a search for solutions is activated, is left out here.

There are many libraries and toolkits extending languages like JAVA and C++ to support constraint programming as referenced above. Such CP libraries

Program 5.6.5 The 8-queens problem using IBM ILOG OPL

```
1   int n = 8;
2   var int queens[1..n] in 1..n;
3   solve {
4     forall(ordered i,j in 1..n) {
5       queens[i] <> queens[j];
6       queens[i] + i <> queens[j] + j;
7       queens[i] - i <> queens[j] - j
8     };
9   };
```

keep the programmer in a familiar language and offer the possibility to extend their functionalities e.g. by new problem-tailored search techniques.

On the negative side, the syntax drifts away from the mathematical description and becomes less readable due to the fact that things like environments, models, and even solvers must be handled explicitly in an object-oriented environment.

The Optimization Programming Language IBM ILOG OPL [112, 94] is built on top of the IBM ILOG Solver CP library and tries to overcome these problems. It is a domain-specific modeling language for mathematical programming and combinatorial optimization which allows one to use and specify constraints and solvers on the one side and search procedures and strategies on the other side.

OPL models are declarative: The following example demonstrates that, using OPL, we do not describe the solution process but instead the problem or its solutions, resp., in a mathematical form.

Example 32 Program 5.6.5 shows an OPL program describing the n-queens problem (cf. [195]). The goal is to place n (here 8) queens on an n×n chess board such that none of them would be able to attack another.

Since each column of the chess board must hold exactly one queen, it suffices to use a list *queens* of variables representing the columns. The values of the variables stand for the rows on which the queens are placed. The constraints in lines 4–8 describe that no two queens can attack each other.◊

5.7 Further constraint-based paradigms

We sketch three further approaches to multi-domain programming languages with constraints which may be considered as DSLs.

Constraint solver cooperation. The combination of constraint systems and the cooperation of constraint solvers is an established concept for improving efficiency and performance of constraint resolution. We go into detail w. r. t. this topic in Chapter 7, where we present the solver (and language) cooperation system META-S.

To provide an environment for structured programming, solver cooperations are typically integrated into a *host-language* which yields multiparadigm constraint programming languages as discussed in the sections above.

While the META-S approach pursues the idea to integrate languages into a system of cooperating solvers, other approaches typically come from the opposite point of view and extend a programming language by cooperative constraint evaluation. Host-languages of such approaches are mainly logic languages [107, 161, 197] or functional logic languages [131, 57].

The languages discussed in the referenced papers are representatives of the language approach for paradigm integration. The languages FCLL and CLL (as presented in Sections 7.2 and 7.3.2) lie in between the language and the library approach. While they extend the solver cooperation system META-S by particular languages, META-S and the constraint paradigm in general are so expressive that narrowing, residuation, and resolution as evaluation principles can be considered as constraint solving algorithms. As a result, META-S allows one to emulate all the above mentioned approaches as it subsumes them.

Constraint Query Languages and Constraint Databases. There is a close relationship between constraint programming and database query languages. This relies on a simple but fundamental duality: On the one hand, the set of solutions of a constraint formula ϕ with variables $X = \{x_1, \ldots, x_n\}$ can be seen as a set of tuples $(a_1, \ldots, a_n)$ each satisfying ϕ. On the other hand, the description of data objects represented over the variables of X can be interpreted as constraints. There are several approaches to the integration of constraints and database programming. For a survey, discussion, and references on constraint query languages and constraint databases see [126, 33, 226, 191, 53].

The Object Constraint Language (OCL) [227, 170] is an extension of the UNIFIED MODELING LANGUAGE (UML) [221]. OCL constraints are *tell-constraints* and they are used to specify invariants in class diagrams, conditions in sequence diagrams, and pre- and postconditions of methods. While UML tools often allow the *specification* of OCL constraints, most of them do not support their parsing, type-checking, or execution and only recently have approaches to the verification of UML/OCL class diagrams emerged [37, 12]. Typically, these verification approaches transform the diagrams into formalisms where efficient constraint solvers or theorem provers are available. OCL is, in general, more expressive than first-order predicate logic. To avoid undecidability, existing methods usually limit the OCL constructs in the models.

Part II
Case Studies

After having introduced the fundamental notions and the main developments in the areas of programming languages, paradigms and paradigm combinations, and after having investigated constraints in a multiparadigm setting, the second part of this book explores two concrete examples of multiparadigm constraint programming in detail.

The *concurrent constraint-based functional programming language* CCFL is presented in Chapter 6. The language offers constraints for efficient problem modeling, but also for the description of non-deterministic behavior, of systems of concurrent processes, and even of typical parallelization patterns. We present programming with CCFL by example, and discuss the design of the language syntax and semantics, its implementation and extensions.

Chapter 7 introduces a *generic framework for multiparadigm constraint programming*. First of all, it allows the combination of constraint systems and the integration of constraint solvers to solve hybrid constraint problems. But even more interesting, the approach enables the extension of declarative languages by arbitrary constraints by considering the language evaluation mechanisms also as particular constraint solvers. We discuss the combination framework in detail and sketch its implementation, the *multiparadigm constraint programming system* META-S.

Chapter 6
Concurrent Constraint Functional Programming with CCFL

The *Concurrent Constraint Functional Language* CCFL is a multiparadigm constraint programming language combining the functional and the constraint-based paradigms. CCFL allows a pure functional programming style, but also the use of constraints for efficient problem modeling on the one hand and for the description of communication and synchronization of concurrent processes on the other hand.

We describe and discuss design, use, and implementation of CCFL. There exist two implementations, each with a different focus.

In Sections 6.1-6.4 we present basic CCFL and a compiler with target language LMNtal (pronounced "elemental"). This is another multiparadigm language which realizes a concurrent model based on rewriting of hierarchical graphs. According to the creators of LMNtal, one of its major aims is to "unify various paradigms of computation" [219]. This was a main motivation to investigate the application of LMNtal as model and compiler target language for CCFL as multiparadigm language.

The second version of CCFL focuses on parallelization and allows one to express typical parallelization schemes and the evaluation of CCFL programs in a multicore environment. We sketch parallel CCFL in Section 6.5.

Further extensions of CCFL and related work are discussed in Sections 6.6 and 6.7, resp.

6.1 Programming with CCFL

CCFL is a declarative language combining concepts and constructs from the functional and constraint-based paradigms and allowing the description of concurrent computations. We introduce CCFL by examples before formally specifying the language syntax and semantics.

Program 6.1.1 A naive implementation of the Fibonacci function

---

```
1   fun fibonacci :: Int -> Int
2   def fibonacci n =
3     case n of 0 -> 0 ;
4               1 -> 1 ;
5               m -> let f1 = fibonacci (m-1);
6                        f2 = fibonacci (m-2)
7                    in f1 + f2
```

6.1.1 Functional programming

Functions are used to express deterministic computations. The functional sub-language of CCFL partially inherits notions and concepts from the functional languages HASKELL and OPAL (see e.g. [26, 109, 178, 172]). A functional CCFL program is a sequence of data type definitions and functions. A function consists of a type declaration and a definition, allowing typical constructs such as case-expressions, let-expressions, function application, and some predefined infix operation applications, constants, variables, and constructor terms. A function call (without free variables) evokes a computation by reduction.

Program 6.1.1 and the function *length* in Program 6.1.2 give examples of functional programming with CCFL. Program 6.1.2 shows, furthermore, the definition of a data type *MyList a*. In the following, we will, however, use the HASKELL-typical notions for lists, i.e. [] and e.g. [1,6,2,5] for an empty and non-empty list, resp., and ":" as the list constructor. The list data type is denoted by [_].

6.1.2 Free variables

One of the main characteristics of constraints is the use of free variables. In CCFL, expressions in general are allowed to contain free variables; this also applies to function applications. Function applications with free variables are evaluated using the residuation principle (cf. Section 5.4). This means that function calls are suspended until variables are bound to expressions such that a deterministic reduction is possible. For example, a function call $4 + x$ with free variable x will suspend. In contrast, consider Program 6.1.2. The function *main* introduces the free variable y of type *Int* using the with-construct in line 9. Here, a concrete binding of y is not necessary to proceed with the computation of *main* which yields 3.

Program 6.1.2 List length

```
1   data MyList a = [] | a : (MyList a)
2
3   fun length :: [a] -> Int
4   def length list = case list of []      -> 0 ;
5                                  x : xs -> 1 + length xs
6
7   fun main :: Int
8   def main =
9     with y :: Int
10    in length [1,y,4]
```

6.1.3 Constraint programming

User-defined constraints allow one to describe non-deterministic behavior and systems of concurrent cooperating processes. A user-defined constraint is given by a constraint abstraction and a type declaration. A constraint always has result type *C*. A constraint abstraction consists of a head and a body which may contain the same elements as a function definition. Additionally, the body can be defined by several alternatives, the choice of which is decided by guards. A constraint abstraction is allowed to introduce free variables and each body alternative is a conjunction of constraint atoms.

Examples of user-defined constraints are *game*, *dice*, and *member* in Program 6.1.4 and *produce*, *consume*, and *main* in Program 6.1.5. We discuss them in detail subsequently.

6.1.3.1 Ask- and tell-constraints

In CCFL we distinguish constraints with two functionalities: ask-constraints and tell-constraints.

Constraints in the body of a rule are *tell-constraints* (cf. Section 4.3.2). Their propagation generates bindings or incomplete knowledge. Tell-constraints include applications $f\ fexpr_1\ \dots\ fexpr_n$ of *user-defined constraints* and *equality constraints* between a variable and a functional expression. While a satisfiable equality constraint $x =:= fexpr$ produces a binding of the variable x to the expression $fexpr$ and terminates with result value **Success**, an unsatisfiable equality is reduced to the value **Fail** representing an unsuccessful computation.

Example 33 Consider the constraint abstraction *failList*.

```
fun failList :: C
def failList =
  with x :: [Int], y :: Int
  in x =:= [] & x =:= [y]
```

Program 6.1.3 Boolean *or*

```
1   fun or :: Bool -> Bool -> Bool -> C
2   def or x y z =
3     x =:= True  -> z =:= True  |
4     y =:= True  -> z =:= True  |
5     x =:= False -> z =:= y     |
6     y =:= False -> z =:= x     |
7     z =:= False -> x =:= False & y =:= False
```

Its body consists of a conjunction of two conflicting equality constraints such that the derivation of the constraint *failList* yields **Fail** (cf. Example 41).◊

The atoms of the guard of a user-defined constraint are *ask-constraints* (cf. Section 4.3.3). If a guard of a rule with matching left-hand side is entailed, the rule alternative concerned may be chosen for further derivation. In case that the guard fails or cannot be decided (yet), this rule alternative is suspended. If all rule alternatives suspend, the computation waits (possibly indefinitely) for a sufficient instantiation of the variables concerned.

For ask-constraints, we distinguish between *bound-constraints* **bound** x checking whether a variable x is bound to a non-variable term and *match-constraints* x =:= c x_1 ... x_n which test for a matching of the root symbol of a term bound to the variable x with a certain constructor c. Here, the variables $x_1, \ldots, x_n$ are fresh.

Example 34 Program 6.1.3 gives a definition of the Boolean function *or* as CCFL constraint. The guards decide on the choice of a rule alternative dependening on the bindings of the variables **x, y, z**. While an evaluation of the constraint (*or x y True*) suspends until a binding of x or y is provided (by a concurrently working process), the constraint (*or True False z*) evaluates non-deterministically to **Success** and produces the binding $\{z/True\}$ using one of the alternatives at lines 3 and 6.   ◊

6.1.3.2 Non-deterministic computations

User-defined constraints can be used to express non-determinism. While in Example 34 the evaluation of a constraint, like for example (*or True False z*), leads to the same result independent of the chosen alternative, this is not mandatorily the case. By a certain constraint different guards may be entailed, such that their rule alternatives may lead to completely different computation results.

Example 35 Program 6.1.4 shows a game between two players throwing a dice n times. The constraint abstraction *member* in lines 17-20 is the source of non-determinism in this program and it is used to simulate the dice. The

Program 6.1.4 A simple game of dice

```
 1  fun  game  ::  Int  ->  Int  ->  Int  ->  C
 2  def  game  x  y  n  =
 3    case  n  of  0  ->  x  =:=  0  &  y  =:=  0  ;
 4                  m  ->  with  x1  ::  Int,  y1  ::  Int,
 5                             x2  ::  Int,  y2  ::  Int
 6                  in  dice  x1  &  dice  y1  &
 7                      x  =:=  add  x1  x2  &  y  =:=  add  y1  y2  &
 8                      game  x2  y2  (m-1)
 9
10  fun  add  ::  Int  ->  Int  ->  Int
11  def  add  x  y  =  x  +  y
12
13  fun  dice  ::  Int  ->  C
14  def  dice  x  =  member  [1,2,3,4,5,6]  x
15
16  fun  member  ::  [a]  ->  a  ->  C
17  def  member  l  x  =
18      l  =:=  y  :  ys  ->  x  =:=  y  |
19      l  =:=  y  :  ys  ->  case  ys  of  []      ->  x  =:=  y  ;
20                                          z  :  zs  ->  member  ys  x
```

match-constraints of the guards of both alternatives of this constraint are
the same, i.e. l =:= y : ys, while the bodies differ. Thus, the evaluation
of a constraint $member$ $[y_1, y_2, \ldots, y_n]$ x non-deterministically generates a
constraint which binds the variable x to one list element y_i.

The user-defined constraint $game$ describes the game: The constraint applications $dice$ $x1$ and $dice$ $y1$ in line 6 non-deterministically produce values
which are consumed by the applications of the function add in the equality
constraints x =:= add $x1$ $x2$ and y =:= add $y1$ $y2$, resp., in line 7. These
function applications suspend until their arguments are sufficiently instantiated (that is, completely instantiated) for the application of the built-in
function +.

A trace showing a non-deterministic computation with $n = 2$ is given in
Example 39.   ◇

6.1.3.3 Concurrent processes

CCFL allows the description of systems of cooperating and communicating processes. The main idea is to express concurrent processes by means
of conjunctions of tell-constraints. Several tell-constraints combined by the
&-combinator generate a corresponding number of processes and these communicate over common variables.

For example, in Program 6.1.4 both computations of dice values, i.e.
$dice$ $x1$ and $dice$ $y1$, which are independent, could have been computed

Program 6.1.5 A producer and a consumer communicating over a common buffer

```
 1   fun produce :: [a] -> C
 2   def produce buf =
 3          with buf1 :: [a], item :: a
 4          in -- generate item here
 5             ...
 6             -- then put it into the buffer and continue
 7             buf =:= item : buf1 & produce buf1
 8
 9   fun consume :: [a] -> C
10   def consume buf =
11          buf =:= first : buf1 ->
12             -- consume first here
13             ...
14             -- and continue
15             consume buf1
16
17   fun main :: C
18   def main =
19          with buf :: [a]
20          in produce buf & consume buf
```

concurrently. There is no required order of the players in this game. However, the computation of the sum by x =:= add $x1$ $x2$ depends on the computation of the dice values $x1$ and $x2$ which must have been processed in advance.

Example 36 Program 6.1.5 shows a consumer and a producer cooperating over a shared buffer. The *main*-function creates the buffer as a fresh variable *buf* using the with-construct and initiates the computation by two processes *produce* and *consume* communicating over the shared buffer.

The user-defined constraint *consume* (lines 9-15) describes the behavior of the *consume*-process. The consumer must wait until the buffer has been filled with at least one element *first*. This is ensured by the guard of the consumer rule (cf. line 11). In contrast, the *produce* process is not restricted to synchronize with the consumer. This rule is not guarded by any ask-constraint, but produces buffer elements by tell-constraints in its body (line 7).   ◊

6.2 Syntax

In this section we formally specify the syntax of CCFL and underline certain features by means of further examples.

Figure 6.1 presents the syntax of CCFL programs in an EBNF-like notation. A CCFL program is a sequence of data type definitions and declarations

$$
\begin{aligned}
Prog &\rightarrow Def^+ \\
Def &\rightarrow TDef \mid FDecl \mid FDef \\[4pt]
FDef &\rightarrow \textbf{def } FName\ Var^* = Expr \\
FDecl &\rightarrow \textbf{fun } FName :: Type \\
TDef &\rightarrow \textbf{data } TypeName\ TypeVar^* = CType\ (\mid CType)^* \\[4pt]
CType &\rightarrow Constructor\ SType^* \\
SType &\rightarrow (\ SType) \mid TypeVar \mid CType \mid \texttt{Int} \mid \texttt{Float} \mid \texttt{Bool} \\
Type &\rightarrow (\ Type) \mid SType \mid Type\ \texttt{->}\ Type \mid C
\end{aligned}
$$

Fig. 6.1 Syntax of CCFL programs in EBNF-like notation

and of definitions of functions and user-defined constraints. In this context we use the notion "function" for both, i. e. we consider user-defined constraints as functions of result type C.

A data type definition starts with the keyword **data**.[5] A function declaration is indicated by the keyword **fun**, a function definition by the keyword **def**. Of course, the parameter variables of a function must all be different.

As an example consider Program 6.2.1 which shows a definition of a data type *Tree a* containing the empty tree *Nil* and trees consisting of nodes *Node* with a value of (the polymorphic) type *a* and a left and a right subtree. Furthermore, the program declares and defines an arithmetic function *foo* with two arguments.

Program 6.2.1 A tree data type and a simple arithmetic function on floats

```
data Tree a = Node (Tree a) a (Tree a) | Nil

fun foo :: Float -> Float -> Float
def foo x y = y +. (x /. y)
```

Constants, constructors, and variable and function names as used in the following, are defined by the grammar given in Figure 6.3. Names consist of alphanumerical symbols; data type names and constructors start with an upper letter while identifiers of variables and functions start with a lower letter.

Expressions are distinguished into functional, constraint, and guarded expressions. The syntax of expressions is given in Figure 6.2.

---

[5] Note that (currently) function types are excluded from user-defined data types.

Expr	→	*FExpr* | *CExpr* | *GExpr*
FExpr	→	*Appl* | *Infix* | *CaseExpr* | *LetExpr*
Appl	→	[*FExpr*] *SExpr*
SExpr	→	*Var* | *Constant* | (*FExpr*) | *Constructor*
Constant	→	*Float* | *Int* | *Bool*
Infix	→	*FExpr BinOp FExpr*
BinOp	→	*ArithOp* | *RelOp* | *BoolOp*
ArithOp	→	+ | - | * | / | +. | -. | *. | /.
RelOp	→	== | <= | < | > | >= | ~= | ==: | ~=:
		| ==. | <=. | <. | >. | >=. | ~=.
BoolOp	→	&& | ||
CaseExpr	→	**case** *FExpr* **of** *Branch* (; *Branch*) *
Branch	→	*Pat* -> *CExpr*
		| *Var* -> *CExpr* (⋆ *otherwise-branch* ⋆)
Pat	→	*Constructor Var* * | *Int* | *Bool*
LetExpr	→	**let** *Binding* (; *Binding*) * **in** *CExpr*
Binding	→	*Var* = *FExpr*
CExpr	→	*With* | *Conj*
With	→	**with** *Var* :: *CType* (, *Var* :: *CType*) *
		in *Conj*
Conj	→	*Atom* (& *Atom*) *
Atom	→	*Var* =:= *FExpr* (⋆ *tell-equality* ⋆)
		| *FExpr* (⋆ *func. expression* ⋆)
GExpr	→	*GAlt* (| *GAlt*) *
GAlt	→	*Guard* -> *CExpr*
Guard	→	*CPrim* (& *CPrim*) *
CPrim	→	**bound** *Var* (⋆ *bound-constraint* ⋆)
		| *Var* =:= *Pat* (⋆ *match-constraint* ⋆)

Fig. 6.2 Syntax of CCFL expressions

Functional expressions. A functional expression *FExpr* is either a function application, a basic infix operator application, a case-expression, or a let-expression.

A function application consists of a (optional) functional expression and a simple expression, like a variable, a constant, a parenthesised functional expression or a constructor (expression).

A number of basic binary arithmetic and Boolean operations and relations can be used in infix notation. Operations on floating point numbers are followed by a dot ".", comparison operations on Booleans by a colon ":".

Case-expressions use the keywords **case** and **of** and the different branches are separated by a semicolon ";". Different cases are distinguished by their top constructor symbols, where the following variables must be fresh and they must match the arity of the constructor. We allow branching on integer numbers and

Program 6.2.2 if-alternatives are realised using the case-construct

```
fun if :: Bool -> a -> a -> a
def if c t e = case c of True  -> t ;
                         False -> e

fun depth :: Tree a -> Int
def depth tree =
  case tree of
     Nil -> 0 ;
     Node left value right ->
         let ldepth = depth left ;
             rdepth = depth right
         in if (ldepth >= rdepth) (ldepth + 1) (rdepth + 1)
```

Program 6.2.3 A function *bar* using local definitions

```
fun bar :: Int -> Int -> Int

def bar a b = a + (let a = b;
                       b = a + 2;
                       a = a * b
                   in (let a = a + b
                       in b + a))

-- or semantically equivalent:
def bar a b = a + (let a0 = b;
                       b0 = a0 + 2;
                       a1 = a0 * b0
                   in (let a2 = a1 + b0
                       in b0 + a2))
```

Booleans by considering them as (0-ary) constructors. An *otherwise-branch* (with a fresh variable as pattern) can be defined for case alternatives on integer numbers as shown for the naive implementation of the function *fibonacci* in Program 6.1.1 in line 5.

An if-construct is realised as a function using the case-construct of basic CCFL as shown in Program 6.2.2. Function *depth* calculates the depth of a tree of type *Tree a* as defined in Program 6.2.1.

Local definitions are introduced by let-expressions. They are allowed to refer to previously defined let-elements; thus, their order is crucial. Program 6.2.3 shows two semantically equivalent versions of a function *bar* illustrating the effect of shadowing variables.

Constraint expressions. The second form of expressions are constraint expressions *CExpr*. These may introduce new logical variables (annotated with their type) using the with-construct and consist in general of a conjunction

Bool	$\rightarrow$	**True** | **False**
Int	$\rightarrow$	([*Sign*] *Digit* $^+$) | *Digit* $^+$
Float	$\rightarrow$	([*Sign*] *Digit* $^+$. *Digit* $^+$ [*Ext*])
		| *Digit* $^+$. *Digit* $^+$ [*Ext*]
Ext	$\rightarrow$	(**e** | **E**)[*Sign*] *Digit* $^+$
Var	$\rightarrow$	*LowerId*
TypeVar	$\rightarrow$	*LowerId*
FName	$\rightarrow$	*LowerId*
Constructor	$\rightarrow$	*UpperId*
TypeName	$\rightarrow$	*UpperId*
LowerId	$\rightarrow$	*LAlpha* (*Alpha* | *Digit*) *
UpperId	$\rightarrow$	*UAlpha* (*Alpha* | *Digit*) *
Alpha	$\rightarrow$	*UAlpha* | *LAlpha*
LAlpha	$\rightarrow$	**a** | ... | **z**
UAlpha	$\rightarrow$	**A** | ... | **Z**
Digit	$\rightarrow$	**0** | ... | **9**
Sign	$\rightarrow$	**+** | **-**

Fig. 6.3 CCFL constants, constructors, variable and function names

of atoms. An atom is either a tell-equality constraint or a functional expression (including applications of user-defined constraints).

Guarded expressions. Finally, there are guarded expressions *GExpr*: They consist of a disjunction of constraint expressions, each with a preceding guard which is a conjunction of constraint primitives. While constraint expressions may be looked at as tell-constraints, guard atoms represent ask-constraints. They include a test **bound** x of a variable x to be bound to a non-variable term and a match-constraint x =:= $c\ x_1\ \ldots\ x_n$ of a variable x to be bound to a term with constructor root symbol c (including Booleans and integer numbers) and fresh variables $x_1, \ldots, x_n$.

The producer and the consumer processes of Program 6.1.5 were defined using constraint and guarded expressions.

6.3 Semantics

In a nutshell, CCFL expressions are evaluated using a lazy strategy. For function applications with free variables, however, the residuation principle is used. Equality constraints are interpreted as strict. That is, the constraint t_1 =:= t_2 is satisfied if both expressions can be reduced to the same ground data term [82].

We give a formal presentation of the *operational semantics* of CCFL and illustrate it by means of examples.

Let P be a CCFL program. Let X be a set of variables, let $F = \Delta \cup \Gamma$ denote the set of function symbols according to P, where Δ is the set of (data) constructors and Γ is the set of defined functions. By $Val \subseteq \Delta$ we denote the union of the sets of Booleans and integer and floating point numbers according to the CCFL types **Bool**, **Int**, and **Float**, resp.

We extend substitutions for application on CCFL expressions (i.e. *Expr* according to Figure 6.2).

Definition 39 (application of a substitution on CCFL expressions)
Presuppose the definition of a substitution σ as given in Definition 10. We extend σ to $\tilde{\sigma} : Expr \to Expr$, i.e. for application on a CCFL expression *Expr*, by the following case distinction:

let-in:

$\tilde{\sigma}(\textbf{let } v_1 = e_1; v_2 = e_2; \ldots; v_n = e_n \textbf{ in } cexpr)$
$= \textbf{let } v_1 = \tilde{\sigma}(e_1); v_2 = \tilde{\sigma}(e_2); \ldots; v_n = \tilde{\sigma}(e_n) \textbf{ in } \tilde{\sigma}(cexpr)$

case-of:

$\tilde{\sigma}(\textbf{case } fexpr \textbf{ of}$
$\qquad c_1 \; v_{1,1} \; \cdots \; v_{1,n_1} \texttt{->} \; cexpr_1 \; ;$
$\qquad \ldots$
$\qquad c_k \; v_{k,1} \; \cdots \; v_{k,n_k} \texttt{->} \; cexpr_k)$
$= \textbf{case } \tilde{\sigma}(fexpr) \textbf{ of}$
$\qquad c_1 \; v_{1,1} \; \cdots \; v_{1,n_1} \texttt{->} \; \tilde{\sigma}(cexpr_1) \; ;$
$\qquad \ldots$
$\qquad c_k \; v_{k,1} \; \cdots \; v_{k,n_k} \texttt{->} \; \tilde{\sigma}(cexpr_k)$

This holds similarly for otherwise-branches.

constraint expression:

$\tilde{\sigma}(\textbf{with } v_1 :: \tau_1, \ldots, v_n :: \tau_n \textbf{ in } conj)$
$= \textbf{with } v_1 :: \tau_1, \ldots, v_n :: \tau_n \textbf{ in } \tilde{\sigma}(conj)$

$\tilde{\sigma}(atom_1 \; \& \; \ldots \; \& \; atom_m)$
$= \tilde{\sigma}(atom_1) \; \& \; \ldots \; \& \; \tilde{\sigma}(atom_m)$

constraint:

$\tilde{\sigma}(v \; \texttt{=:=} \; fexpr)$
$= \tilde{\sigma}(v) \; \texttt{=:=} \; \tilde{\sigma}(fexpr)$

guarded expression:

$$\tilde{\sigma}(a_{1,1} \ \& \ \dots \ \& \ a_{1,n_1} \quad \text{-> } \ cexpr_1 \ |$$

$$\dots$$

$$a_{m,1} \ \& \ \dots \ \& \ a_{m,n_m} \text{-> } \ cexpr_m)$$

$$= \tilde{\sigma}(a_{1,1}) \ \& \ \dots \ \& \ \tilde{\sigma}(a_{1,n_1}) \quad \text{-> } \ \tilde{\sigma}(cexpr_1) \ |$$

$$\dots$$

$$\tilde{\sigma}(a_{m,1}) \ \& \ \dots \ \& \ \tilde{\sigma}(a_{m,n_m}) \text{-> } \ \tilde{\sigma}(cexpr_m)$$

We identify a substitution σ with its extension $\tilde{\sigma}$ and write σ instead of $\tilde{\sigma}$. $\lhd$

We presuppose a *constraint solver* with functions *solve*, *entail*, and *proj* as introduced in Section 4.2, in general. Currently, CCFL only supports equality constraints on terms and user-defined constraints, both as tell-constraints, and match- and bound-constraints as ask-constraints. Thus, the *constraint store* just holds equality constraints $x =:= t$, $x \in X, t \in \mathcal{T}(\Delta, X)$ on functional expressions, which are expressed by means of substitutions. Accordingly, the constraint solver can be based on the parallel composition $\uparrow$ of substitutions (cf. Section 2.3).

Let C be a conjunction of equality constraints representing a substitution σ_C. We define the solver operations as follows:

satisfiability:

$$solve(C \wedge v =:= w) = \begin{cases} true & \text{if } \sigma_C \uparrow \{v/w\} \neq \emptyset \\ false & \text{if } \sigma_C \uparrow \{v/w\} = \emptyset \end{cases}$$

entailment:

Bound-constraints are used to check whether a variable is bound to a non-variable constructor term or value.

$$entail(C, \mathbf{bound}(v)) = \begin{cases} true & \text{if } \sigma_C(v) \notin X \\ delay & \text{otherwise} \end{cases}$$

A match-constraint checks on the matching of two constructor terms or values. Let $v, v_1, \dots, v_n \in X$, $c, d \in \Delta$, $t_1, \dots, t_m \in Expr$.

$$entail(C, v =:= c \ v_1 \dots v_n) = \begin{cases} true & \text{if } \sigma_C(v) = c \ t_1 \dots t_n \\ delay & \text{otherwise} \end{cases}$$

and resp.

$$entail(C, d \ t_1 \dots t_m =:= c \ v_1 \dots v_n) = \begin{cases} true & \text{if } d = c \text{ and } m = n \\ delay & \text{otherwise} \end{cases}$$

The entailment of a conjunction of constraints can be tested by checking the constraints individually, because the variables on the right-hand side of the match-constraints are all fresh.

$$entail(C, a_1 \& \ldots \& a_n) = \begin{cases} delay & if\ \exists i \in \{1, \ldots, n\} : entail(C, a_i) = delay \\ true & otherwise \end{cases}$$

projection:

$$proj(C, \{x\}) = (x \; \texttt{=:=} \; \sigma_C(x))$$

We define the *operational semantics* of CCFL by means of a derivation relation $\leadsto_P$ on system states. A *system state* $Z = \langle A, C \rangle$ consists of a multi-set A of expressions and a conjunction of constraints $C \in \Delta Cons$, i.e. the constraint store. The function of the constraint store C is to collect constraints computed during the program evaluation. We use multi-sets A of expressions to describe their concurrent computation. The multi-set operation union is denoted by $\uplus$. The empty multi-set $\{\}$ of (constraint or guarded) expressions is also denoted by $\{\textbf{Success}\}$. The multi-set $\{\textbf{Fail}\}$ is a derivation result of an unsatisfiable set of constraints.

Definition 40 (derivation relation $\leadsto_P$) Let P be a CCFL program. Let $Z = \langle \{p\} \uplus A, C \rangle$ be a system state, where p is an expression. The derivation relation $\leadsto_P$ is composed of the following subrelations:

let-in: Let-expressions introduce local definitions of variables which may refer to previously defined let-elements. Thus, the right-hand sides of the local definitions are stepwise substituted into the subsequently following local definitions and constraint expression.

Here, we assume that shadowing variables of different local definitions have already been disambiguated by renamings (as shown in Program 6.2.3).

Let p be an expression of the following form:

  let $v_i = e_i; \ldots; v_n = e_n$ **in** *cexpr*

The following holds:

$$\langle \{p\} \uplus A, C \rangle \leadsto_P \langle \{p'\} \uplus A, C \rangle, \text{ where } \sigma = \{v_i/e_i\} \text{ and}$$

- $p' = \sigma(\textbf{let } v_{i+1} = e_{i+1}; \ldots; v_n = e_n \text{ in } cexpr)$ for $i < n$,
- $p' = \sigma(cexpr)$ for $i = n$.

case-of: A case-expression drives the evaluation of the distinguishing functional expression $fexpr$ to normal form and applies the substitution emerging from the matching with the corresponding alternative.

- Let p be an expression of the following form:

    case $fexpr$ **of**
       $c_1\ v_{1,1} \ \ldots\ v_{1,n_1}$ -> $cexpr_1$;
       $\ldots$
       $c_k\ v_{k,1} \ \ldots\ v_{k,n_k}$ -> $cexpr_k$

If $\langle fexpr, C \rangle \leadsto_P^* \langle c_i \, t_{i,1} \, \ldots \, t_{i,n_i}, C \rangle$, where $c_i \, t_{i,1} \, \ldots \, t_{i,n_i}$ is in normal form and $i \in \{1, \ldots, k\}$, then

$$\langle \{p\} \uplus A, C \rangle \leadsto_P \langle \{p'\} \uplus A, C \rangle,$$

where $p' = \sigma(cexpr_i)$ with $\sigma = \{v_{i,1}/t_{i,1}, \ldots, v_{i,n_i}/t_{i,n_i}\}$.

- Let p be an expression of the following form (with otherwise-branch):

  case $fexpr$ **of**
  $\quad c_1$ -> $cexpr_1$;
  $\quad \ldots$
  $\quad c_k$ -> $cexpr_k$;
  $\quad m$ -> $cexpr_{k+1}$

  with $c_1, \ldots, c_k \in \mathbf{Int}$ and $m \in X$.

  If $\langle fexpr, C \rangle \leadsto_P^* \langle c, C \rangle$, where $c = c_i$ with $i \in \{1, \ldots, k\}$, then

  $$\langle \{p\} \uplus A, C \rangle \leadsto_P \langle \{cexpr_i\} \uplus A, C \rangle.$$

  If $\langle fexpr, C \rangle \leadsto_P^* \langle c, C \rangle$ and $\not\exists i \in \{1, \ldots, k\} : c = c_i$, then

  $$\langle \{p\} \uplus A, C \rangle \leadsto_P \langle \{\sigma(cexpr_{k+1})\} \uplus A, C \rangle,$$

  where $\sigma = \{m/c\}$.

apply: The application of a function realizes a call-by-name evaluation strategy. Actually, CCFL evaluates lazily, which, however, cannot be expressed accordingly, here.

Let p be an expression of the following form:

$f \, t_1 \, \ldots \, t_n$ with $n \geq 0$.

If there is a rule **def** $f \, v_1 \, \ldots \, v_n$ = $expr$ in the program, then

$$\langle \{p\} \uplus A, C \rangle \leadsto_P \langle \{p'\} \uplus A, C \rangle,$$

where $p' = \sigma(expr)$ with $\sigma = \{v_1/t_1, \ldots, v_n/t_n\}$.

var: A variable is evaluated by a lookup in the constraint store for its current binding.

Let $p = v$ be a variable.

If $proj(C, \{v\}) = (v \; \texttt{=:=} \; t)$, where $t \neq v$ and $t \in \mathcal{T}(\Delta, X)$, then

$$\langle \{p\} \uplus A, C \rangle \leadsto_P \langle \{t\} \uplus A, C \rangle.$$

built-in operators: A built-in operator initiates the evaluation of its arguments to normal form.

Let p be an expression of the following form:

$$fexpr_1 \oplus fexpr_2,$$

where $\oplus$ is a built-in operator $BinOp$ according to Figure 6.2.

If $\langle fexpr_1, C \rangle \leadsto_P^* \langle w_1, C \rangle$ and $\langle fexpr_2, C \rangle \leadsto_P^* \langle w_2, C \rangle$ with $w_1, w_2 \in Val$, then

$$\langle \{p\} \uplus A, C \rangle \leadsto_P \langle \{p'\} \uplus A, C \rangle,$$

where $p' = eval(w_1 \oplus w_2)$ is the result of the application of the operator $\oplus$ on w_1 and w_2.

constraint expression: The with-construct in a constraint expression only introduces fresh logical variables. Thus, the derivation just unfolds the atoms of the constraint expression.

Let p be an expression of the form

with $v_1 :: \tau_1, \ldots, v_n :: \tau_n$ **in** $atom_1$ & ... & $atom_m$ or

$atom_1$ & ... & $atom_m$, resp.,

where $n, m \geq 1$.

The following holds:

$$\langle \{p\} \uplus A, C \rangle \leadsto_P \langle \{atom_1, \ldots, atom_m\} \uplus A, C \rangle.$$

tell: A tell-constraint $v \mathrel{=:=} fexpr$ introduces an equality between the expression bound to the variable v and the functional expression $fexpr$. Since both are functional expressions (of base type) their evaluation is deterministic.

The constraint $v \mathrel{=:=} fexpr$ is satisfied if both expressions can be reduced to the same ground data term (*strict equality*, [82]). Thus, we evaluate both expressions to data terms and then perform a unification of the resulting expressions. The evaluation to constructor terms is interleaved with unification.

We distinguish four cases concerning the propagation of equality constraints:
Let p be an expression of the form $v \mathrel{=:=} fexpr$.

- If $\langle fexpr, C \rangle \leadsto_P^* \langle w, C \rangle$, where $w \in X \cup \Delta$, and $solve(C \wedge v \mathrel{=:=} w) = true$, then

$$\langle \{p\} \uplus A, C \rangle \leadsto_P \langle A, C' \rangle,$$

where $\mathcal{D} \models \forall (C' \longleftrightarrow (C \wedge v \mathrel{=:=} w))$.

- If $\langle fexpr, C \rangle \rightsquigarrow_P^* \langle w, C \rangle$, where $w \in X \cup \Delta$, and $solve(C \wedge v =:= w) = false$, then

$$\langle \{p\} \uplus A, C \rangle \rightsquigarrow_P \langle \{\boldsymbol{Fail}\}, false \rangle.$$

- If $\langle fexpr, C \rangle \rightsquigarrow_P^* \langle c\ t_1 \ldots t_n, C \rangle$, with $c \in \Delta$, $t_i \in \mathcal{T}(F, X)$, $i \in \{1, \ldots, n\}$, and $solve(C \wedge v =:= c\ v_1 \ldots v_n) = true$, where v_i, $i \in \{1, \ldots, n\}$, are fresh, then

$$\langle \{p\} \uplus A, C \rangle \rightsquigarrow_P \langle \{v_1 =:= t_1, \ldots, v_n =:= t_n\} \uplus A, C' \rangle,$$

where $\mathcal{D} \models \forall (C' \longleftrightarrow (C \wedge v =:= c\ v_1 \ldots v_n))$.

- If $\langle fexpr, C \rangle \rightsquigarrow_P^* \langle c\ t_1 \ldots t_n, C \rangle$, with $c \in \Delta$, $t_i \in \mathcal{T}(F, X)$, $i \in \{1, \ldots, n\}$, and $solve(C \wedge v =:= c\ v_1 \ldots v_n) = false$, where v_i, $i \in \{1, \ldots, n\}$, are fresh, then

$$\langle \{p\} \uplus A, C \rangle \rightsquigarrow_P \langle \{\boldsymbol{Fail}\}, false \rangle.$$

guarded expression: Guards are used for a conditional choice of alternatives within the definition of a user-defined constraint. If more than one guard is entailed by the constraint store, then the choice of the alternative to be applied is non-deterministic. If none of the guards of a rule is entailed, the computation suspends, either indefinitely or until another concurrent process provides a sufficient binding.

Let p be a guarded expression:

$$a_{1,1}\ \&\ \ldots\ \&\ a_{1,n_1}\quad \text{->}\ cexpr_1\ |$$

$$\ldots$$

$$a_{m,1}\ \&\ \ldots\ \&\ a_{m,n_m}\ \text{->}\ cexpr_m$$

If there is an $i \in \{1, \ldots, m\}$ such that we can successfully check the guard's $a_{i,1}\ \&\ \ldots\ \&\ a_{i,n_i}$ entailment, i.e.:

- For every ask-constraint $a_{i,j}$ holds:
  - Either it is a match-constraint of the form $fexpr =:= c\ v_1 \ldots v_k$ and $\langle \{fexpr\}, C \rangle \rightsquigarrow_P^* \langle \{d\ t_1, \ldots t_m\}, C \rangle$ with $c = d$ and $m = k$,

    then $a'_{i,j} = (d\ t_1 \ldots t_m =:= c\ v_1 \ldots v_k)$,
    and $\sigma_j = \{v_1/t_1, \ldots, v_k/t_k\}$.
  - Or $a_{i,j}$ is of the form $\boldsymbol{bound}\ v$.
    In this case, $a'_{i,j} = a_{i,j}$ and $\sigma_j = id$.

- The entailment of the guard (in normal form) is checked successfully:
  $entail(C, a'_{i,1}$ & ... & $a'_{i,n_i}) = true.$

then a derivation step

$$\langle\{p\} \uplus A, C\rangle \rightsquigarrow_P \langle\{p'\} \uplus A, C\rangle,$$

is possible, where $p' = \sigma(cexpr_i)$ with $\sigma = \uparrow_{j\in\{1,...,n_i\}} \sigma_j$ resulting from the evaluation of the match-constraints of the chosen alternative's guard.

If P is clear from the context, we just write $\rightsquigarrow$.   ◁

The computation of a CCFL expression e is described by means of a derivation sequence using the $\rightsquigarrow_P$ relation starting with the *initial state* $\langle\{e\}, true\rangle$. In the initial situation, the constraint store is empty which is denoted by the constraint *true*. In general, for a system state there may be more than one applicable rule for a $\rightsquigarrow_P$ step which choice is non-deterministic. There are two forms of final states:

- A state $S = \langle\{\textbf{Fail}\}, false\rangle$ is a *failed final state*.
- A state $S = \langle A, C\rangle$ with $C \neq false$ such that no derivation on S is possible anymore, is called a *successful final state*.

Note that we do not explicitly distinguish between successful and suspended final states (or deadlocked final states, resp.). The result of the evaluation of a *functional expression* remains in the multi-set A of expressions of a successful final state $\langle A, C\rangle$. The application of a *(user-defined) constraint* may yield a successful final state $\langle A, C\rangle$ with empty multi-set $A = \{\}$ (or $A = \{$ *Success* $\}$, resp.) which represents a successful computation. If, in contrast, there remain expressions (different from **Fail**) in the multi-set component A of the final state, then this indicates a suspended computation. We discuss relevant examples in the following.

Example 37 We consider the *derivation of a functional expression* **bar 1 4** w. r. t. Program 6.2.3. We denote the name of each applied rule as the subscript of the $\rightsquigarrow$ relation.

⟨ { **bar 1 4** }, *true* ⟩

$\rightsquigarrow_{apply}$ ⟨ { 1 + (**let** a0 = 4; b0 = a0 + 2; a1 = a0 * b0
                        in (**let** a2 = a1 + b0 **in** b0 + a2)) }, *true* ⟩

The built-in operator + enforces the derivation of the let-expression:

⟨ { **let** a0 = 4; b0 = a0 + 2; a1 = a0 * b0
      in (**let** a2 = a1 + b0 **in** b0 + a2) }, *true* ⟩

$\rightsquigarrow_{let-in}$ ⟨ { **let** b0 = 4 + 2; a1 = 4 * b0
                        in (**let** a2 = a1 + b0 **in** b0 + a2) }, *true* ⟩

$\leadsto^*_{let-in}$ $\langle$ { let $a2$ = $(4 * (4 + 2)) + (4 + 2)$
                        in $(4 + 2) + a2$ }, $true$ $\rangle$

$\leadsto_{let-in}$ $\langle$ { $(4 + 2) + ((4 * (4 + 2)) + (4 + 2))$ }, $true$ $\rangle$

$\leadsto^*_{built-in}$ $\langle$ { 36 }, $true$ $\rangle$

Now, the original computation continues:

. . .

$\leadsto_{apply}$ $\langle$ { $1 +$ (let $a0$ = 4; $b0$ = $a0 + 2$; $a1$ = $a0 * b0$
                        in (let $a2$ = $a1 + b0$ in $b0 + a2$)) }, $true$ $\rangle$

$\leadsto^*$ $\langle$ { 37 }, $true$ $\rangle$

Observe that the evaluation of a functional CCFL program does not influence the constraint store. $\Diamond$

Example 38 *Lazy evaluation* is a strategy combining call-by-name evaluation and sharing of variable bindings such that an expression is only evaluated once and copies originating from this expression are not reevaluated but just replaced by the result (cf. Section 3.2.3). This is, however, not explicitly expressed by the rules of the $\leadsto_P$ relation.

We consider a program *square* which builds the square value of an integer number.

```
fun square :: Int -> Int
def square x = x * x
```

The evaluation of the expression *square* $(3 + 1)$ illustrates lazy behavior. The term $3 + 1$ is unevaluatedly substituted into the function's body according to the call-by-name strategy. Thereby, the term appears twice, where it is actually shared between its occurrences, represented by the grey color.

$\langle$ { *square* $(3 + 1)$ }, $true$ $\rangle$

$\leadsto_{apply}$ $\langle$ { $(3 + 1)$ * $(3 + 1)$ }, $true$ $\rangle$

$\leadsto_{built-in}$ $\langle$ { 16 }, $true$ $\rangle$

Here, the evaluation of the built-in function * requires the computation of $3 + 1$ which is performed only once for the shared term.

$\langle$ { $(3 + 1)$ }, $true$ $\rangle$

$\leadsto_{built-in}$ $\langle$ { 4 }, $true$ $\rangle$ $\Diamond$

Example 39 Now, consider our game of dice from Example 35, Program 6.1.4. We show a derivation of the constraint *game a b* 2.

⟨ { *game a b 2* }, *true* ⟩

⤳*apply*   ⟨ { **case** 2 **of** 0 -> *a* =:= 0 & *b* =:= 0 ;
                    m -> **with** *x1* :: Int, *y1* :: Int,
                                 x2 :: Int, *y2* :: Int
                         in *dice x1* & *dice y1* &
                             a =:= *add x1 x2* & *b* =:= *add y1 y2* &
                             game x2 y2 (*m*-1) },
         true ⟩

⤳*case-of* ⟨ { **with** *x1* :: Int, *y1* :: Int, *x2* :: Int, *y2* :: Int
            in *dice x1* & *dice y1* &
                a =:= *add x1 x2* & *b* =:= *add y1 y2* &
                game x2 y2 (2-1) },
         true ⟩

⤳*with-in* ⟨ { *dice x1*, *dice y1*,
            a =:= *add x1 x2*, *b* =:= *add y1 y2*, *game x2 y2* (2-1) },
         true ⟩

⤳$^2_{apply}$ ⟨ { *member* [1,2,3,4,5,6] *x1*,
            member [1,2,3,4,5,6] *y1*,
            a =:= *add x1 x2*, *b* =:= *add y1 y2*, *game x2 y2* (2-1) },
         true ⟩

⤳*apply*   ⟨ { ([1,2,3,4,5,6] =:= *y* : *ys* -> *x1* =:= *y* |
                [1,2,3,4,5,6] =:= *y* : *ys*
                                 -> **case** *ys* **of** [] -> *x1* =:= *y* ;
                                                z : *zs* -> *member ys x1*),
                member [1,2,3,4,5,6] *y1*,
                a =:= *add x1 x2*, *b* =:= *add y1 y2*, *game x2 y2* (2-1) },
         true ⟩

⤳*guarded expression*
              ⟨ { *x1* =:= 1,
                member [1,2,3,4,5,6] *y1*,
                a =:= *add x1 x2*, *b* =:= *add y1 y2*, *game x2 y2* (2-1) },
         true ⟩

⤳*   ⟨ { *x1* =:= 1, *y1* =:= 5,
                a =:= *add x1 x2*, *b* =:= *add y1 y2*, *game x2 y2* (2-1) },
         true ⟩

⤳$^2_{tell}$ ⟨ { *a* =:= *add x1 x2*, *b* =:= *add y1 y2*, *game x2 y2* (2-1) },
            x1 = 1 ∧ *y1* = 5 ⟩

⤳*   ⟨ { *a* =:= *add x1 x2*, *b* =:= *add y1 y2* },
            x1 = 1 ∧ *y1* = 5 ∧ *x2* = 5 ∧ *y2* = 3 ⟩

⤳*   ⟨ { *a* =:= 6, *b* =:= 8 },

$$x1 = 1 \wedge y1 = 5 \wedge x2 = 5 \wedge y2 = 3\ \rangle$$

$\leadsto^2_{tell}$ $\langle\ \{\ Success\ \},$
$\qquad\qquad x1 = 1 \wedge y1 = 5 \wedge x2 = 5 \wedge y2 = 3 \wedge a = 6 \wedge b = 8\ \rangle$

The derivation yields the empty multi-set of expressions represented by { *Success* } and a constraint store which holds bindings of the variables a and b of the initial constraint *game a b* 2. The non-deterministic computation shown above represents a game between two players each throwing a dice twice, where the overall score of player 1 is 6 and of player 2 is 8, resp.   ◊

Example 40 We consider the producer-consumer setting of Program 6.1.5 to provide an example of a (successful but) *suspending* computation.

A consumer working on a list (1 : x) consumes the first element 1 and suspends afterwards, because (resp. in case that) x remains unbound.

$\langle\ \{\ consume\ (1\ :\ x)\ \},\ true\ \rangle$

$\leadsto_{apply}$ $\langle\ \{\ 1\ :\ x\ =:=\ first\ :\ buf1\ ->\ \ldots\ \&\ consume\ buf1\ \},\ true\ \rangle$

$\leadsto_{guarded\ expression}$
$\qquad\qquad \langle\ \{\ \ldots\ \&\ consume\ x\ \},\ true\ \rangle$

$\leadsto^*$ $\langle\ \{\ consume\ x\ \},\ \ldots\ \rangle$

If, in contrast, there is a concurrent (producer) process (as part of the multi-set A', see below) which instantiates the remaining buffer x with new elements, then the consumer can proceed.

$\langle\ A,\ true\ \rangle$

$\leadsto^*$ $\langle\ \{\ consume\ x\ \} \uplus A',\ true\ \rangle$

$\leadsto^*$ $\langle\ \{\ consume\ x\ \} \uplus A'',\ x\ =\ 1\ :\ y \wedge \ldots\ \rangle$

$\leadsto_{apply} \leadsto_{guarded\ expression}$
$\qquad\qquad \langle\ \{\ \ldots\ \&\ consume\ y\ \} \uplus A'',\ x\ =\ 1\ :\ y \wedge \ldots\ \rangle$

$\leadsto$ $\ldots$ ◊

Example 41 The derivation of the expression *failList* using the rules of Example 33 yields a *failed final state*.

$\langle\ \{\ failList\ \},\ true\ \rangle$

$\leadsto_{apply}$ $\langle\ \{\ with\ x\ ::\ [Int],\ y\ ::\ Int$
$\qquad\qquad in\ x\ =:=\ []\ \&\ x\ =:=\ [y]\ \},$
$\qquad\quad true\ \rangle$

$\leadsto_{with-in}$ $\langle\ \{\ x\ =:=\ []\ \&\ x\ =:=\ [y]\ \},\ true\ \rangle$

$\leadsto_{tell}$ $\langle\ \{\ x\ =:=\ [y]\ \},\ x\ =\ []\ \rangle$

$\leadsto_{tell}$ $\langle\ \{\ Fail\ \},\ false\ \rangle$ ◊

6.4 Compiling CCFL into LMNTAL

CCFL programs are translated into code of another multiparadigm language, LMNtal (pronounced "elemental") [219, 220, 139]. LMNtal was designed and developed by Kazunori Ueda and his group at Waseda University in Tokyo. Translation between high-level languages is not unusual, in particular in cases where the languages come from similar paradigms and where a mapping of constructs from the source language to those of the target language seems natural.

The main constructs of our target language LMNtal are not functions, constraints, statements and procedures, or objects and methods as typical for most higher-level languages, but hierarchical graphs and rules to describe the graphs' (concurrent) rewriting. Based on these concepts the designers of LMNtal intend to provide a model and language to "unify various paradigms of computation" [219].

Taking LMNtal as target language of the compilation of a multiparadigm language which, like CCFL, provides popular as well as new constructs and ideas, allows one to discuss the adequacy of the LMNtal language approach and aims. If successful it could, moreover, support the definition of clear, simple, and extendable compilation schemata.

We briefly discuss the target language LMNtal and the structure and particular phases of the CCFL compiler in the following.

6.4.1 LMNTAL

LMNtal [139] is a concurrent graph rewriting language. An LMNtal program describes a *process* as a multiset of *atoms, cells, logical links,* and *rules.*

An *atom* $p(X_1, \ldots, X_n)$ has a name p and *logical links* $X_1, \ldots, X_n$ which may connect to other atoms and build graphs in this way. For example, the atoms $f(A,B,E)$, $A = 7$, $g(D,B)$ are interconnected by the links A and B. Note that the links of an atom are ordered such that the above atoms can also be denoted by $E = f(A,B)$, $A = 7$, $B = g(D)$. As a shortened notation we may also write $E = f(7, g(D))$. A and B are inner links in this example; they cannot appear elsewhere because links are bilateral connections and they can, thus, occur at most twice.

A *cell* $\{a^*, r^*, c^*, l^*\}$ encloses a *process*, i.e. atoms a, rules r (see below), and cells c within a *membrane* "{}" and it may encapsulate computations and express hierarchical graphs in this way. Links l may also appear in cells where they are used to interconnect with other cells and atoms.

Example 42 Consider the following two cells.

$$\{succ(A,B) \;\; :- \;\; B=1+A. \;\; E=5, \;\; \{succ(2,D)\}\}, \;\; \{+E\}$$

Program 6.4.1 LMNtal: non-deterministic bubble sort

```
L=[X,Y|L2]  :- X > Y |  L=[Y,X|L2].
aList = [2,1,5,0,4,6,3].
```

Program 6.4.2 LMNtal: membranes to encapsulate computations

```
1  {@r,{$p},$s}  :- {{@r,$p},$s}.
2  {{@r,$p}/,$s}  :- {@r,$p,$s}.
3
4  {append([],Y,Z)  :- Y = Z.
5   append([XH|XT],Y,Z)  :- Z = [XH|ZT],  append(XT,Y,ZT).
6   {R = append([1,2],[4])}},  {P = append([9],[8,1])}
7  }
```

The first cell encloses a rule $succ(A,B)$:- $B=1+A$., an atom $E=5$, and an inner cell $\{succ(2,D)\}$ enclosing an atom itself. The second (outer) cell just contains a link $+E$ connecting into the first cell on the value 5.   ◇

Rules have the form lhs :- rhs and they are used to describe the rewriting of graphs. Both the left-hand side lhs and the right-hand side rhs of a rule are process templates which may contain atoms, cells, rules, and further special constructs (see e.g. [219]), among them process contexts and rule contexts. Contexts may appear within a cell, when they refer to the rest of the entities of this cell. *Rule contexts* $@r$ are used to represent multisets of rules, *process contexts* $\$p$ represent multisets of cells and atoms.

Consider the bubble sort rule and a list to sort in Program 6.4.1 as a first and simple example. In the rule, link L connects to a graph $[X,Y\ |L2]$ representing a list. Thus, $[X,Y\ |L2]$ does not describe the beginning of a list but an arbitrary cut-out such that the rule is in general applicable on every list position where $X > Y$ holds. Since LMNtal does not fix an evaluation strategy, the sorting process is non-deterministic.

As a second example consider Program 6.4.2. Lines 4–7 show a cell, i. e. a process encapsulated by a membrane "{}". It consists of two *append*-rewrite rules for list concatenation in a PROLOG-like syntax and two cells each enclosing an *append*-atom by membranes in line 6. Y, Z, XH, XT, ZT, R, and P are links. The *append*-rewrite rules cannot be applied on the *append*-atoms in line 6 because these are enclosed by extra membranes which prevent them from premature evaluation. The rules in lines 1 and 2, however, operate on a higher level and they allow one to describe the shifting of the *append*-rules into the inner cells and backwards. Here, the expression $@r$ is a rule-context denoting a (multi)set of rules, and $\$p$ and $\$s$ are process-contexts which stand for (multi)sets of cells and atoms. The template $\{@r,\ \$p\}/$ in line 2 has a stable flag "/" which denotes that it can only match with a stable cell, i.e. a cell containing no applicable rules.

We show a reduction sequence of the cell of lines 4–7 (in the context of the rules of lines 1–2). We denote the LMNtal derivation relation by $\longmapsto$ and we underline the elements reduced in the respective steps.

In the initial situation, the rule in line 1 is applicable where @r matches the *append*-rules, $p matches one of the inner *append*-atoms (the choice of which is non-deterministic) and $s stands for the rest of the cell contents. As the result of the rewrite step the *append*-rules are shifted into one of the inner cells such that a reduction of the corresponding inner atom becomes possible in the second step.

```
{ append([],Y,Z) :- Y = Z.
  append([XH|XT],Y,Z) :- Z = [XH|ZT], append(XT,Y,ZT).
  {R = append([1,2],[4])}, {P = append([9],[8,1])}
}
```

$\longmapsto$(1)

```
{{ append([],Y,Z) :- Y = Z.
   append([XH|XT],Y,Z) :- Z = [XH|ZT], append(XT,Y,ZT).
   P = append([9],[8,1])},
 { R = append([1,2],[4])}
}
```

$\longmapsto^*$

```
{{ append([],Y,Z) :- Y = Z.
   append([XH|XT],Y,Z) :- Z = [XH|ZT], append(XT,Y,ZT).
   P = [9,8,1]},
 { R = append([1,2],[4])}
}
```

The first inner cell is now stable, i.e. no rule is applicable inside it. Thus, we can apply the rule from line 2 which unpacks this cell.

. . .

$\longmapsto$(2)

```
{ append([],Y,Z) :- Y = Z.
  append([XH|XT],Y,Z) :- Z = [XH|ZT], append(XT,Y,ZT).
  P = [9,8,1],
  { R = append([1,2],[4])}
}
```

In this state, again the first outer rule (line 1) is applicable and allows a reduction of the second atom R = append([1,2],[4]). The subsequent derivation yields the following final state:

```
{ append([],Y,Z)  :- Y = Z.
  append([XH|XT],Y,Z)  :- Z = [XH|ZT], append(XT,Y,ZT).
  P = [9,8,1], R = [1,2,4]
}
```

As one can see by the example, LMNtal supports a PROLOG-like syntax. However, there are fundamental differences. The above example already demonstrated the use of process-contexts, rule-contexts, membrane-enclosed cells, and the stable flag. In contrast to other languages, the head of a rule may contain several atoms, even cells, rules, and contexts.

A further important difference to other declarative languages is the logical links of LMNtal. What one may take for variables in our program, e.g. Y, Z, XH, are actually logical links. Their intended meaning strongly differs from that of variables. Declarative variables stand for particular expressions or values and, once bound, they stay bound throughout the computation and are indistinguishable from their value. Links in LMNtal also connect to a structure or value. However, link connections may change. While this is similar to imperative variables, links are used to interconnect exactly two atoms, two cells, or an atom and a cell to build graphs, and they have, thus, at most two occurrences. The links P and R in the above example occur only once and, thus, link to the outside environment. In rules, logical links must occur exactly twice.

Semantically, LMNtal is a concurrent language realizing graph rewriting. It inherits properties from concurrent logic languages (cf. Section 5.3). The rule choice is non-deterministic, but can be controlled by guards (not shown in Program 6.4.2).

For a detailed description of LMNtal we refer to [219, 220, 139].

6.4.2 The structure of the compiler

The general structure of the CCFL compiler is shown in Figure 6.4. It starts, as usual, with the syntactic and semantic analyses of a CCFL program which result in an annotated abstract syntax tree (AST). This is the starting point of the code generation.

Code generation is separated into several segments: In the first step (phase 1), we generate basic LMNtal code from the AST subtrees for the semantic program components, where we map CCFL functions to LMNtal rules, CCFL function applications, data terms, and guards to LMNtal atoms and guards, and so on. Furthermore, we generate an additional rule-set per function to realize the handling of higher-order functions and partial applications. Since LMNtal does not a priori fix a particular evaluation strategy, the generated LMNtal programs are evaluated non-deterministically. The resulting

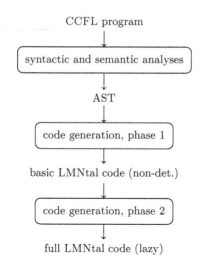

Fig. 6.4 Overview of the CCFL compiler

code is transformed in the second step (phase 2) to realize the complete CCFL functionality including free variables, constraints, and lazy evaluation.

In the following, we briefly discuss the syntactic and semantic analyses in Section 6.4.3 and sketch the code generation for CCFL in Section 6.4.4.

6.4.3 The syntactic and semantic analyses

The implementation of the *syntactic analysis* of the CCFL compiler relies on the monadic parser combinator library Parsec [137].

The *semantic analysis* mainly comprises scope and type checking. Actually, scope checking and type checking can both be considered as constraint solving problems.

The *scoping* constraints derived from the program are simple set constraints which are collected and their solution process is folded into one AST traversal.

In CCFL programs, the user must give types for functions and constraints and for free constraint variables. We distinguish the built-in data types as given in Figure 6.5, functional data types which map from types to types, and user-defined data types built by means of alternatives and products, e.g. the data type *Tree a* in Program 6.2.1. Figure 6.6 shows the types of predefined functions and built-in constraints in CCFL.

The compiler performs *type checking*, and – because of the use of polymorphism – *type inference* in certain cases. The type constraints are collected from the AST of the program. They are equality constraints over terms which

Int	Integer numbers $-2147483648, \ldots, -1, 0, 1, \ldots, 2147483647$
Float	Floating point numbers
Bool	*True* and *False*
C	*Success* and *Fail*

Fig. 6.5 Built-in data types of CCFL

```
fun   +   -   *   /   ::    Int -> Int -> Int
fun   +.  -.  *.  /.  ::    Float -> Float -> Float
fun   ~=  <=  >=  <   >   ==     ::   Int -> Int -> Bool
fun   ~=.  <=.  >=.  <.  >.  ==.   ::   Float -> Float -> Bool
fun   ~=:  ==:  &&  ||  ::   Bool -> Bool -> Bool
fun   not  ::   Bool -> Bool

fun   =:=  ::   a -> a -> C
fun   &  ::  C -> C -> C
fun   bound  ::   a -> C
```

Fig. 6.6 Types of predefined functions and built-in constraints

can be solved using unification according to Hindley-Milner type inference [50, 156].

The result of the semantic analysis phase is an AST annotated with additional information, in particular, types, and it is used as the starting point of the code generation phase.

6.4.4 Encoding CCFL *into* LMNTAL

The code generation starts from the annotated CCFL AST and generates a corresponding LMNtal AST from which we finally derive valid LMNtal code.

We consider the basic translation of functions and functional expressions in Section 6.4.4.1 and the handling of higher-order functions and partial applications in Section 6.4.4.2. This mainly corresponds to the code generation phase 1 in Figure 6.4. The introduction of heap structures as discussed in the third subsection enables one to deal with free variables and to represent sharing of subexpressions. This is the basis of the second code generation phase (see Figure 6.4) and it allows one to realize the complete CCFL functionality, including constraints and lazy evaluation (see Sections 6.4.4.4 and 6.4.4.5).

The transformation of CCFL functions (and constraints) is partially based on translation techniques [41, 166, 167, 228] for functional into logic languages.

Program 6.4.3 LMNtal program as compilation result: list length

```
1    length(List,VO)  :-
2      case__length(List,List,VO).
3
4    case__length(V1,List,VO),  nil(V1)  :-
5      VO = 0.
6
7    case__length(V1,List,VO),  cons(X,XS,V1)  :-
8      VO = 1 + V3,  app(length,XS,V3).
9
10   app(length,X1,X2)  :-  length(X1,X2).
```

6.4.4.1 Functional elements

Let us first consider the functional sublanguage of CCFL. A CCFL function definition is translated into a set of LMNtal rules. Here, there is one initial rule and possibly a set of subordered rules realizing e.g. pattern matching as necessary for case-constructs.

CCFL data elements and variables are represented and processed by means of heap structures during run-time. However, to clarify the presentation in this subsection, we represent CCFL variables directly by LMNtal links[6] instead and data structures by LMNtal atoms. We concentrate on the heap structures later on.

The right-hand side of a CCFL function definition is an expression composed of the typical constructs such as function applications, infix operator applications, let- and case-constructs, variables, constants, and constructors. CCFL infix operations are mapped onto their LMNtal counterparts. Function applications are realized by an atom *app(...)* and an according *app*-rule which is also used for higher-order functions as discussed in the next subsection. Case-expressions generate extra LMNtal rules for pattern matching; let-constructs are straightforwardly realized by equality constraints.

Example 43 Consider Program 6.4.3 as compilation result of the list length function from Program 6.1.2.

The LMNtal program illustrates the generation of different rule alternatives from the case-construct and the handling of function applications and predefined infix operations. Also note the additional link argument *VO* of the *length*-rewrite rule. This link is used to access the result of the rule application, which is necessary because LMNtal explicitly deals with graphs while a computation with a functional language like CCFL yields an expression as result.   ◇

---

[6] Moreover, we tolerate n-fold occurrences of links in rules, where $n \neq 2$. This does not conform with LMNtal, where links must occur exactly twice in a rule, but the problem disappears with the introduction of heap data structures as well.

6.4.4.2 Higher-order functions and partial application

We use a transformation scheme from [228] to allow *higher-order function application* in CCFL. For every CCFL function $f\ x_1 \ldots x_n = expr$ a rewrite rule $app(f, X_1, \ldots, X_n, Y) :- f(X_1, \ldots, X_n, Y)$ is generated, which in combination with the generation of an *app*-atom for a function application realizes higher-order function application.

Example 44 Let the following simple CCFL program be given:

```
fun  double  ::  Int  ->  Int
def  double  x  =  2  *  x

fun  foo  ::  (Int  ->  Int)  ->  Int  ->  Int
def  foo  f  val  =  f  (val  +  5)
```

By the compilation process we obtain the LMNtal rules:

```
double(X, V0)  :-
    V0  =  2  *  X.

foo(F, Val, V0)  :-
    V1  =  Val  +  5,  app(F, V1, V0).

app(double, X1, X2)  :-  double(X1, X2).

app(foo, X1, X2, X3)  :-  foo(X1, X2, X3).
```

Notice that the atom $app(F, V1, V0)$ on the right-hand side of the *foo* rule has been generated from the CCFL function application $f\ (val\ +\ 5)$ as described above.

We show a CCFL reduction of the functional expression *foo double 3* and a corresponding derivation of the LMNtal atom $foo(double, 3, Z)$.[7]

A CCFL derivation:

$\langle\ \{\ foo\ double\ 3\ \}, true\ \rangle \rightsquigarrow \langle\ \{\ double\ (3+5)\ \}, true\ \rangle$
$\rightsquigarrow \langle\ \{\ 2*(3+5)\ \}, true\ \rangle \rightsquigarrow \langle\ \{\ 2*8\ \}, true\ \rangle \rightsquigarrow \langle\ \{\ 16\ \}, true\ \rangle$

A corresponding LMNtal derivation:

$foo(double, 3, Z) \rightarrowtail app(double, 3+5, Z) \rightarrowtail double(3+5, Z)$
$\rightarrowtail Z = 2*(3+5) \rightarrowtail Z = 2*8 \rightarrowtail Z = 16$ ◇

The *partial application* of functions in CCFL is enabled by a number of additional LMNtal rules per CCFL function, where we adopt a transformation given in [41, 166]. To simplify the rule generation, the CCFL compiler performs

---

[7] We have not yet fixed a strategy for the evaluation of the generated LMNtal code (cf. Section 6.4.4.5). Thus, we consider one derivation (of possibly several) here.

an η-enrichment, i.e. additional arguments are appended to the left-hand sides and right-hand sides of a function definition where necessary to meet the type declaration.

Example 45 Let *add* and *addOne* be CCFL functions, where the latter is defined by a partial application of the former.

```
fun add :: Int -> Int -> Int
def add a b = a + b
fun addOne :: Int -> Int
def addOne = add 1
```

The η-enrichment of the function *addOne* within the compilation process yields the following intermediate representation.

```
def addOne x = (add 1) x
```

$\diamond$

The method to enable the partial application of functions from [41, 166] generates $\frac{n\times(n+1)}{2}$ rules for every n-ary function. In [100] we give a detailed presentation of the rule-set; we show an illustrative example here instead.

Example 46 Consider again the functions *add* and *addOne* from Example 45. A CCFL derivation sequence is the following:

$\langle \{ \text{addOne } 2 \}, \text{true} \rangle \rightsquigarrow \langle \{ (\text{add } 1) \text{ } 2 \}, \text{true} \rangle \rightsquigarrow \langle \{ 1 + 2 \}, \text{true} \rangle$
$\rightsquigarrow \langle \{ 3 \}, \text{true} \rangle$

The functions *add* and *addOne* are translated into LMNtal rules as discussed in Section 6.4.4.1. Additionally, we generate rules for each function for all possible cases of its partial application. These rules just generate constructor terms with the function name at root position; in this way the data may be kept and the computation suspended until the function is fully applied. Program 6.4.4 shows the rule set generated from the functions *add* and *addOne* from Example 45.

Now, we can rewrite the LMNtal atom *addOne(2,R)* which corresponds to the CCFL expression *addOne 2*:

```
addOne(2,R)
↦ app(add,1,Y), app(Y,2,R)
↦ add(1,Y), app(Y,2,R) ≡ app(add(1),2,R)
↦ add(1,2,R)
↦ R = 1+2
↦ R = 3
```

$\diamond$

The representation of data and variables by heap structures as discussed subsequently allows one to fuse the set of $\frac{n\times(n+1)}{2} + 1$ rules for handling partial applications and higher-order functions from the original approaches [41, 166, 228] into *one* unified rule.

Program 6.4.4 Generated LMNtal rules for the handling of partial applications and higher-order function applications

```
add(A,B,VO) :-
  VO = A + B.

addOne(X,VO) :-
  app(add,1,Y), app(Y,X,VO).

// handling a CCFL expression add
app(add,VO) :- add(VO).

// handling (add v₀)
app(add,VO,V1) :- add(VO,V1).

// handling ((add v₀) v₁)
app(add (VO),V1,V2) :- add(VO,V1,V2).

// handling add as argument of a higher-order function
app(add,VO,V1,V2) :- add(VO,V1,V2).

// handling addOne
app(addOne,VO) :- addOne(VO).

// handling addOne as argument of a higher-order function
app(addOne,VO,V1) :- addOne(VO,V1).
```

6.4.4.3 Representing CCFL expressions by heap structures

While links in LMNtal look similar to variables, they have a different functionality (cf. Section 6.4.1). In [100] we show in detail that a direct translation of CCFL variables into LMNtal links (and, thus, of CCFL data structures into LMNtal atoms) would not be successful. Since links connect exactly two elements, i.e. cells or atoms, a representation of variables by links would disallow the representation of free variables and the sharing of data structures as needed for lazy evaluation. At least it can be shown [100] that a direct simulation is possible for a functional language (without constraints) using a call-by-value evaluation strategy, where multiply used data structures are just completely copied.

The introduction of a heap as run-time environment enables the representation of free variables and the sharing of common data by different structures. This allows the compilation of user-defined constraints and rule guards on the one hand and the implementation of evaluation strategies using sharing of data structures on the other hand.

The generation and transformation of heap structures is directly incorporated into the generated LMNtal rules as a result of the compilation process.

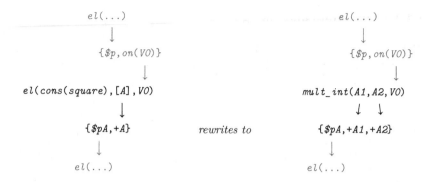

Fig. 6.7 A graph rewriting rule *square*

Example 47 Consider the arithmetic function *square*.

```
fun  square  ::  Int  ->  Int
def  square  a = a * a
```

The compilation according to our translation scheme yields the following code.

```
square(A,VO)  :- VO = A * A.
```

Taking the handling of heap data structures into consideration we obtain the following LMNtal rule, where the atom *mult_int(A1,A2,VO)* calls the LMNtal infix operator "*".

```
el(cons(square),[A],VO),  {$pA,+A}  :-
  mult_int(A1,A2,VO),  {$pA,+A1,+A2}.
```

Figure 6.7 visualizes the generated LMNtal rewrite rule.

In general, built-in operators, like *, are represented by corresponding atoms, e.g. *mult_int*, and they are handled by specific prelude rules. All other non-variable CCFL-expressions are represented by atoms *el(cons(f),OL,I)*, where *f* is the function or constructor name, *OL* is a list of (*o*utgoing) links to cells connecting to structures which represent the arguments according to the original CCFL expression, and *I* is a(n) (*i*ncoming) link from a cell which manages links onto this term. For example, the CCFL term (*square a*) yields the atom *el(cons(double),[A],VO)* with outgoing link *A* and incoming link *VO*. Variables are handled by a similar scheme.

In the heap structures, cells containing links, like *{$p,on(VO)}*, are used to connect between the atoms to build structures. In this way it is possible to realize sharing as illustrated by the cell *{$pA,+A1,+A2}* which holds two incoming links *+A1* and *+A2* and one outgoing link onto the common shared structure (indicated by the gray outgoing link onto the atom *el(...)*). ◊

6.4.4.4 Constraints and rule guards

CCFL integrates functional and constraint programming. Since user-defined constraints can be considered as particular functions, the code generation treats them uniformly such that we reach a proper unification of both paradigms.

User-defined constraints in CCFL support all the constructs as introduced for functions, but additionally allow free variables, a with-construct for their introduction, ask-constraints in the rule guard and tell-constraints in the rule body.

Just like LMNtal rules for CCFL functions, rules for user-defined constraints must hold an additional link in the rule head to connect to the computation result because constraints must be accessible as elements, e.g. for partial application.

Ask-constraints, i.e. bound- and match-constraints, are realized by additional atoms in the heads of the generated LMNtal rules matching the corresponding heap structures.

Example 48 The user-defined constraint *member* from Program 6.1.4 non-deterministically chooses values from a given list $(y : ys)$. We either take the first element y as result value or initiate a further computation on the rest ys of the list.

The CCFL rule guards consist of identical match-constraints l =:= y : ys (cf. Program 6.1.4, lines 18 and 19) to realize the non-deterministic choice. The compilation yields, thus, identical rule heads matching the list structure $(y : ys)$ or $cons(Y, Ys)$, resp., as given below for both alternatives. The corresponding heap structure is shown for illustration in Figure 6.8.

```
el(cons(member),[L,X],VO),
el(cons(cons),[Y,Ys],LO),
{on (LO),$pL,+L} :-
    . . .
```

$\diamond$

For *tell-constraints* we distinguish between applications of user-defined constraints which are just handled like function applications and equality constraints t_1 =:= t_2. The latter is based on a unification of the constraint subexpressions t_1 and t_2. We provided a unification mechanism for heap data in LMNtal: *unify(L1,L2,R)* unifies the heap structures connected to the links $L1$ and $L2$ and yields a result structure linked to R. The transformation of a CCFL equality constraint into LMNtal code, thus, produces a *unify*-atom over both heap structures which initiates the unification process.

Example 49 Consider the producer-consumer example in Program 6.1.5 and a cut-out of an LMNtal rule for *produce* as compilation result given in Program 6.4.5.

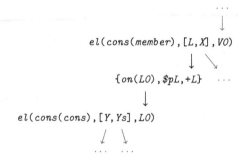

Fig. 6.8 A heap structure representing the expression *member* (*y* : *ys*) *x*

Program 6.4.5 LMNtal compilation result: produce

```
 1  el(cons(produce),[Buf],VO) :-
 2     // generate a fresh variable buf1
 3     el(var(...),OnBuf1,InBuf1), ..., {on(InBuf1),+Buf1},
 4     // generate structure for item
 5     ...
 6     // generate expression (item:buf1)
 7     el(cons(cons),[Item,Buf1],V3), {on(V3),+V2},
 8     // unify call: buf =:= item:buf1
 9     unify(Buf,V2,VO),
10     ...
```

The constraint *buf* =:= *item* : *buf1* in line 7, Program 6.1.5, generates a corresponding *unify*-atom in line 9, Program 6.4.5. This atom *unify(Buf, V2, VO)* initiates the unification of the two structures connected to the links *Buf* and *V2* which yields a result structure with link *VO*. While the first structure (connected to *Buf*) is passed as an argument of the rule, the second structure (connected to *V2*) is created by the code of lines 2-7. ◊

6.4.4.5 Evaluation strategies

LMNtal evaluates non-deterministically, and a priory it does not support certain evaluation strategies. Thus, the control of evaluation strategies for CCFL is directly integrated into the compilation schemes. Here, we use the ability of LMNtal to express hierarchical computation spaces and code migration between them (as shown in Program 6.4.2) which enables a clear and simple strategy description. The use of the membrane construct of LMNtal plays an essential role for the encoding and allows a significantly simpler than previous encodings, e.g. that of the lambda calculus by Sinot [208] based on token passing in interaction nets.

We discussed the fundamental ideas, concepts, and the implementation in detail in [101].

The main idea when encoding evaluation strategies is a destructuring of expressions into subexpressions, their encapsulation by membranes into separate computation spaces, and their interconnection by links. This allows one to express dependencies between subexpressions on the one hand, but to hold the computations apart from each other, on the other hand.

Expressions to be reduced (e.g. innermost for eager strategies or outermost for call-by-name and lazy strategies) are provided with the rule-set such that their reduction becomes possible. Other calls are delayed by holding them apart from the rules until the computation of the redexes they depend on is finished. Then a reorganization of computation spaces takes place.

Thus, the control of the order of subexpression evaluation according to a strategy within the CCFL compilation schemes is based on two main concepts:

1. The destructuring of expressions within the LMNtal rules generated from the CCFL program which realize local computations.
2. A general LMNtal rule set which reorganizes the computation spaces when local computations have been finished.

We refrain from a detailed presentation and refer to [101] which discusses the compilation schemes including a presentation of the general rule sets for concurrent eager and lazy strategies, resp.

6.5 Parallel programming with πCCFL

While they are broadly handled similarly in the compilation process, functions and user-defined constraints serve different purposes in CCFL. Functions can be considered as the computational core and constraints as the coordinational core of the language, resp. This combination can be used to control concurrency in CCFL programs and even to express typical parallelization schemes.

Beside the implementation presented in Section 6.4, there exists a second compiler with focus on parallelization as presented in [103]. The compiler target is an abstract machine ATAF that can be efficiently implemented on multicore architectures. ATAF implements a G-machine [21, 122] to evaluate functional expressions and provides facilities to run multiple cooperating processes on a fixed set of CPUs.

To distinguish between the approaches, we will use the name πCCFL when talking about the parallel version in the following.

We discuss examples taken from [103] to underline techniques for parallel programming using πCCFL.

Example 50 Consider Program 6.5.1 defining a function *map* and a constraint abstraction *farm*. Both have the same general structure, i.e. a function f

Program 6.5.1 πCCFL: functional *map* and constraint-based *farm*

```
1   fun  map  ::  (a -> b) -> [a] -> [b]
2   def  map  f  l  =
3     case  l  of  []        -> [];
4                  x  :  xs -> (f x) : (map f xs)
5
6   fun  farm  ::  (a -> b) -> [a] -> [b] -> C
7   def  farm  f  l  r  =
8     case  l  of  []        -> r =:= [];
9                  x  :  xs -> with  rs  ::  [b]
10                            in  r =:= (f x) : rs & farm f xs rs
```

is applied to every element of a given list *l* and the results are composed
into a new list. However, there is one fundamental difference: Since *map* is a
function, it is evaluated sequentially. On the other hand, *farm* is a user-defined
constraint. Its evaluation yields two concurrently working processes generated
from the constraint conjunction in line 10.   ◊

While this uncontrolled form of parallelization as demonstrated in Example 50 may yield a huge number of, possibly computationally light-weight,
concurrent processes, selective control of the degree of parallelization of computations is possible in πCCFL, too.

We consider modeling of data and task parallelism, resp. While *data parallelism* describes the distribution of data across (different) parallel computing
nodes, where each node executes the same instructions on the different items
from the data set, *task parallelism* concerns the distribution of execution
processes.

Example 51 Program 6.5.2 shows a data parallel farm skeleton *pfarm* with
granularity control. Here, the number of processing elements *noPE* determines
the number of generated processes. The abstraction *pfarm* calls *nfarm* which
splits the list to be processed into *noPE* sublists and generates an appropriate
number of processes for list processing. These are distributed across the
parallel computing nodes by the run-time system of πCCFL.   ◊

Example 52 As a second example of typical parallelization patterns in
πCCFL consider Program 6.5.3. It realizes a data parallel fold skeleton.

In functional languages like HASKELL or ML, fold is typically a higher-
order built-in function which, starting from an initial value and using a binary
function, reduces a list to one value.

The data parallel skeleton *pfold* partitions a list into sublists according
to the number of available processing nodes *noPE*. The run-time system of
πCCFL manages the parallel processing of the sublists. In a final step, the
overall result *r* is computed by a (sequential) fold function *foldl* of the list
rs of intermediate results.   ◊

Program 6.5.2 πCCFL: farm parallelization with granularity control

```
1    fun nfarm :: Int -> (a -> b) -> [a] -> [b] -> C
2    def nfarm n f l r =
3      with rs :: [[b]]
4      in let parts = partition n l;
5             pf    = map f
6         in farm pf parts rs & r =:= concat rs
7
8    fun pfarm :: (a -> b) -> [a] -> [b] -> C
9    def pfarm f l r = nfarm noPE f l r
```

Program 6.5.3 πCCFL: parallel fold

```
fun pfold :: (a -> a -> a) -> a -> [a] -> a -> C
def pfold f e l r =
  with rs :: [[a]]
  in let parts = partition noPE l
     in farm (foldl f e) parts rs &
        r =:= foldl f e rs

fun foldl :: (b -> a -> b) -> b -> [a] -> b
def foldl f e l =
  case l of []        -> e;
            x : xs -> foldl f (f e x) xs
```

As we can see from these examples, πCCFL does not feature specialized data structures to support data parallelism. Instead, the user provides a regular splitting of the data structure controlling the granularity of parallelism in this way, while the run-time system is responsible for an equitable distribution of the data (and tasks) onto the processing nodes. Thus, the step from data to task parallel skeletons is smooth in πCCFL.

Example 53 In Program 6.5.4 a formulation of a parallel mergesort is given. The list to sort is partitioned into subparts to be sorted on the individual processing elements. However, we observe two things: 1) The list partitioning is performed in a tree-like fashion, i.e. each *pmsort* process bears two *pmsort* child processes. 2) There are two *pmsort* processes *and* a third concurrent sibling process, namely *r =:= merge sl sr* which realizes a merge of the sorted result lists.[8] Thus, Program 6.5.4 is actually an example of the simultaneous use of data and task parallelism within a user-defined constraint.   ◇

---

[8] Note, that *msort* and *merge* are just functions and, thus, they are evaluated sequentially.

Program 6.5.4 πCCFL: parallel mergesort

```
fun pmergesort :: [Int] -> [Int] -> C
def pmergesort l r = pmsort noPE l r

fun pmsort :: Int -> [Int] -> [Int] -> C
def pmsort n l r =
  case l of
    []      -> r =:= [];
    x : xs -> case n > 1 of
               True  -> let (first, second) = split l;
                            n1 = n/2
                        in with sl, sr :: [Int]
                           in pmsort n1 first sl       &
                              pmsort (n-n1) second sr &
                              r =:= merge sl sr;
               False -> r =:= msort l

fun msort :: [Int] -> [Int]
def msort l = ...

fun merge :: [Int] -> [Int] -> [Int]
def merge l r = ...
```

6.6 Integration of external constraints into CCFL

Currently, constraint programming in CCFL is based on equality constraints over functional expressions. In this section, we sketch concepts for the introduction of new constraint domains (and solvers) into CCFL, as is realized in many declarative languages [217, 1, 148, 68].

CCFL provides ask-constraints in the guards of rules and tell-constraints in the rule bodies. We discuss the extension of both in the subsequent sections.

6.6.1 External tell-constraints

Tell-constraints appear in the body of user-defined constraints. Up to now we have distinguished applications of user-defined constraints and equality constraints on functional expressions. The integration of external constraints into the body of user-defined constraints allows one to express typical constraint-problems, like the well-known Send-More-Money problem and the 8-queens problem, in a simple way.

We consider another example which is inspired by [148]. Program 6.6.1 combines external arithmetic constraints and user-defined constraints in

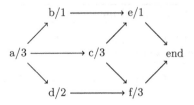

Fig. 6.9 Tasks and durations, ordered from left to right

Program 6.6.1 Computation of a schedule

```
1    fun schedule :: [Int] -> C
2    def schedule [a,b,c,d,e,f,end] =
3      with max :: Int
4      in a+3 ≤# b  &  a+3 ≤# c  &  b+1 ≤# e  &  e+1 ≤# end  & ... &
5         a =# 0  &  end ≤# max  &  max =:= Σ [3,1,3,2,1,3]  &
6         cfarm (∈# {0..max}) [a,b,c,d,e,f,end]
7
8    fun cfarm :: (a -> C) -> [a] -> C
9    def cfarm c (x : xs) =
10     case xs of []      -> c x ;
11                y : ys  -> c x & cfarm c xs
```

CCFL. The constraints of the external domain are indicated by a subscript "#".

The user-defined constraint *schedule* takes the variables $a, \ldots, f$, and *end* representing starting times of tasks to be scheduled. The tasks must be performed in the left-to-right order given in Figure 6.9, where each task takes a certain time as given. Task *a* starts at time 0. The user-defined constraint *cfarm* takes a constraint, actually a partial application ($\in_\# \{0..max\}$ :: **Int -> C**) of an external constraint in our example, applies it to a list of variables, and generates a constraint conjunction in this way. In line 5 we compute an upper bound *max* of the finishing time of the schedule as the sum of the task durations.

We show a derivation of the constraint *schedule* $[a,b,c,d,e,f,end]$ using the CCFL derivation relation ⤳ (cf. Section 6.3), where we assume an additional constraint solver which propagates the external constraints using ⤳$_{tell}$ to its constraint store. This store is just represented as part of the second component C of a system state $\langle A, C \rangle$.

$\langle$ { *schedule* $[a,b,c,d,e,f,end]$ }, *true* $\rangle$

⤳ $\langle$ { $a+3 \leq_\# b$, $a+3 \leq_\# c$, $\ldots$, $a =_\# 0$, $end \leq_\# max$,
           $max =:= \Sigma [3,1,3,2,1,3]$, $cfarm(\in_\# \{0..max\})$ $[a,b,\ldots,end]$ },
        true $\rangle$

⤳$^*_{tell}$ $\langle$ { $cfarm$ $(\in_\# \{0..max\})$ $[a,b,\ldots,end]$ },

$$3 \leq b, \ 3 \leq c \ \wedge \ \ldots \ \wedge \ a = 0 \ \wedge \ end \leq 13 \ \wedge \ max = 13 \ \rangle$$

$\leadsto^* \quad \langle \ \{ \ a \in_{\#} \{0 \ldots max\}, \ b \in_{\#} \{0 \ldots max\}, \ \ldots, \ end \in_{\#} \{0 \ldots max\} \ \},$
$\qquad 3 \leq b, \ 3 \leq c \ \wedge \ \ldots \ \wedge \ a = 0 \ \wedge \ end \leq 13 \ \wedge \ max = 13 \ \rangle$

$\leadsto^*_{tell} \ \langle \ \{ \ \textbf{\textit{Success}} \ \}, 3 \leq b, \ 3 \leq c \ \wedge \ \ldots \ \wedge \ a = 0 \ \wedge \ max = 13 \ \wedge$
$\qquad b \in \{3 \ldots 11\} \ \wedge \ c \in \{3 \ldots 7\} \ \wedge \ \ldots \ \wedge \ end \in \{9 \ldots 13\} \ \rangle$

The derivation highlights two important issues:

- The external constraint store must exchange bindings and other constraints on the variables of common sorts with the CCFL runtime system.
- In out example, we just check the satisfiability of the constraints and narrow the domains of the variables. However, the user will typically be interested in finding one or a number of concrete solutions or a solution optimal w.r.t. a certain objective function. There are several approaches to this including encapsulated search [82, 148] and monads [147].

6.6.2 External ask-constraints

In CCFL ask-constraints appear in the forms of match- and bound-constraints which perform an entailment test of constraints on the structure of (potentially incompletely bound) terms. An extension of the rule guards by arithmetic constraints realizes similar tests on arithmetic expressions which can be used for the process coordination as well.

In Program 6.6.2 we provide an insertion sort algorithm as user-defined constraint. In contrast to a corresponding function definition, a sorting of lists containing potentially unbound variables of type $\textbf{\textit{Int}}$ is possible. For such list elements, however, there must be sufficient information to decide about their position within the ordered result list.

Again, we indicate external constraints by a subscript "#". The function ins inserts an element a into a sorted list il at the appropriate position. Arithmetic ask-constraints control the insertion process and allow to deal with unbound variables as long as enough information about the variables' relations is available to decide about their list positions.

We consider two derivations for illustration. In the first computation, let a be a free variable.

$\langle \ \{ \ isort \ [7,a,2] \ r \ \}, \ true \ \rangle$

$\leadsto \quad \langle \ \{ \ ins \ 7 \ s \ r, \ isort \ [a,2] \ s \ \}, \ true \ \rangle$

$\leadsto^* \langle \ \{ \ ins \ 7 \ s \ r, \ ins \ a \ s' \ s, \ ins \ 2 \ s'' \ s', \ s'' =:= [] \ \}, \ true \ \rangle$

$\leadsto^* \langle \ \{ \ ins \ 7 \ s \ r, \ ins \ a \ s' \ s \ \}, s'' = [] \ \wedge \ s' = [2] \ \rangle$

Program 6.6.2 Insertion sort with arithmetic ask-constraints

```
1   fun isort :: [Int] -> [Int] -> C
2   def isort il out =
3     with s :: [Int]
4     in case il of []        -> out =:= [];
5                    x : xs -> ins x s out & isort xs s
6
7   fun ins :: Int -> [Int] -> [Int] -> C
8   def ins a il out =
9       il =:= []                    -> out =:= [a] |
10      il =:= x : xs & a ≤# x -> out =:= a : il |
11      il =:= x : xs & a ># x -> with s :: [Int]
12                                 in out =:= x : s & ins a xs s
```

$\rightsquigarrow$ ⟨ { *ins 7 s r*,

　　　$s' =:= []$　　　　　　　　-> $s =:= [a]$ |

　　　$s' =:= x : xs$ & $a \leq_{\#} x$ -> $s =:= a : s'$ |

　　　$s' =:= x : xs$ & $a >_{\#} x$ -> ... }, $s'' = []$ ∧ $s' = [2]$ ⟩

The *isort*-constraint is completely unwound but finally the computation suspends when the unbound variable a is to be inserted into the list [2], because its position cannot be decided yet.

Now, let us add further information about the variable a, namely $a >_{\#} 8$. This yields the following successful derivation.

⟨ { *isort* [7,a,2] r, $a >_{\#} 8$ }, *true* ⟩

$\rightsquigarrow^*$ ⟨ { *ins 7 s r*, *ins a s' s* }, $s'' = []$ ∧ $s' = [2]$ ∧ $a > 8$ ⟩

$\rightsquigarrow^*$ ⟨ { *Success* }, $s'' = []$ ∧ $s' = [2]$ ∧ $s = [2,a]$ ∧ $a > 8$ ∧ ... ∧ $r = [2,7,a]$ ⟩

6.6.3 Evaluation of external constraints

The integration of external constraints into CCFL requires an extension of the compilation scheme and of the runtime system. There are two main approaches for the evaluation of external constraints in CCFL programs.

Firstly, the solution mechanisms of certain constraint domains can comfortably be implemented using the CCFL compiler target language LMNtal. For example, set-constraints [4, 174] can be expressed in LMNtal in a natural way. We also followed this approach when providing equality constraints on functional expressions as tell-constraints for CCFL, where we implemented a unification algorithm for terms in LMNtal and incorporated *unify*-atoms into the compilation result. Even the arithmetic built-in functions can be considered as representatives of this approach in its simplest case, because they are based on their equivalents in LMNtal.

The second approach is to integrate external constraints resp. solvers into both languages LMNtal and CCFL. However, this demands an extension of syntax and semantics not only of CCFL but of *both* languages.

LMNtal allows one to use processes in rule bodies which build on inline code [139]. An implementation of external CCFL tell-constraints based on this option seems reasonable. However, ask-constraints may require an actual extension of the LMNtal compiler.

An external solver to be integrated into LMNtal to provide the basis of CCFL constraints needs a constraint propagation function for the CCFL tell-constraints, (preferably) an entailment test (otherwise implemented on top of the propagation function or satisfiability test, see Section 4.2) for the ask-constraints, and functions to handle the constraint store. Constraint solving libraries appropriate for an integration would be e.g. the CHOCO constraint solver [44] on finite domain constraints written in JAVA or GECODE [73] for finite domain constraints and finite set constraints implemented in C++.

6.7 Conclusion and related work

The implementation of CCFL based on LMNtal demonstrates the embedding of the concurrent functional paradigm into the LMNtal language model. This enabled to equip CCFL with advanced language features, like constraints for communication and synchronization of process systems, and to express non-deterministic computations and even typical parallelization schemes. Moreover, LMNtal supports a clear and simple encoding of typical evaluation strategies [101].

Functional languages allowing for concurrent computation of processes are e.g. EDEN [141] and ERLANG [19, 20], both languages using explicit notions for the generation of processes and their communication, and CONCURRENT HASKELL [179] which supports threads via the IO monad. DATA PARALLEL HASKELL [40] targets multicore architectures and allows nested data parallel programming based on a built-in type of parallel arrays.

As multiparadigm language representatives combining the functional and the constraint-based or logic programming paradigms we mention the constraint functional language GOFFIN [39], which strongly separates the functional sublanguage from the constraint part, and CURRY [82], combining the functional and the logic paradigms and building on the evaluation principle narrowing (in contrast to residuation and non-deterministic choice in CCFL). A language similar to CURRY is TOY [57, 217] for which the integration of different arithmetic constraint domains has been examined over recent years.

The CCFL coordination of concurrent processes is based on the concurrent constraint programming (CCP) model [199, 200] (cf. Section 5.3).

Chapter 7
A Generic Framework for Multiparadigm Constraint Programming

In this chapter we present a framework for the integration of arbitrary declarative programming languages and constraints. This approach goes beyond the methods presented so far and tackles the subject of language integration from a completely different point of view: Our main concept is *constraint solver cooperation.*

As discussed in Section 4, constraint solving algorithms are typically limited to restricted domains, e.g. linear or non-linear arithmetics, Boolean constraints, finite domain constraints etc. to allow efficient processing. However, many interesting problems are intuitively expressed as multi-domain descriptions. Since the cost and time for developing new constraint solvers that are able to handle such problems are significant, (preexisting) constraint solvers are combined to tackle multi-domain constraint problems in collaboration. In Section 7.1 we present a *framework for cooperating constraint solvers* which allows the integration of arbitrary black-box solvers. We discuss its model and preconditions, and present illustrative examples.

We take an important step forward in Section 7.2: By considering language evaluation mechanisms (in combination with programs) as constraint solvers we can integrate them with other solvers within the solver cooperation framework. This allows us to equip the languages with constraints from multiple domains which yields *multiparadigm constraint programming languages.* We discuss the integration of a logic and a functional logic language, resp., into the cooperation framework.

Finally, in Section 7.3 we sketch the implementation of the theoretical concepts in the multiparadigm constraint programming system META-S and evaluate example computations.

7.1 Constraint solver cooperation

In this section we introduce the theoretical and conceptual background of our system of cooperating constraint solvers. We introduce the general model, give formal requirements for the interface functions of the solvers to be integrated, and show an example to illustrate the approach.

The framework for *cooperating constraint solvers* as presented here was initially introduced and formally described in [97]. We examined termination and confluence, as well as soundness and completeness restrictions in [98]. The representation of Sections 7.1.1 – 7.1.3 is partially taken from [105].

7.1.1 The general model

The basic architecture of a single constraint solving system is a *solver algorithm* CS associated to a *constraint store* C and a *constraint pool* (see Figure 7.1(a)). A constraint pool is a set (resp. conjunction) of (basic) constraints. While a store is mostly also a conjunction (cf. Section 4.2), for reasons of generality we allow a store to be a disjunction of constraint conjunctions in our model.

Given a constraint problem, the solving system performs as follows. Initially the constraint store of a solver is empty: more precisely, it contains only the constraint *true*; the constraint pool contains the constraint problem to solve. By *constraint propagation* the solver adds constraints from the pool to its store while ensuring that the constraints in the store remain satisfiable. In this way the set of possible valuations for the variables of the constraint store is successively narrowed. If the solver detects an inconsistency, the corresponding constraint is rejected. In this case, the initial conjunction of constraints is unsatisfiable.

When constraints from *different* domains are used together, we have two possibilities. Either we develop a new solver that is capable of handling all constraints of the different realms. Or we take several existing solvers, one for each realm, and coordinate them by some mediating program. The former approach usually generates more efficient solvers, but the amount of implementation work becomes prohibitive, when more and more kinds of constraints must be integrated. Therefore we focus on the second approach, which is more flexible and more economical.

Figure 7.1(b) shows the architecture of our system for cooperating solvers. In the following let L with $\mu, \nu \in L$ denote the set of indices of constraint solvers. The system constitutes of the following parts:

- The *stores* C_ν of the individual *constraint solvers* CS_ν hold the constraints which have been propagated so far. Initially they are all empty, i.e. they contain the constraint *true*.

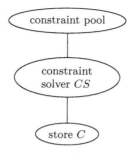

(a) A solver with pool and store

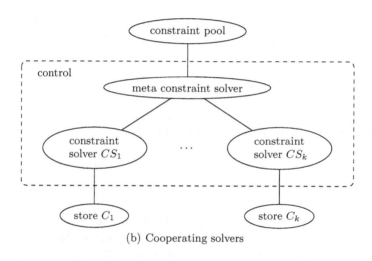

(b) Cooperating solvers

Fig. 7.1 General architecture for (cooperating) constraint solvers

- The *constraint pool* is again the set of constraints that still need to be considered. Initially it contains the constraint problem to be solved.
- The *meta constraint solver* (MCS) coordinates the work of the individual solvers. It distributes the constraints from the pool to the appropriate solvers, which add them to their stores by *constraint propagation* and use them for their local computations. Conversely, constraints in the local stores may be *projected* to the pool in order to make them available as new information to other solvers.

The constraint computation is a process of sequent propagations and projections which ends when no more information interchange takes place. Then the contents of the stores (and of the pool) together represent the result: It indicates whether the initial constraint conjunction was unsatisfiable or not and shows constraints (if any) which could not be handled because of incomplete solvers. Restrictions of the solution space, which may even provide a full solution of the problem, are provided by means of *projections* of the stores.

Details of the cooperation and communication of the solvers are determined by their *cooperation strategy*. We consider this aspect in Sections 7.1.5 and 7.3.3.

At the heart of our approach are the requirements for the *interfaces* by which the solvers are integrated into the system. There are essentially two kinds of operations that constitute this interface (cf. Sections 7.1.2 and 7.1.3):

- For every solver CS_ν there is a function $tell_\nu$ for *propagating* constraints from the pool to the store C_ν.
- For every pair of solvers CS_ν and CS_μ there is a *projection* function $proj_{\nu \to \mu}$ for providing information from the store C_ν to the solver CS_μ (via the constraint pool). Note that this entails translation into the other solver's signature.

7.1.2 Constraint propagation (tell$_\nu$)

Constraint propagation is one important interface function which is a precondition for the integration of a constraint solver into our solver cooperation framework. It is based on a satisfiability test on the constraint store.

Consider a constraint system $\zeta_\nu = (\Sigma_\nu, \mathcal{D}_\nu, \mathcal{T}_\nu, X_\nu, \mathcal{C}ons_\nu)$ and a corresponding solver CS_ν with constraint store C_ν. The function $tell_\nu$, $\nu \in L$, takes a constraint $c \in \mathcal{C}ons_\nu$ (i.e. a basic constraint of the constraint system of CS_ν) from the pool and adds it to the constraint store C_ν, which leads to a new store C'_ν. There may also be a remaining part c'' of c, which is moved back into the pool. At the same time, the *satisfiability* of C'_ν is ensured.

Figure 7.2 shows the requirements for the function $tell_\nu$. Let $Store_\nu = \bigvee \bigwedge \mathcal{C}ons_\nu$ denote disjunctions of constraint conjunctions. Our propagation function returns three values. The first one is a Boolean indicator of success or failure. The second one is the modified store. And the third value is a possibly remaining constraint $c'' \in \bigvee \bigwedge \mathcal{C}ons_\nu$, which is given back to the pool.

When the solver *successfully* propagates a constraint c to a store C_ν (Case 1), then it must be ensured that the overall knowledge of the system, that is of the store and of the constraint together, is neither lost nor increased (a). It is only possible to add constraints to a store, but not to delete them. Thus, the new store C'_ν must imply the old one (b). Of course, the new store C'_ν has to be satisfiable in the domain $\mathcal{D}_\nu$ as it is a constraint store (c).

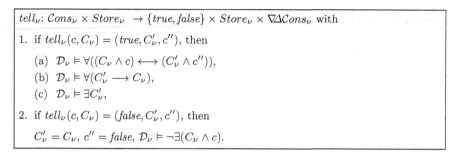

$tell_\nu: Cons_\nu \times Store_\nu \rightarrow \{true, false\} \times Store_\nu \times \nabla\!\!\!\!\triangle Cons_\nu$ with

1. if $tell_\nu(c, C_\nu) = (true, C'_\nu, c'')$, then

   (a) $\mathcal{D}_\nu \models \forall((C_\nu \wedge c) \longleftrightarrow (C'_\nu \wedge c''))$,
   (b) $\mathcal{D}_\nu \models \forall(C'_\nu \longrightarrow C_\nu)$,
   (c) $\mathcal{D}_\nu \models \exists C'_\nu$,

2. if $tell_\nu(c, C_\nu) = (false, C'_\nu, c'')$, then

   $C'_\nu = C_\nu$, $c'' = false$, $\mathcal{D}_\nu \models \neg\exists(C_\nu \wedge c)$.

Fig. 7.2 Interface function $tell_\nu$, $\nu \in L$ (requirements)

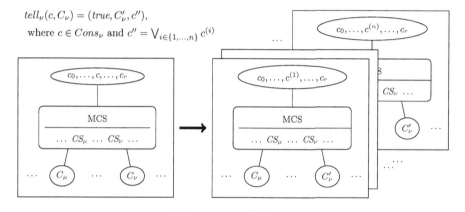

$tell_\nu(c, C_\nu) = (true, C'_\nu, c'')$,
where $c \in Cons_\nu$ and $c'' = \bigvee_{i \in \{1,...,n\}} c^{(i)}$

Fig. 7.3 Application of the interface function $tell_\nu$

This first case also covers the situation that a solver is not able to handle a certain constraint c, i.e. that the solver is incomplete. In this case the store C_ν does not change and $c = c''$ remains in the pool.[9]

If $tell_\nu(c, C_\nu)$ fails (Case 2) because c and C_ν are *contradictory*, then *false* is added to the constraint pool and the constraint store C_ν does not change.

Figure 7.3 visualizes the state change of the system when a solver performs a successful constraint propagation. The left side shows the system before the propagation, the right side afterwards. When we propagate a constraint c to a store C_ν by $tell_\nu(c, C_\nu)$, c is deleted from the pool and propagated to the store. The remaining constraint c'' may in general be a disjunction of constraint conjunctions, i.e. $c'' = \bigvee_{i \in \{1,...,n\}} c^{(i)}$. Since the pool is a set of basic constraints, this causes a splitting of the system state as shown in Figure 7.3.

---

[9] To ensure termination of the overall system, this particular case must be detected by the overall machinery and the treatment of the constraint must be suspended (cf. [97]). We omit this technical detail in favor of readability.

Example 54 The interface function $tell_A$ of a rational arithmetic solver CS_A could work as follows. Let a store $C = (1/X + 1/Y =_A 1/200)$ be given.

We propagate a constraint $(X =_A 300)$:

$tell_A((X =_A 300), C) = (true, C', true)$.

The solver CS_A computes a new simplified store $C' = (X =_A 300 \wedge Y =_A 600)$.

On the other hand, now propagating a constraint $(Y >_A 600)$ yields a failing propagation:

$tell_A((Y >_A 600), C') = (false, C', false)$.   ◇

Example 55 Suppose we have the constraint $\sqrt{X} = Y$ in the pool. An arithmetic solver might not be able to handle this constraint completely, but to add $Y \geq 0$ to its store and keep the constraint $X = Y^2$ in the pool for later consideration, i.e.

$tell_A((\sqrt{X} = Y), C) = (true, C', X = Y^2)$,

where $\mathcal{D}_A \models \forall((C \wedge Y \geq 0) \longleftrightarrow C')$.   ◇

For each solver CS_ν to be integrated into the overall cooperating system a suitable function $tell_\nu$ must be provided. However, this is unproblematic for the following reasons: 1) Constraint propagation is mainly based on the *satisfiability test* which is the main operation of a constraint solver. 2) Moreover, the requirements in Figure 7.2 are fulfilled by many existing solvers because they take particular properties of solvers (like their incompleteness or an existing entailment test) into consideration.

Further examples of constraint propagations and concrete propagation functions will be shown in Section 7.1.4, where we examine an example computation in our cooperation framework, and in Sections 7.2.1 and 7.2.2 for the special cases of functional logic and logic languages, when they are viewed as solvers.

7.1.3 Projection of constraint stores ($proj_{\nu \to \mu}$)

The second interface function for solvers to be integrated into our cooperation framework is projection. It is used for information interchange between constraint solvers CS_ν and CS_μ, $\nu \neq \mu$, $\mu, \nu \in L$.

Figure 7.4 shows the requirements for the projection function. The function $proj_{\nu \to \mu}$ takes a set of common variables of the two solvers and the local store C_ν and returns (a disjunction of conjunctions of) constraints to the pool. The projection $proj_{\nu \to \mu}(X, C_\nu) = c$ of a store C_ν w.r.t. common variables (i.e. $X \subseteq X_\nu \cap X_\mu$) provides constraints c of another solver CS_μ. These constraints represent knowledge implied by the store C_ν. Projection does not change the stores but only extends the pool by the projected constraints.

$proj_{\nu \to \mu} : \wp(X_\nu \cap X_\mu) \times Store_\nu \to \nabla\!\!\!\!\Delta Cons_\mu$, where $var(proj_{\nu \to \mu}(X, C_\nu)) = Y \subseteq X$,

must be *sound*, i.e. for every valuation σ_ν for the variables of Y must hold:

If $(\mathcal{D}_\nu, \sigma_\nu) \vDash \exists\_\tilde{Y} C_\nu$, then $(\mathcal{D}_\mu, \sigma_\nu) \vDash proj_{\nu \to \mu}(X, C_\nu)$, where

$\exists\_\tilde{Y} C_\nu$ denotes the existential closure of formula C_ν except for the variables of Y.

Fig. 7.4 Interface function $proj_{\nu \to \mu}$, $\mu \neq \nu$, $\mu, \nu \in L$ (requirements)

To ensure that no solution is lost, a projection c must provide (at least) every satisfying valuation of the current store C_ν. That is, $proj_{\nu \to \mu}$ must be defined in such a way that every solution σ_ν of C_ν is a solution of its projection c in $\mathcal{D}_\mu$ (soundness).

Example 56 Consider an arithmetic solver $CS_\mathcal{A}$ and a finite domain solver $CS_{\mathcal{FD}}$. Let $C_{\mathcal{FD}}$ be the store of the finite domain solver with

$$C_{\mathcal{FD}} = X \in_{\mathcal{FD}} \{300, 600, 900, \ldots, 2700, 3000\} \wedge$$
$$Y \in_{\mathcal{FD}} \{300, 600, 900, \ldots, 2700, 3000\}.$$

Define $proj_{\mathcal{FD} \to \mathcal{A}}$ (as a *weak* projection, see below) such that

$$proj_{\mathcal{FD} \to \mathcal{A}}(\{X\}, C_{\mathcal{FD}}) = (X \geq_\mathcal{A} 300 \wedge X \leq_\mathcal{A} 3000).   \diamond$$

Again, the projection function $proj_{\nu \to \mu}$ must be given for every pair of solvers. For many pairs of solvers it is possible to automatically provide simple projection functions generating equality constraints which at least express variable bindings. Also it is often sufficient to provide actual projection functions only for particular pairs of solvers and to reduce superfluous communication. (Note that *true* is always a valid projection, too.)

Examples of projection functions and their applications will also be shown in Section 7.1.4 in an example and in Sections 7.2.1 and 7.2.2 in connection with language-based solvers.

Weak vs. strong projection. In general, a constraint solver may provide several projection functions. In the practical implementation META-S (cf. Section 7.3) of our approach we found it useful to introduce the concept of *weak* and *strong* projections.

Weak projection is allowed to generate constraint conjunctions only, while *strong projection* may produce disjunctions as well. Thus, weak projection may result in more unspecific constraints. For example for a store which allows only certain discrete values for a variable X, strong projection may express this by enumerating all alternatives, like $X = 1 \vee X = 3 \vee X = 7$, whereas weak projection results in a less precise conjunction $1 \leq X \wedge X \leq 7$.

Typically, this concept can be used as follows: During the evaluation of a constraint problem by a sequence of propagations and projections (cf. Section 7.1.1), the meta constraint solver performs weak projections until a fixed point is reached. Then the solvers switch to strong projection and allow the creation of disjunctions. This technique results in significantly fewer disjunctions and, thus, a slimmer search-tree and less cloning of stores. This behavior corresponds to the Andorra principle [229].

7.1.4 An example

For better understanding of the approach we present an example. It illustrates the cooperation of an *arithmetic solver* CS_A and a *finite domain solver* $CS_{\mathcal{FD}}$. We sketch the way in which our approach may handle a given multi-domain constraint problem.

The following notation is used to illustrate snapshots from an evaluation sequence (a branch of a *search-tree*), where the stores C_A and $C_{\mathcal{FD}}$ belong to the arithmetic solver and the finite domain solver, resp.

constraint pool	
store C_A	store $C_{\mathcal{FD}}$

Initially, the constraint pool contains the constraint conjunction C to solve, the stores are initially empty. We start from the constraint conjunction

$$C = 1/X + 1/Y =_A 1/200 \land$$
$$X \in_{\mathcal{FD}} \{300,600,900,\ldots,2700,3000\} \land$$
$$Y \in_{\mathcal{FD}} \{300,600,900,\ldots,2700,3000\}.$$

The domains of the variables X and Y each contain the multiples of 300 between 300 and 3000.

$1/X + 1/Y =_A 1/200$, $X \in_{\mathcal{FD}} \{300,600,\ldots,3000\}$, $Y \in_{\mathcal{FD}} \{300,\ldots,3000\}$	
true	*true*

In the first step, the constraints of the pool are propagated to the stores of the solvers using the respective propagation functions:

$tell_A((1/X + 1/Y =_A 1/200), C_A) = (true, C_{A,1}, true)$, where
$C_{A,1} = (1/X + 1/Y =_A 1/200)$.

$tell_{\mathcal{FD}}(c, C_{\mathcal{FD}}) = (true, C_{\mathcal{FD},1}, true)$, where
$c = C_{\mathcal{FD},1} = (X \in_{\mathcal{FD}} \{300,600,\ldots,3000\} \land Y \in_{\mathcal{FD}} \{300,600,\ldots,3000\})$.

In the following, we leave out the indices of constraint relations indicating their domains, as soon as they enter their associated stores. We reach the following system state:

true
$1/X+1/Y=1/200$ $\qquad$ $X\in\{300,\ldots,3000\}\wedge$ $Y\in\{300,\ldots,3000\}$

In the next step, let $CS_{\mathcal{FD}}$ perform *weak* projections of its current store $C_{\mathcal{FD},1}$ w.r.t. the variables X and Y as discussed in Example 56:

$$proj_{\mathcal{FD}\to\mathcal{A}}(\{X\},C_{\mathcal{FD},1}) = (X \geq_{\mathcal{A}} 300 \wedge X \leq_{\mathcal{A}} 3000)$$
$$proj_{\mathcal{FD}\to\mathcal{A}}(\{Y\},C_{\mathcal{FD},1}) = (Y \geq_{\mathcal{A}} 300 \wedge Y \leq_{\mathcal{A}} 3000)$$

The resulting constraints are transferred to the constraint pool which yields the following new state.

$X \geq_{\mathcal{A}} 300,\ X \leq_{\mathcal{A}} 3000,\ Y \geq_{\mathcal{A}} 300,\ Y \leq_{\mathcal{A}} 3000$
$1/X+1/Y=1/200$ $\qquad$ $X\in\{300,\ldots,3000\}\wedge$ $Y\in\{300,\ldots,3000\}$

The propagation of the constraints of the pool yields – after some computation by the arithmetic solver $CS_{\mathcal{A}}$ – a new augmented store $C_{\mathcal{A},2}$:

true
$X\geq 300 \wedge X\leq 600 \wedge Y\geq 300 \wedge$ $Y\leq 600 \wedge 1/X+1/Y=1/200$ $\qquad$ $X\in\{300,\ldots,3000\}\wedge$ $Y\in\{300,\ldots,3000\}$

There follows a projection of the arithmetic solver's store $C_{\mathcal{A},2}$ and a propagation of the received constraints restricting X and Y for the finite domain solver $CS_{\mathcal{FD}}$:

true
$X\geq 300 \wedge X\leq 600 \wedge Y\geq 300 \wedge$ $Y\leq 600 \wedge 1/X+1/Y=1/200$ $\qquad$ $X\in\{300,600\}\wedge Y\in\{300,600\}$

Now, the finite domain solver performs a *strong* projection of its current store $C_{\mathcal{FD},2}$, generating a disjunction of four constraint conjunctions.

$$proj_{\mathcal{FD}\to\mathcal{A}}(\{X,Y\},C_{\mathcal{FD},2})$$
$$= (X=_{\mathcal{A}} 300 \vee X=_{\mathcal{A}} 600) \wedge (Y=_{\mathcal{A}} 300 \vee Y=_{\mathcal{A}} 600)$$
$$= (X=_{\mathcal{A}} 300 \wedge Y=_{\mathcal{A}} 300) \vee (X=_{\mathcal{A}} 300 \wedge Y=_{\mathcal{A}} 600) \vee$$
$$(X=_{\mathcal{A}} 600 \wedge Y=_{\mathcal{A}} 300) \vee (X=_{\mathcal{A}} 600 \wedge Y=_{\mathcal{A}} 600)$$

Due to this disjunction, the system generates four instances of its system state but with different pools, each representing one of the choices. The constraints of the pool are then propagated, which finally yields two failing computation branches and two successful branches with final states representing solutions.

Final state 1:

true	
$C_{A,3} = (X = 300 \wedge Y = 600)$	$C_{\mathcal{FD},3} = (X = 300 \wedge Y = 600)$

Final state 2:

true	
$C_{A,4} = (X = 600 \wedge Y = 300)$	$C_{\mathcal{FD},4} = (X = 600 \wedge Y = 300)$

Solutions of the initial multi-domain constraint problem C can be gained by projection of one of the stores, e.g.:

$$proj_{\mathcal{FD} \to A}(\{X, Y\}, C_{\mathcal{FD},3}) = (X =_A 300 \wedge Y =_A 600).$$

7.1.5 Cooperation strategies

The order of actions in a solver cooperation may affect the efficiency of the solution process dramatically. It is defined by the *solver cooperation strategy.*
    While in the above example in Section 7.1.4 we did not explicitly fix any such strategy for the cooperating solvers, we implicitly presupposed one, which e.g. decides the order of propagations and projections, the choice of variables and stores for projections and the transition from weak to strong projection of the finite domain solver.
    A solver cooperation strategy may influence the solution process mainly on two levels and with regard to different criteria:

1. The choice and handling of system states or copies of the architecture during computation affects the form and traversal of the search-tree. We refer to these aspects in Section 7.3.3 by the subject of *general strategies.*

2. Besides, there are *heuristics and choice criteria* which allow one to refine and optimize the general strategies. This concerns among other things

   - preferences for particular operations, like $tell_\nu$ and $proj_{\nu \to \mu}$, and transitions between weak and strong projection,
   - preferences concerning the invocation of solvers,
   - ordering and choice of constraints for propagation according to their kind, per solver or globally for all solvers, and
   - variable ordering heuristics.

For a detailed discussion concerning the definition of cooperation strategies for our architecture in theory we refer to [98]. We consider the strategy definitions in practice for our implementation META-S in Section 7.3.3, where we also show examples of the above concepts.

7.2 Language integration

Our framework of cooperating solvers allows the integration of different host-languages. The main idea behind this is to consider *declarative programming as constraint programming* and treating the language evaluation mechanisms as constraint solving. This kind of consideration opens an interesting potential: The integration of language solvers into our solver cooperation framework allows us to extend the languages by constraint systems and, thus, to *build constraint languages customized for a given set of requirements for comfortable modeling and solving of many problems.*

We show the idea and procedure for an integration of declarative languages into the cooperation framework. For a discussion of semantic aspects like soundness and completeness or concerning language evaluation strategies we refer to [98, 99, 105].

The feasibility of our idea is based on three main observations: *First,* expressions in a declarative language naturally are or can be transformed into constraint expressions. For example, logic languages are based on predicates, and goals (on these predicates) are constraints; for functional (logic) languages the underlying equality relations can be regarded as constraints as well. *Second,* the evaluation of expressions in declarative languages consists of their stepwise transformation to a normal form while particular knowledge (in the form of substitutions) is collected. *Third,* this way of proceeding is similar to a stepwise propagation of constraints to a store, which is simplified in doing so.

In the following, we consider the integration of a logic language and of a functional logic language, resp., into our framework for cooperating solvers. Syntactically, we extend the languages by constraints, but their evaluation mechanisms are nearly unchanged: they are only extended by a mechanism for collecting constraints from the domains of other constraint solvers.

A four-step-process. The integration of a declarative language into our system of cooperating solvers requires four activities:

1. The inherent constraints of the language must be identified.
2. Conversely, the constraints from the other domains must be integrated into the syntax of the language.
3. The language evaluation mechanism (e.g. reduction or resolution) must be extended by gathering constraints from the other domains.

Program 7.2.1 Sequential and parallel composition of resistors

```
1   res(simple(W),W)  :- W ∈_FD {300,600,900,...,2700,3000}.
2   res(seq(R,S),Z)   :- X + Y =_A Z, res(R,X), res(S,Y).
3   res(par(R,S),Z)   :- 1/X + 1/Y =_A 1/Z, res(R,X), res(S,Y).
```

---

4. Finally, one needs to carefully define the interface functions $tell_\nu$ and $proj_{\nu \to \mu}$ of the new language solver.

7.2.1 A logic language as constraint solver

In Sections 3.2.4 and 5.2 we introduced the syntax and semantics of logic programming and of constraint logic programming, resp. The integration of a logic language into the system of cooperating solvers yields a constraint logic programming language. We follow the four-step-process.

(1) Identifying language constraints

It is widely accepted that logic programming can be interpreted as constraint programming over the Herbrand universe. The appropriate constraint solving mechanism $CS_\mathcal{L}$ is *resolution*.

The goals according to a given constraint logic program are the natural constraints of a logic language solver. Furthermore, the set $Cons_\mathcal{L}$ of constraints must contain equality constraints $Y =_\mathcal{L} t$ between variables Y and terms t to represent substitutions.

(2) Extending the language by constraints from other domains

We extend the syntax of the logic language by constraints from other constraint systems of the cooperation which yields the typical CLP syntax (cf. Section 5.2). Thus, the set $Cons_\mathcal{L}$ must furthermore include all constraints of the incorporated solvers.

Example 57 Program 7.2.1 shows a constraint logic program which describes resistors of between 300 Ω and 3000 Ω and defines the sequential and parallel composition of resistors.

The formulation is a mixture of logic and constraint programming. The first clause uses the membership test $\in_{FD}$ from a constraint system for finite domains; the other two clauses use the equality $=_A$ from an arithmetic constraint solver and goals as constraints of the logic language solver.   ◊

$tell_{\mathcal{L}}$: Let P be a constraint logic program, let $C_{\mathcal{L}} = \phi$ be the current store of $CS_{\mathcal{L}}$.

1. Let $R = p(t_1, \ldots, t_m)$ be a constraint (i. e. a goal) which is to be propagated. Let $\hat{R} = \phi(R)$. We use the following notion: A rule $p = (Q_p \; :\text{-} \; rhs_p)$ *applies to* $\hat{R}$, if there is a unifier $\sigma_p = mgu(\hat{R}, Q_p)$.

   a. If the set $P_R \subseteq P$ of applicable rules is non-empty, then
   $$tell_{\mathcal{L}}(R, C_{\mathcal{L}}) = (true, \; C_{\mathcal{L}}, \; \bigvee_{p \in P_R}(\sigma_p \wedge \sigma_p(rhs_p))).$$

   b. If there is no applicable rule in P, then
   $$tell_{\mathcal{L}}(R, C_{\mathcal{L}}) = (false, C_{\mathcal{L}}, false).$$

2. Let $c = (Y =_{\mathcal{L}} t)$ be a constraint which is to be propagated.

   a. If $(\{Y = t\} \uparrow C_{\mathcal{L}}) \neq \emptyset$, then
   $$tell_{\mathcal{L}}(c, C_{\mathcal{L}}) = (true, \{Y = t\} \uparrow C_{\mathcal{L}} \;, true).$$

   b. If $(\{Y = t\} \uparrow C_{\mathcal{L}}) = \emptyset$, then
   $$tell_{\mathcal{L}}(c, C_{\mathcal{L}}) = (false, C_{\mathcal{L}}, false).$$

Fig. 7.5 Interface function $tell_{\mathcal{L}}$

(3) Extending the language evaluation mechanism by gathering constraints

Gathering constraints during resolution is realized by the extension of the resolution step (cf. Definition 19) such that a rule body may include constraints from other domains.

(4) Define the interface functions of the logic language solver $CS_{\mathcal{L}}$

For the integration of the new constraint solver $CS_{\mathcal{L}}$ into the cooperation framework the interface functions $tell_{\mathcal{L}}$ and $proj_{\mathcal{L} \to \nu}$, $\nu \in L$, must be defined. We discuss this procedure in the following.

Propagation. The propagation function $tell_{\mathcal{L}}$ emulates resolution steps (including gathering constraints). Its formal definition is given in Figure 7.5.

Since the constraint store $C_{\mathcal{L}}$ of the logic language solver collects solely substitutions, in the following we denote it as such for better reading.

Case 1a represents a *resolution step* on a goal R as a successful propagation, where for every applicable rule we get a newly created constraint pool and, thus, a new instantiation of the architecture. If there is no applicable rule for a goal (Case 1b), then the propagation fails.[10]

The remaining cases describe the propagation of equality constraints by parallel composition $\uparrow$ of substitutions (Case 2) which realizes a *satisfiability test*.

---

[10] Undefinedness of a predicate is regarded as failure.

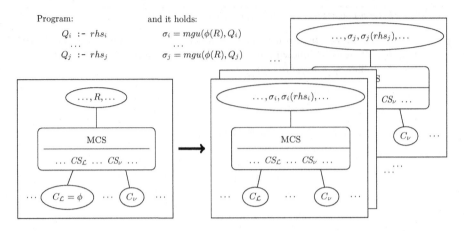

Fig. 7.6 Application of the interface function $tell_{\mathcal{L}}$ (Case 1a)

$proj_{\mathcal{L}\to\nu}$: The projection of a store $C_{\mathcal{L}} = \phi$ w.r.t. a constraint system ζ_ν and a set of variables $X \subseteq X_{\mathcal{L}} \cap X_\nu$ makes the substitutions for $\mathbf{x} \in X$ explicit (and yields equality constraints):

$$proj_{\mathcal{L}\to\nu}(X, \phi) = \phi|_X$$

Fig. 7.7 Interface function $proj_{\mathcal{L}\to\nu}, \nu \in L$

Figure 7.6 illustrates how the interface function $tell_{\mathcal{L}}$ is used to simulate a resolution step with constraints (corresponding to Figure 7.5, Case 1a).

Initially, the constraint pool contains the constraint R (a goal), the constraint store $C_{\mathcal{L}}$ contains a substitution ϕ. The successful propagation of R corresponds to a resolution step on R: For $\hat{R} = \phi(R)$ and for every rule Q_i :- rhs_i with unifiable left-hand side, the corresponding most general unifier σ_i is built. Goal R in the pool is replaced by the right-hand side rhs_i of the rule under σ_i, i.e. by $\sigma_i(rhs_i)$, and by the newly build unifier σ_i (in the form of equality constraints). If there is more than one matching rule, then we get a number of instantiations of the architecture with alternative constraint pools.

Projection. The projection function provides equality constraints representing the substitution from the store which has been computed during resolution. The definition of the function $proj_{\mathcal{L}\to\nu}$ is given in Figure 7.7.

Since the interface functions $tell_{\mathcal{L}}$ and $proj_{\mathcal{L}\to\nu}$ fulfill the requirements given in Sections 7.1.2 and 7.1.3, it can be shown that the soundness and completeness results (cf. [98]) of the cooperation framework hold for the integration of a logic language solver.

By the integration of a logic language as constraint solver into the overall solver cooperation framework we reach CLP syntax and semantics. The definition of $tell_{\mathcal{L}}$ and $proj_{\mathcal{L}\to\nu}$ as given in Figures 7.5 and 7.7, resp., realize (together with the handling of constraints from other domains by additional solvers) the CLP derivation relation as given in Definition 31.

Example 58 We consider the cooperation of the *logic language solver* $CS_{\mathcal{L}}$ with an *arithmetic solver* $CS_{\mathcal{A}}$ and a *finite domain constraint solver* $CS_{\mathcal{FD}}$ to illustrate the approach.

We evaluate the goal $res(par(A,B),200)$ w.r.t. the CLP clauses given in Program 7.2.1, i.e. we ask for resistors A and B connected in parallel such that their overall resistance value is 200 Ω.

Again, we use the diagrammatic notation of Section 7.1.4 to denote snapshots of the computation. Initially, the constraint pool contains the goal to solve, the stores of the participating solvers are empty. We denote the substitution contained in the constraint store $C_{\mathcal{L}}$ of the logic language solver by equality constraints.

constraint pool $= res(par(A,B),200)$		
store $C_{\mathcal{L}} = true$	store $C_{\mathcal{A}} = true$	store $C_{\mathcal{FD}} = true$

The first step is a propagation of the constraint of the pool by applying $tell_{\mathcal{L}}$. This corresponds to a resolution step using the third program clause.

$$tell_{\mathcal{L}}(res(par(A,B),200),C_{\mathcal{L}}) = (true, C_{\mathcal{L}},$$
$$A =_{\mathcal{L}} R \wedge B =_{\mathcal{L}} S \wedge Z =_{\mathcal{L}} 200 \wedge 1/X+1/Y =_{\mathcal{A}} 1/200 \wedge res(A,X) \wedge res(B,Y))$$

This yields the following new system state.

$A =_{\mathcal{L}} R,\ B =_{\mathcal{L}} S,\ Z =_{\mathcal{L}} 200,\ 1/X+1/Y =_{\mathcal{A}} 1/200,\ res(A,X),\ res(B,Y)$		
true	true	true

The propagation of the equality constraints of the logic language solver and the constraints of the other solvers yields a new system state. Again, we leave out the indices of the relations indicating their domains, as soon as they enter their associated stores.

	$res(A,X),\ res(B,Y)$	
$A = R \wedge B = S \wedge Z = 200$	$1/X+1/Y = 1/200$	true

Next, the goal $res(A,X)$ is chosen for a resolution step. By $C_{\mathcal{L},1}$ we denote the current store of $CS_{\mathcal{L}}$.

$$tell_{\mathcal{L}}(res(A,X),C_{\mathcal{L},1}) = (true, C_{\mathcal{L},1},$$
$$(A =_{\mathcal{L}} simple(W) \wedge X =_{\mathcal{L}} W \wedge X \in_{\mathcal{FD}} \{300,600,900,\ldots,2700,3000\}) \vee$$
$$(A =_{\mathcal{L}} seq(\ldots) \wedge \ldots) \vee (A =_{\mathcal{L}} par(\ldots) \wedge \ldots))$$

There are three alternative computation branches according to the three clauses of the constraint logic program 7.2.1. In the following, we only derive the first alternative and leave the others out.

$A =_\mathcal{L} simple(W)$, $X =_\mathcal{L} W$, $X \in_{\mathcal{FD}} \{300,600,900,\ldots,2700,3000\}$, $res(B,Y)$		
$A = R \wedge B = S \wedge Z = 200$	$1/X + 1/Y = 1/200$	$true$

Again, we propagate the equalities of $CS_\mathcal{L}$ and the constraints of the other domains from the pool. In the new system state, we leave out constraints in the store $C_{\mathcal{L},2}$ which do not play a further role in the computation and denote them by "...".

$res(B,Y)$		
$A = simple(X) \wedge \ldots$	$1/X + 1/Y = 1/200$	$X \in \{300,600,\ldots,3000\}$

A corresponding expansion of the remaining goal $res(B,Y)$ of the pool yields the next snapshot.

$true$		
$A = simple(X) \wedge \ldots \wedge$ $B = simple(Y) \wedge \ldots$	$1/X + 1/Y = 1/200$	$X \in \{300,\ldots,3000\} \wedge$ $Y \in \{300,600,\ldots,3000\}$

All constraints or goals, resp., of the logic language solver have now been propagated. If we only consider the stores of the finite domain solver and the arithmetic solver then the current situation corresponds to the second system state in the example of Section 7.1.4 (cf. page 131). Thus, we can assume a corresponding computation sequence to follow with final solutions $(X = 300 \wedge Y = 600)$ and $(X = 600 \wedge Y = 300)$.   ◇

7.2.2 A functional logic language as constraint solver

A functional logic language can be considered as a constraint solver $CS_{\mathcal{FL}}$ and can be integrated into our cooperation framework. This yields constraint functional logic programming as implemented e.g. in the languages CURRY [82] or TOY [57]. We investigated this approach in detail in [105] including a thorough discussion of semantic aspects. In this section, we briefly discuss the main ideas, where we follow again the four-step-process.

(1) Identifying language constraints

In Section 5.4 we introduced the syntax and semantics of functional logic programming. Equalities $t_1 =_{\mathcal{FL}} t_2$ on terms t_1, t_2 are the natural constraints of a functional logic programming language. To ease the following presentation, constraints of the form $t_1 =_{\mathcal{FL}} t_2$ such that t_1 and t_2 are non-variable terms, are decomposed into $(W =_{\mathcal{FL}} t_1) \wedge (W =_{\mathcal{FL}} t_2)$ where $W \in X$ is a fresh variable.

(2) Extending the language by constraints from other domains

The extension of functional logic programming languages by constraints was considered in Section 5.5. Recall that the basic syntactic construct is rules of the form $f(t_1, \ldots, t_n) \to t$ where G. The set G of constraints includes constraints from other domains. When performing a narrowing step, the functional logic language solver $CS_{\mathcal{FL}}$ must collect constraints from the other domains within the cooperation (cf. step (3)). Thus, the set $Cons_{\mathcal{FL}}$ of constraints of $CS_{\mathcal{FL}}$ also contains the constraints from these other domains.

To get a clean separation of concerns for our approach we flatten hybrid terms from different domains. Suppose, for example, that we have a functional logic program corresponding to the CLP program 7.2.1, where the third rule is in the hybrid form:

$res(par(R,S)) \to Z$ where $1/res(R)+1/res(S) =_{\mathcal{A}} 1/Z$

Then we transform this rule into a separated form such that all constraints in G are *homogeneous*, that is, each is built from the signature of one solver, including equalities $t_1 =_{\mathcal{FL}} t_2$ of the functional logic language:

$res(par(R,S)) \to Z$ where
$\qquad 1/X+1/Y =_{\mathcal{A}} 1/Z, \quad X =_{\mathcal{FL}} res(R), \quad Y =_{\mathcal{FL}} res(S)$

(3) Extending the language evaluation mechanism by gathering constraints

The evaluation mechanism of a functional logic language as constraint solver $CS_{\mathcal{FL}}$ is basically *narrowing*. But in addition to performing narrowing steps, the solver must collect constraints from other domains occurring in the rule part ... where G. This is realized by means of the concept of a *narrowing step with constraints* as defined by Definition 38 in Section 5.5. We apply this principle in the definition of the interface function $tell_{\mathcal{FL}}$ in step (4) (see below).

Note that we do not consider particular evaluation strategies, like innermost or lazy narrowing, here and refer to [105] for a discussion of this subject.

(4) Defining the interface functions $tell_{\mathcal{FL}}$ and $proj_{\mathcal{FL} \to \nu}$ of the functional logic language solver $CS_{\mathcal{FL}}$

This final step integrates the functional logic solver into the framework, i.e. it defines the interplay between narrowing, constraint accumulation, and constraint solving.

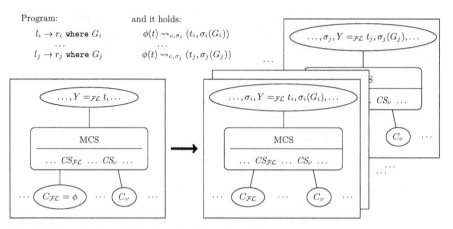

Fig. 7.8 Application of the interface function $tell_{\mathcal{FL}}$

Propagation. Figure 7.8 illustrates the interface function $tell_{\mathcal{FL}}$ simulating a *narrowing step with constraints*, Figure 7.9 gives the formal definition of the pertinent requirements.

Like all solvers, $CS_{\mathcal{FL}}$ propagates constraints to its store $C_{\mathcal{FL}}$, thereby checking the satisfiability of $C_{\mathcal{FL}}$ in conjunction with the new constraints. Therefore, the function $tell_{\mathcal{FL}}$ incorporates the principle of narrowing.

Let us suppose that all constraints which enter the pool (either as part of the initial problem to solve or as results of propagations or projections) have been decomposed with the help of auxiliary variables such that all subterms of the form $f(t_1, \ldots, t_n)$, where f is a defined function, are extracted. The definition of $tell_{\mathcal{FL}}$, thus, only needs to consider narrowing steps on outermost terms. The distinction between e.g. a *call-by-value* and a *call-by-name* evaluation must therefore be based on an external choice mechanism respecting dependency relations among variables (cf. [105]).

We distinguish two kinds of constraints $Y =_{\mathcal{FL}} t$ (see Figure 7.9):

When the term t still contains defined functions (Case 1), a narrowing step is applied as part of $tell_{\mathcal{FL}}$. This is only reflected by a change of the constraint pool. The store does not change in this case. Note that due to the flattening, the term t contains exactly one defined function f, and this function is the outermost symbol in t. Moreover, since the substitution ϕ, i.e. the constraint store $C_{\mathcal{FL}}$, only contains constructor terms, $\hat{t} = \phi(t)$ retains this property.

When the term t is a constructor term (Case 2), then the constraint $Y =_{\mathcal{FL}} t$ is added to the store if possible. Thereby, the *satisfiability test* is realized again by the parallel composition $\uparrow$ of substitutions.

Projection. As for $C_{\mathcal{L}}$ in Section 7.2.1, the constraint store $C_{\mathcal{FL}}$ only contains substitutions. Thus, again, the projection generates equality constraints as their representation.

$tell_{\mathcal{FL}}$: Let P be a functional logic program with constraints, let $C_{\mathcal{FL}} = \phi$ be the current constraint store of $CS_{\mathcal{FL}}$. (Recall that the constraint store $C_{\mathcal{FL}}$ is nothing but a substitution ϕ from variables to constructor terms, which is written in the form of equations and thus can be treated like constraints.) Let $c = (Y =_{\mathcal{FL}} t)$ be the constraint to be propagated. Let $\hat{t} = \phi(t)$.

We use the following notion: A rule $p = (l_p \rightarrow r_p \text{ where } G_p)$ *applies to* $\hat{t}$, if for $\hat{t} \notin X$ there is a unifier $\sigma_p = mgu(\hat{t}, l_p)$.

We distinguish the following cases:

1. Let $\hat{t}$ contain defined functions; that is, $\hat{t}$ is of the form $f(\dots)$ with f being the only defined function (due to the maximal flattening). If the set $P_c \subseteq P$ of applicable rules is non-empty, then

$$tell_{\mathcal{FL}}(c, C_{\mathcal{FL}}) = (true,\ C_{\mathcal{FL}},\ \bigvee_{p \in P_c} (\sigma_p \wedge Y =_{\mathcal{FL}} \sigma_p(r_p) \wedge \sigma_p(G_p))).$$

2. Let $\hat{t}$ be a constructor term, i.e. $\hat{t} \in \mathcal{T}(\Delta, X_{\mathcal{FL}})$.

   a. If $(\{Y = t\} \uparrow C_{\mathcal{FL}}) \neq \emptyset$, then
      $tell_{\mathcal{FL}}(c, C_{\mathcal{FL}}) = (true,\ \{Y = t\} \uparrow C_{\mathcal{FL}},\ true)$.

   b. If $(\{Y = t\} \uparrow C_{\mathcal{FL}}) = \emptyset$, then
      $tell_{\mathcal{FL}}(c, C_{\mathcal{FL}}) = (false, C_{\mathcal{FL}}, false)$.

Fig. 7.9 Interface function $tell_{\mathcal{FL}}$

The definition of the projection function $proj_{\mathcal{FL} \rightarrow \nu}$ resembles $proj_{\mathcal{L} \rightarrow \nu}$ of the logic language solver $CS_{\mathcal{L}}$ in Figure 7.7.

Since the interface functions $tell_{\mathcal{FL}}$ and $proj_{\mathcal{FL} \rightarrow \nu}$ of our functional logic language solver again fulfill the requirements given in Sections 7.1.2 and 7.1.3, the soundness and completeness results of the cooperation framework (given in [98]) hold for the integration of a functional logic language – however, only relative to the completeness of the narrowing strategy encoded within $tell_{\mathcal{FL}}$ (for a detailed discussion see [105]).

7.3 Implementation

META-S [64, 65, 66, 67, 68] is an efficient and flexible solver cooperation system that implements the solver cooperation approach described theoretically in the previous sections. It allows the integration of external black-box constraint solvers which extend the META-S base syntax by their constraints. The system provides the users with a flexible strategy definition framework to enable efficient problem computation. Moreover, it is possible to integrate declarative languages and constraints within META-S as discussed conceptually in Section 7.2.

We present the structure of the META-S system and the implementation in Section 7.3.1. We introduce the integrated constraint solvers and languages in

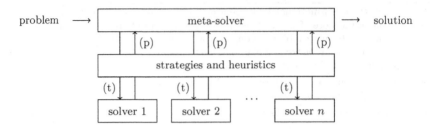

Fig. 7.10 Structure of META-S

Section 7.3.2. Section 7.3.3 is dedicated to the strategy definition framework of META-S. We discuss the advantages and results of certain evaluation strategies in Section 7.3.4.

7.3.1 The architecture of META-S

The structure of the META-S system is given in Figure 7.10; it reflects the general architecture of the theoretical solver cooperation framework (cf. Figure 7.1(b)).

A coordination mechanism – the *meta-solver* – treats the different applied *solvers as black boxes*. It receives the problem to solve in the form of mixed-domain constraints, analyzes them and splits them up into single-domain constraints processable by the individual solvers. These problem constraints are held in a *global pool*, which is managed by the meta-solver. Constraints are taken from this pool and propagated to the individual solvers. These solvers collect the constraints in their *constraint stores*, thereby ensuring their satisfiability. In return the solvers are requested to provide newly gained information (i.e. constraints) back to the meta-solver to be added to the pool and propagated to other solvers during the following computation. This communication is handled via the *solver interface* functions *tell* and *project*. These are based on typical solver functions provided by most preexisting solvers or which can be implemented by very little glue code, hence allowing simple integration into our system.

- The function *tell* (denoted by (t) in Figure 7.10) for *constraint propagation* allows an individual solver to add constraints taken from the global pool to its store, narrowing the solution set of the store's constraints.
- The *projection* function *project* (denoted by (p)) provides constraints implied by a solver's store for information interchange between the solvers. They are added to the pool of the solver cooperation system and later propagated to another solver.

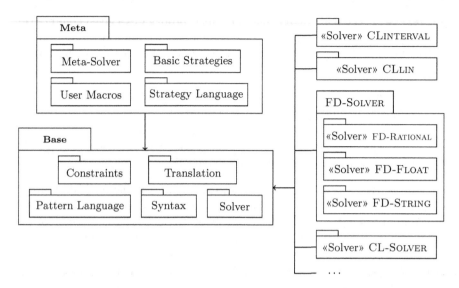

Fig. 7.11 The module structure of META-S

The meta-solver performs the overall *tell–projection* cycle guided by a *solver cooperation strategy and heuristics* until a failure occurs or the global pool is emptied. Problem solutions can then be retrieved by projection.

The module structure of the META-S implementation is given in Figure 7.11. It was kept highly modular to allow radical changes in one module without negative influences in others. It consists of three main modules: the *Base* module, the *Meta* module and any number of pluggable external constraint solvers.

The *Base* module is the common foundation of the META-S system and contains the internal and external constraint representations and means for translations between them, a syntax extension facility, a pattern matching facility for constraints, and the abstract interface between the framework and the integrated solvers. The *Meta* module implements mainly the meta solver functionalities and the strategy framework as discussed in Section 7.3.3. Several solvers have been integrated into META-S using the abstract interface of the *Base* module. We consider these in the subsequent Section 7.3.2.

7.3.2 Solvers

META-S provides an interface for the integration of constraint solvers. Essentially three functions must exist in a solver to be integrated [69]:

`solver-tell (solver store constraint)` propagates a given `constraint` to the `store` of the `solver`. It corresponds to the interface function *tell* (see Section 7.1.2), but is allowed to generate (besides `true` and `false`) two additional answers, namely

> `redundant`   in case of a successful propagation, where the constraint was, however, redundant w.r.t. the store and
>
> `delayed`   if the solver is not able to handle the given constraint yet. This is a request to the meta-solver to hold back the constraint and re-offer it for propagation if the store has changed.

`solver-project (solver store variable ...)`   is the realization of the projection operation (see Section 7.1.3). The `solver` is requested to project the `store` w.r.t. to the given `variable`. To support incomplete solvers which do not always detect inconsistencies during propagation, solvers are allowed to project the contradictory constraint `false`.

`solver-clone (solver store)`   clones a solver `store`. This is needed to allow the computation of alternative solutions resp. solution sets by traversing a search-tree.

There are three kinds of *constraint solvers* which have been integrated into META-S. We distinguish

1. "proper" constraint solvers,
2. declarative programs together with the language evaluation mechanism considered as solvers, and
3. the generic solver CL-SOLVER which allows the user to define operators and relations based on normal COMMON LISP functions.

(1)   META-S allows the integration of arbitrary black-box solvers providing the common solver interface as discussed above. It comes with an external solver LINAR [133], implemented in C, for linear equations, inequalities and disequations over rational numbers which uses a variant of the Simplex algorithm to incrementally compute solutions for a given constraint system. Since META-S itself is implemented in COMMON LISP, the interface can, thus, be best served by COMMON LISP-implemented solvers, e.g. CLLIN which is also a linear solver for rational numbers based on the Simplex algorithm (cf. Section 4.1.1) and which allows (like LINAR) the handling of non-linear constraints using a delay mechanism. CLINTERVAL is a COMMON LISP-based interval arithmetic solver on real numbers using the *smath* library of Hickey *et al.* [96]. The solvers FD-RATIONAL, FD-FLOAT, and FD-STRING are instances of a generic finite domain solver FD-SOLVER using the techniques of the well-known library CSPLIB [222].

Consider Program 7.3.1 as an example. It shows a META-S program for the Send-More-Money problem variant with 25 solutions (i.e. leading zeros

Program 7.3.1 A Send-More-Money problem definition

```
 1   (define-meta-solver *smm*              ; problem definition
 2
 3      (meta-solver eager-strategy         ; select strategy
 4                  :variable-ordering
 5                  '(SEND MORE MONEY M O N E Y R S D))
 6
 7      ((my-fd-rational fd-rational)       ; solver integration
 8       (my-linar cllin))
 9
10                                          ; constraints
11      (((in S, E, N, D, M, O, R, Y #{0 1 2 3 4 5 6 7 8 9})
12       (alldifferent {S E N D M O R Y})
13       ((= my-linar)
14        SEND
15        (+ (* (+ (* (+ (* S 10) E) 10) N) 10) D))
16        (= MORE (+ (* (+ (* (+ (* M 10) O) 10) R) 10) E))
17        (= MONEY (+ (* ... (* M 10) O) 10) N) 10) E) 10) Y))
18        (= (+ SEND MORE) MONEY)))))
```

are allowed). It uses the cooperation of the linear solver CLLIN and the finite domain solver FD-RATIONAL (lines 7 and 8).

(2) By considering declarative programs together with the associated language evaluation mechanism as constraint solver it is possible to integrate declarative languages and constraints within META-S [67, 68, 66, 105]. We discussed the integration of logic and functional (logic) languages into our theoretical framework in Sections 7.2.1 and 7.2.2.

We investigated the practical integration of a logic language which allows CLP-like programming with the *constraint logic language* CLL in META-S. In the same way we extended META-S by a *constraint functional logic language* FCLL. By utilizing the strategy definition framework (see Section 7.3.3) the user is able to define strategies and heuristics for the evaluation of programs in these languages.

Program 7.3.2 gives a CLL program describing edges and paths with costs in directed graphs. For better understanding we give a PROLOG equivalent in Program 7.3.3. A CLL rule consists of a declaration and a corresponding definition. A declaration (lines 1 and 7 in Program 7.3.2) is composed of the key symbol *rl*, the name of the rule and a list of parameter types. A rule definition is a list of at least three elements: the key symbol <-, a list of variable declarations, and the rule head. If these are the only elements, the rule definition is a fact (e.g. lines 3 and 4), otherwise the remainder of the list forms the rule body.

In the rule definitions for the predicate *path/4* (beginning at lines 9 and 13) the variable *N1* is the origin of the path, *N2* is its end node, the third

---

Program 7.3.2 CLL: edges and paths with costs in directed graphs

```
1    (rl edge (cll-term cll-term rational))
2
3    (<- () (edge (a) (b) 75))
4    (<- () (edge (b) (e) 50))
5    ...
6
7    (rl path (cll-term cll-term cll-term rational))
8
9    (<- ((cll-term N1 N2) (rational COST))
10        (path N1 N2 (list N1 (list N2 (empty))) COST)
11       (edge N1 N2 COST))
12
13   (<- ((cll-term N1 N2 X REST)
14        (rational COST EDGE_COST REST_COST))
15       (path N1 N2 (list N1 REST) COST)
16       (edge N1 X EDGE_COST)
17       (> EDGE_COST 0)
18       (> REST_COST 0)
19       (= COST (+ EDGE_COST REST_COST))
20       (path X N2 REST REST_COST))
```

Program 7.3.3 PROLOG: edges and paths

```
1    edge (a,b,75).
2    edge (b,e,50).
3    ...
4
5    path (N1,N2,[N1,N2],COST) :-
6        edge (N1,N2,COST).
7
8    path (N1,N2,[N1|REST],COST) :-
9        edge(N1,X,EDGE_COST),
10       EDGE_COST > 0,
11       REST_COST > 0,
12       COST = EDGE_COST + REST_COST,
13       path(X,N2,REST,REST_COST).
```

---

argument describes the path itself and the fourth argument is the cost of the path. The path is either defined by a direct edge between $N1$ and $N2$ or recursively by an edge and a path.

Programs 7.3.4 and 7.3.5 illustrate the use of the functional constraint logic language FCLL. Program 7.3.4 shows an alternative definition of the Send-More-Money problem, where we additionally use FCLL as constraint solver for functional equations (line 6). While the equation in line 12 is handled by the linear arithmetic solver as before, lines 13–15 describe three goals for the functional logic language solver.

Program 7.3.4 The Send-More-Money problem using FCLL

```
1   (define-meta-solver *smm*
2     (meta-solver depth-first)
3
4     ((my-fd-rational fd-rational)      ; solver   integration
5      (my-linar cllin)
6      (my-fcll fcll-solver :file "word.fcll"
7                           :redex 'innermost))
8
9                                        ; constraints
10    (((in S, E, N, D, M, O, R, Y #{0 1 2 3 4 5 6 7 8 9})
11     (alldifferent {S E N D M O R Y})
12     (= (+ SEND MORE) MONEY)
13     (= (word [S,E,N,D] 0) SEND)
14     (= (word [M,O,R,E] 0) MORE)
15     (= (word [M,O,N,E,Y] 0) MONEY)))))
```

Program 7.3.5 Functional logic combination of letters to words (file word.fcll)

```
1   (fn word (cll-term rational) rational)
2
3   (== (word [] ACC) ACC)                ; word [] ACC = ACC
4   (== (word [FT|RT] ACC)                ; word [FT|RT] ACC =
5       (word RT (+ (* 10 ACC) FT)))      ;    word RT 10*ACC+FT
```

The function *word* combines a sequence of digits into a number as given in Program 7.3.5. A function consists of a declaration (line 1) with key symbol *fn* and a definition by rules using the equality symbol "==".

(3) The CL-SOLVER is a generic solver that gives the user the opportunity to define operators and relations based on normal COMMON LISP functions. Contrary to most other solvers, the operators and relations of the CL-SOLVER are not fixed, but can be specified by the user.

The solver uses *residuation* [9] for constraint evaluation, i. e. all non-binding constraints are delayed until all variables in the constraint have been bound, at which time they can easily be evaluated for their truth value. Only equality constraints, i. e. binding-constraints, between a variable and fully bound terms are not delayed but evaluated.

The CL-SOLVER can be used e.g. to define conversion functions for the transformation between disjoint but still fairly compatible value types or even for the definition of rewriting rules for constraint conjunctions and disjunctions. Both are typical applications in multi-domain applications.

Program 7.3.6 shows the extract of a constraint problem definition that defines a CL-SOLVER instance *my-conversions* with two operators *to-dfloat* and *to-rat* (lines 3–5) which convert from double-floats to rationals and

Program 7.3.6 A solver for converting double-float to rational numbers and vice versa

```
1    (my-conversions cl-solver
2       :operators
3        '((to-dfloat (rational) double-float
4           (lambda (x) (coerce x 'double-float)))
5          (to-rat (double-float) rational cl:rationalize))
6       :relations
7        '((= (rational rational) cl:=)
8          (= (double-float double-float) cl:=)))
```

vice versa, resp., using the standard COMMON LISP functions *coerce* and *rationalize*. Additionally the appropriate equality relations are declared (lines 7 and 8). These ensure that the CL-SOLVER receives all bindings and can thus react on all variables captured in *to-dfloat* and *to-rat* applications.[11]

7.3.3 The strategy definition framework

The flow of information between the participating solvers greatly influences the overall efficiency of the solution process. Unfortunately, an effective co-operation strategy depends on the problem (and its modeling) as well as on the number and capabilities of the cooperating solvers and can thus not be generally formulated.

Thus, META-S provides the user and strategy developer with facilities to develop solving strategies within different levels of abstraction and detail. We distinguish *general strategies* on the one hand, and *constraint and variable selection strategies and heuristics* on the other hand.

7.3.3.1 General strategies

META-S provides three predefined general strategies. They emphasize the handling of the system states as nodes in the overall search-tree and of returned disjunctions within the projection phase. On top of the general strategies, the user can add and replace code by deriving new classes for more fine-grained action-oriented strategy definitions.

---

[11] Of course, this approach is fraught with problems when the coercions involved are imprecise, i.e. result in loss of information, which is the case with the numeric types mentioned. Nevertheless, the easy conversion of more abstract data types is still an interesting option.

For an illustration of the behavior of the general strategies see Figure 7.12. To depict a system state, we again use tables showing the pool in the first row, and the solver's stores in the second row, divided by vertical bars.

eager   The *eager* strategy propagates all constraint information as early as possible in the solving process. Returned disjunctions (during projection) lead to immediate spawning of cloned system states.

Consider the system behavior according to the *eager* strategy in Figure 7.12(a). Assuming a pool containing the conjunction $A \land B$ and a store containing the constraint S (further stores are not considered in this example), the next constraint propagated is A. Suppose that only a part of this constraint can be handled by the solver, i.e. A_3, and the disjunction $A_1 \lor A_2$ is put back into the pool. To ensure correctness, $S \land A$ must be equivalent to $(A_1 \lor A_2) \land (S \land A_3)$. In the next step the system state is cloned. To find all solutions of the constraint problem both resulting states must be processed further.

lazy   The *lazy* (cloning) strategy is comparable to the *eager* strategy with the major difference that the backtrack-branches of disjunctions (returned by projections) are not created immediately but possibly remaining constraint conjunctions are propagated first to the solvers. This is done in the hope that it will help to reduce the lifetime of dead-end backtracking branches. Once all conjunctions are processed the cloning actions for the disjunction branches are initiated.

This is illustrated in Figure 7.12(b). The approach is related to the *Andorra principle* as described in [229]. The idea behind this strategy is to propagate common constraints only once. The first step in the figure is the same as for the *eager* strategy, but the next step differs. The cloning is delayed, and the constraint B is propagated first. Obviously, B is propagated only once, while it had to be propagated twice in Figure 7.12(a).

heuristic   The *heuristic* (search) strategy is related to the *first-fail principle* [27] which tries to minimize the expanded search-tree size and has proved to be beneficial in solving constraint satisfaction problems. The idea of the first-fail principle is to choose the variable with the smallest domain size for value assignment. This choice is the one most likely to fail and hence will cut away failing branches very fast. Furthermore, variables with large domains may get restricted further such that unnecessary search can be avoided. The *heuristic* strategy uses this selection heuristic for choosing between several queued disjunctions while performing *lazy* cloning. We dequeue a disjunction with the least number of constraint conjunctions. As a further optimization we throw away all other disjunctions. To ensure that no knowledge is lost, all solvers are marked in order to project them again later. For illustration see Figure 7.12(c). Here, the disjunction $(A_1 \lor A_2 \lor A_3)$ is removed, but can be reproduced later since it originates from a projection. Of course, this schema can only be used when propagation does not return disjunctions, because they cannot be reproduced in this way. Thus, in

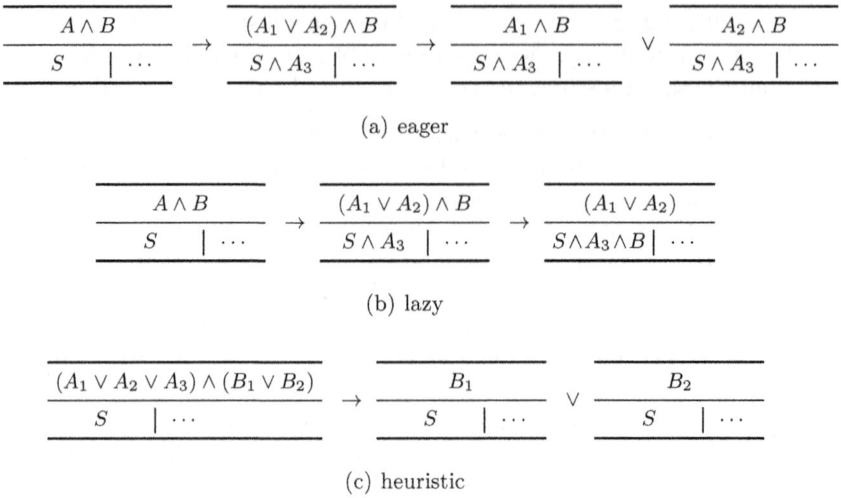

$$\frac{A \wedge B}{S \quad | \; \cdots} \;\rightarrow\; \frac{(A_1 \vee A_2) \wedge B}{S \wedge A_3 \quad | \; \cdots} \;\rightarrow\; \frac{A_1 \wedge B}{S \wedge A_3 \quad | \; \cdots} \;\vee\; \frac{A_2 \wedge B}{S \wedge A_3 \quad | \; \cdots}$$

(a) eager

$$\frac{A \wedge B}{S \quad | \; \cdots} \;\rightarrow\; \frac{(A_1 \vee A_2) \wedge B}{S \wedge A_3 \quad | \; \cdots} \;\rightarrow\; \frac{(A_1 \vee A_2)}{S \wedge A_3 \wedge B \quad | \; \cdots}$$

(b) lazy

$$\frac{(A_1 \vee A_2 \vee A_3) \wedge (B_1 \vee B_2)}{S \quad | \; \cdots} \;\rightarrow\; \frac{B_1}{S \quad | \; \cdots} \;\vee\; \frac{B_2}{S \quad | \; \cdots}$$

(c) heuristic

Fig. 7.12 META-S: general solver cooperation strategies

general the *heuristic* strategy cannot be used in cooperations with the CLL and FCLL solvers, but typically in ordinary solver cooperations.

7.3.3.2 Refinement of general strategies and heuristics

Since the control of information flow can achieve important performance increases, META-S provides a *strategy language* that allows the user to devise new more efficient strategies by extending generic strategies with problem and domain specific knowledge to speed up the solving process.

The design of our strategy language anticipates that the user wants to control the exact order of constraint propagations, based on different criteria like the target solver and the structure or properties of constraints. Additionally, rewriting of returned constraints and influence on the projection sequencing should be possible. Founded on these considerations the strategy language provides the following set of constructs and properties:

- Primitives for the propagation of sets of constraints as well as for the projection of specific or all solvers against a given set of variables and terms support a detailed information flow control.
- An integrated pattern language allows the classification, destructuring (i.e. splitting into subparts matching specified patterns), and rewriting of constraints based on their structure by using positional pattern expressions.

Program 7.3.7 Definition of the *heuristic-solver-flow* strategy

```
1   (define-strategy heuristic-solver-flow
2       (heuristic-strategy)              ; heuristic as basis
3       (:step
4       (select
5           ((eq-constraints (= t t))      ; patterns for
6            (in-constraints (in t t))     ;   =/in constraints
7            (rest t))
8           (tell-all in-constraints)      ; first propagate in-
9           (tell-all eq-constraints)      ;   and eq-constraints
10          (tell-all rest)                ; then all others
11          (project-one my-lin)           ; project from my-lin
12          (tell-all)                     ;   and propagate
13          (project-all))))               ; project from
14                                         ;   all other solvers
```

- Due to the integration of the strategy language into the COMMON LISP environment, additionally all normal COMMON LISP constructs can be applied.

Figure 7.3.7 presents a strategy called *heuristic-solver-flow*. It was derived by extending the general *heuristic* strategy (line 2) with a more optimized information flow. The :*step* clause initiates the inner strategy control loop definition. We start by partitioning all the constraints of the global pool into three groups based on their structure using the pattern matching facility (lines 5–7): *eq-constraints* are constraints with an equality relation (=), *in-constraints* match constraints with the *in*-relation, *rest* match all other constraints. This is expressed by the wildcard *t*.

The classified constraints are then propagated to the external solvers in the order of the groups given in lines 8–10. This is supported by the user knowledge about the particular solvers of the application and the problem structure. In the next step a linear arithmetic solver instance *my-lin* taking part in this particular cooperation is requested to project its knowledge (line 11). The received constraints are again removed from the pool and propagated to the other solvers (line 12). Finally, the remaining solvers are requested to project their derived constraints (line 13). This solving step is repeatedly initiated by the controlling strategy until certain termination conditions are satisfied.

The order of variable projection is often tremendously important for the overall performance in solving a constraint problem. However, a "good" variable order is not always available, e.g. when feeding machine generated problem descriptions to the meta-solver, or when the user does not want to perform an in-depth analysis of the problem at hand. META-S allows the user to give a static *variable ordering* for projection as shown in Program 7.3.1 in lines 4 and 5. In general, one may implement more sophisticated heuristics, like *first-fail* or *most-constrained* (see [27, 134, 198, 106]) using the COMMON LISP interface of META-S.

7.3.3.3 Strategies in the context of language solvers

The application of the strategy definition framework to cooperations with participating language solvers allows one to define language evaluation strategies and classical and new search strategies for an efficient evaluation of hybrid constraint declarative programs. We briefly sketch typical strategies in the context of language evaluation.

depth/breadth-first search   These strategies can be applied e.g. for the constraint logic language solver CLL to emulate a CLP- or PROLOG-like evaluation. They are variants of the classical ones: A propagation phase performing *depth/breadth-first search* until the pool is emptied alternates with a projection phase, where all solvers are projected and the results are added to the constraint pool. These strategies can be defined on top of the *eager* strategy (see Section 7.3.3.1) by specifying the evaluation order within the search-tree.

lazy   This strategy has already been described in the previous section. It proved very advantageous when applied using CLL (cf. Section 7.3.4).

heuristic   For the integration of language solvers we use the solver interface functions for realizing program evaluation, like a reduction step, a resolution step, or a narrowing step (see Section 7.2). The propagation of an atom from the constraint pool using *tell* generates (in general) a disjunction of constraints (in the third element of the answer tuple), again to deposit in the pool. Thus, the *heuristic* strategy and its descendants cannot be used for a cooperation where language solvers participate. This is caused by the fact that these strategies may delete disjunctions in the pool resulting from propagations which cannot be reproduced later on.

residuation   This is a method to cope with indeterminism caused by insufficiently bound variables (cf. Section 5.4). The concept of residuation, as defined for logic languages in [210], divides all rules into two groups. *Residuating rules* may be applied only when their application is deterministic, i.e. only one rule matches the goal that is subject to resolution. *Generating rules* do not need to be deterministic, but may only be used when no residuating rule is applicable. CLL supports both residuating and generating rules.

narrowing/reduction strategies   In [188] it is shown how to define redex selection strategies, like innermost and lazy narrowing, for the evaluation of programs of the functional logic language FCLL.

Program 7.3.4 is an example of the use of the FCLL solver applying innermost narrowing (line 7) and a *depth-first search* strategy (line 2).

example	strategy	clones	prop.	resolutions	weak proj.	strong proj.
dag	*bfs/dfs*	6143	24575	14335	24576	24576
	lazy	6143	22528	10241	24576	24576
cgc	*bfs/dfs*	9540	53426	12402	3027	3027
	lazy	9540	19082	12404	3027	3027
hamming	*lazy*	148	2141	895	266	266
smm	*lazy*	135	6550	19	456	148
	bfs/dfs	3	3333	19	902	105
nl-csp	*lazy*	35352	109852	0	285	192
	bfs/dfs	493	118751	0	34758	2614
	heuristic	345	109121	0	31485	4944

Table 7.1 META-S: experimental results

7.3.4 Performance evaluation

To round out the picture we present benchmark results of five illustrative examples (cf. Table 7.1) to investigate the effects of different strategies for multi-domain constraint problems. As an example of language integration we used the CLL solver. Our examples feature varying extents of logic predicates and multi-domain constraints.

Our solvers are proof-of-concept implementations, their performance is, of course, not comparable to advanced solvers of modern systems like ECL^{i}PS^e-PROLOG. Thus, we were mainly interested in a comparison of the reduction steps (i.e. propagations, projections and resolutions) to enable a discussion and evaluation of the effects of solver cooperations and strategies. Using the solver integration mechanism and strategy framework of META-S thus allows for prototyping of solver cooperations and constraint integration into languages, as well as for the exploration of cooperation and evaluation strategies of such systems.

Table 7.1 captures the following key values:

- the number of *clones*, i.e. copies of the system state as nodes of a search-tree generated during the computation,
- the number of *propagations* covers resolution steps and the propagation of equality constraints resulting from substitutions computed during resolution, both for CLL, as well as constraint propagation steps for other incorporated solvers,
- the number of resolution steps (already covered in the number of propagations, but separated out for better understanding), and
- the number of weak and strong projections (cf. Section 7.1.3).

In the following, we briefly sketch example programs and discuss their performance results.

A directed acyclic graph (`dag`). Our first example concentrates on logic language evaluation without constraints of other domains. It searches for paths in a directed acyclic graph with 13 nodes. Since a full graph traversal is necessary, all strategies sooner or later create all the clones for the possible edges. Thus, the number of clones (and for similar reasons, the number of projections) do not differ between the strategies. The wanted effect of the *lazy* strategy first to propagate pending constraints of a conjunction before cloning stores (due to disjunctions produced by projections), yields an explicitly smaller number of resolution steps (and thus propagations) here, and explains why *lazy* search is eventually the fastest strategy in this scenario.

Path costs in a complete graph (`cgc`). A complete graph (i.e. with bidirectional edges between every pair of nodes) is traversed. Again, the graph is described by logic facts, but this time each edge is annotated with random costs between 1 and 100. Rules for a path search additionally contain arithmetic cost constraints (cf. Program 7.3.2).

The structure and results of this problem are similar to the previous one. The only remarkable difference is the number of resolution steps, being nearly the same now for all strategies, although the number of overall propagations is lower for the *lazy* strategy.

Again the reason is the delay of disjunction splitting (and thus the delay of cloning constraint stores) while preferring the propagation of pending constraints. While in the `dag` example this concerned goals, i.e. logic language constraints, in `cgc` arithmetic constraints are prioritized. This causes the significantly smaller number of propagations for *lazy* search.

Experiments with different goal sequences in the rules of this example led to another observation (not documented in Table 7.1): Since the *lazy* strategy prefers conjunctions, while delaying the evaluation of disjunctive goals, it may reorder goals in the right-hand side of rules in favor of the more deterministic ones. This causes situations where the *lazy* strategy "stepping over" a disjunction and evaluating deterministic goals first terminates, while *depth/breadth-first search* produce infinite resolution derivations.

The Hamming numbers (`hamming`). This example was chosen to show that META-S allows the combination of *residuating* and *generating* rules (cf. Section 7.3.3.3). A residuating CLL rule computes (in cooperation with an arithmetic solver) multiples of 2, 3 and 5; its results are requested by generating CLL rules and merged into a common list of Hamming numbers.

The user formulates residuating and generating rules which are accessed in the solver cooperation definition as shown in Program 7.3.8, lines 3 – 6.

Table 7.1 shows the results of the computation of the first 20 Hamming numbers. In the table we only give the results for the *lazy* strategy. The other strategies behave similarly because of the highly deterministic nature of the rule choice here.

Program 7.3.8 Integration of residuating and generating rules

```
1    (define-meta-solver *hamming*
2            (meta-solver residuating-strategy ...)
3            ((res cll-solver :file "residuating.cll"
4                                 :residuating-p t)
5             (gen cll-solver :file "generating.cll"
6                                 :residuating-p nil)
7             (lin cllin))
8
9            ... ; constraints
```

Send-More-Money (smm). While it is well known that this problem can be solved by a typical finite domain solver providing arithmetic, we nevertheless found it appropriate as a short and simple example to illustrate general strategy effects for a cooperation of different solvers and domains.

The problem is constructed by a CLL predicate *word* describing the composition of letters into words and constructing the respective equality constraint, i.e. $S*1000 + E*100 + N*10 + D = SEND$ (similarly as given for FCLL in Program 7.3.5). This is done in a few deterministic evaluation steps, where only one rule definition at a time matches the goals to solve. Thus, the influence of language evaluation is surpassed by constraint solving. Besides the CLL solver, two other solvers cooperate in this example. A linear arithmetic solver is supported by a finite domain solver. These two solvers rely on information interchange by projection, and hence the overall effort is greatly affected by the timing when switching from propagation to projection.

The *lazy* strategy avoids projection as long as possible, which means propagating conjunctions first, then breaking disjunctions and switching to projection only when the constraint pool is completely empty. While this is often advantageous, it has a tradeoff which becomes obvious and hindering here: It implies a higher number of clones, because a projection might disclose inconsistencies between two solvers before a queued disjunction is split into several clones. This shows that mainly problems with a larger portion (and allowing alternative steps) of language evaluation (different to *smm*) profit from *lazy* cloning.

A nonlinear constraint satisfaction problem (nl-csp). Like the previous example, this is a crypto-arithmetic puzzle. We want to replace different letters by different digits, s.t. $ABC * DEF = GHIJ$ holds. This problem is given without any CLL rules or facts, so that it shows the consequences of our cooperation strategies for a pure constraint problem.

The effect of the increased cloning rate for the *lazy* strategy becomes enormous here. However, since the CLL solver is not used in this example, the application of the *heuristic* strategy was allowed (cf. Section 7.3.3, pages 150 and 152) and the reordering of disjunctions is decisive in this case.

Overall evaluation. Our examples show that in problems with a large amount of logic language evaluation, the strategy *lazy* gives the best results. This strategy reorders goals in favor of deterministic ones and thus prevents a lot of propagations. An evaluation using the *lazy* strategy may even terminate in circumstances where *depth/breadth-first search* produce infinite resolution derivations. In problems dominated by constraint solving most disjunctions are already avoided by the weak/strong projection schema. Hence the overhead of the *lazy* strategy outweighs its advantages here and *depth/breadth-first search* are more appropriate. Problems described without use of the CLL solver may benefit from the *heuristic* strategy, which gives near optimal results in many situations.

7.4 Conclusion and related work

In this section, we presented a general approach for the integration of declarative languages and constraint systems. The main idea is to combine several constraint systems and the associated constraint solving techniques to allow the solution of hybrid constraint problems. The basis of our approach is a uniform interface for constraint solvers which enables a fine-grained formal specification of information interchange between constraint solvers. On top of this interface, an open and flexible combination mechanism for constraint solvers was developed. By considering declarative programming languages as constraint solvers for specific language constraints we were eventually able to integrate these languages and constraint systems to build *multiparadigm constraint programming languages.*

The meta-solver system META-S implements the framework. This system integrates several constraint solvers, among them an interval arithmetic solver, a linear solver and several finite domain solvers, and a logic and a functional logic language, resp. The system is equipped with an advanced strategy description framework to influence the efficiency of the cooperative solution process. We investigated classical and new search and evaluation strategies for the integrated solvers and declarative programming languages.

META-S allows the user to integrate new black-box solvers and languages and supports the definition of new cooperation strategies. It is, thus, very well suited for the prototyping of new solver cooperations and new multiparadigm constraint programming languages.

The general schemes *CLP(X)* [116, 115] and *CFLP(X)* [144] for constraint logic programming and constraint functional logic programming, resp., both over a constraint system X, are covered by the presented approach. Since our general framework, moreover, provides mechanisms for the definition of cooperation strategies, it can, thus, be instantiated by three parameters: a *strategy definition* S, a *set* X *of constraint systems* and a *host-language* Y. In this way, the presented approach enables the building of constraint languages customized for a given set of requirements for comfortable modeling and the solution of many problems.

Based on CFLP(X), functional logic programming has been integrated with arithmetic constraint domains in the context of the TOY language [57, 217]. Lux [147, 148] integrates linear constraints over real numbers into the functional logic language CURRY in a similar way. OPENCFLP [131] combines a functional logic host-language with collaborating equational solvers which may be distributed in an open environment. It provides the user with a declarative strategy definition for the cooperating solvers based upon a set of basic operators. However, the strategy language of META-S gives more subtle control over the individual collaboration steps because of its well considered solver interface on the one hand and its structural pattern-matching and constraint rewriting facilities which provide a finer and more intuitive control for strategy definition on the other hand.

While our approach pursues the idea to integrate languages (functional logic, logic, and others) into a system of cooperating solvers, the above mentioned approaches come from the opposite point of view and extend the functional logic program evaluation by constraint evaluation. Furthermore, most of them do not consider the integration of several constraint systems in combination.

The opportunity to integrate different host-languages and constraint systems also distinguishes our approach from other existing systems of cooperating solvers [107, 161, 196] that usually have one fixed host-language (a logic language).

Finally, META-S distinguishes itself from other approaches by its sophisticated strategy definition framework.

Chapter 8
Outlook

In this book we investigated the area of *multiparadigm constraint programming languages*. We discussed established and new approaches in the field and presented two concrete approaches in theory and practice.

Multiparadigm programming languages enable comfortable and efficient modeling and implementation of software because they allow the representation of the applications' components by concepts of paradigms according to their particular problem domains. The area of multiparadigm programming languages has yielded many interesting developments in recent years, including languages like ADA or the Microsoft software platform .NET realizing a loose coupling of languages. We expect that research in but also the application of such languages will further increase. In this context, e.g. [31] emphasizes the need for programming languages which allow the programmer to adopt (concepts of) programming paradigms appropriate to the particular subproblem at hand.

Languages from the *constraint-based paradigm* provide a declarative programming style and focus in particular on search and optimization problems. They developed into an established programming paradigm and are used for many application areas in practice and science, e.g. planning and scheduling of tasks, timetabling, optimization of production, configuration of products, program analysis, test data generation for software, and automatic theorem proving. We think that their application and importance in practice in the form of *multiparadigm constraint programming languages* will grow further.

In Chapter 7 we integrate programming language evaluation into constraint evaluation and reach in this way a generic framework for multiparadigm constraint programming, where both constraint domains and programming languages can be instantiated. Thus, our generic framework and its implementation are well suited for prototyping solver cooperations and multiparadigm constraint programming languages. In contrast, the typical and more pragmatic approach in practice is the extension of a host programming language by constraints, often by constraint libraries. The CCFL approach as shown in

Chapter 6 is in between, i.e. the combination of a (functional) programming language and constraints is obtained by unification of both paradigms.

For the short term and in particular for languages widely used in practice (i.e. usually imperative or object-oriented languages) we expect a further consolidation of the use of constraints within multiparadigm programming languages on the basis of (1) the library approach (as introduced in Section 5.1), that is by the integration of constraint libraries, and (2) a loose coupling of concepts as in the .NET approach.

For the longer term we believe that proper representatives of the language approach (cf. again Section 5.1) will also achieve more acceptance, in particular for domain-specific languages and applications. Exemplary developments can be seen e.g. in the current approaches to the evaluation and verification of UML/OCL diagrams and the use of constraint-based annotations in programs or their generation from programs, both for verification and test data generation (for references cf. Sections 4.4 and 5.7).

References

1. Abderrahamane Aggoun, David Chan, Pierre Dufresne, Eamon Falvey, Hugh Grant, Warwick Harvey, Alexander Herold, Geoffrey Macartney, Micha Meier, David Miller, Shyam Mudambi, Stefano Novello, Bruno Perez, Emmanuel van Rossum, Joachim Schimpf, Kish Shen, Periklis Andreas Tsahageas, and Dominique Henry de Villeneuve. ECL^{i}PS^e User Manual. Release 6.0. http://eclipseclp.org/docs/6.0/userman.pdf, 2010. last visited 2010-11-07.
2. Alfred V. Aho, Monica Lam, Ravi Sethi, and Jeffrey D. Ullman. *Compilers. Principles, Techniques, & Tools.* Pearson Education, 2007.
3. Akira Aiba, Kô Sakai, Yosuke Sato, David J. Hawley, and Ryuzo Hasegawa. Constraint Logic Programming Language CAL. In *International Conference on Fifth Generation Computer Systems – FGCS. Institute for New Generation Computer Technology – ICOT*, pages 263–276. OHMSHA Ltd. Tokyo and Springer, 1988.
4. Alexander Aiken. Set Constraints: Results, Applications, and Future Directions. In Alan Borning, editor, *Principles and Practice of Constraint Programming – PPCP*, volume 874 of *Lecture Notes in Computer Science*, pages 326–335. Springer, 1994.
5. Alexander Aiken. Introduction to Set Constraint-Based Program Analysis. *Science of Computer Programming*, 35(2-3):79–111, November 1999.
6. Alexander Aiken, Manuel Fähndrich, Jeffrey S. Foster, and Zhendong Su. A Toolkit for Constructing Type- and Constraint-Based Program Analyses. In Xavier Leroy and Atsushi Ohori, editors, *Second International Workshop on Types in Compilation*, volume 1473 of *Lecture Notes in Computer Science*, pages 78–96. Springer, 1998.
7. Alexander Aiken and Edward L. Wimmers. Type Inclusion Constraints and Type Inference. In *Conference on Functional Programming Languages and Computer Architecture – FPCA*, pages 31–41. ACM Press, 1993.
8. Alexander Aiken, Edward L. Wimmers, and T. K. Lakshman. Soft Typing with Conditional Types. In *ACM SIGPLAN-SIGACT Symposium on Principles of Programming Languages – POPL*, pages 163–173. ACM Press, 1994.
9. Hassan Aït-Kaci and Roger Nasr. Integrating Logic and Functional Programming. *Lisp and Symbolic Computation*, 2(1):51–89, 1989.
10. Yasuhiro Ajiro and Kazunori Ueda. Kima – an Automated Error Correction System for Concurrent Logic Programs. In Mireille Ducassé, editor, *International Workshop on Automated Debugging – AADEBUG*, 2000.
11. Klaus Alber and Werner Struckmann. *Einführung in die Semantik von Programmiersprachen.* Bibliographisches Institut, 1988.
12. Kyriakos Anastasakis, Behzad Bordbar, Geri Georg, and Indrakshi Ray. UML2Alloy: A Challenging Model Transformation. In Gregor Engels, Bill Opdyke, Douglas C. Schmidt, and Frank Weil, editors, *International Conference on Model Driven*

Engineering Languages and Systems – MoDELS, volume 4735 of *Lecture Notes in Computer Science*, pages 436–450. Springer, 2007.

13. Gregory R. Andrews. *Foundations of Multithreaded, Parallel and Distributed Programming*. Addison-Wesley, 2000.

14. Sergio Antoy, Rachid Echahed, and Michael Hanus. A Needed Narrowing Strategy. *Journal of the ACM*, 47(4):776–822, 2000.

15. Krzysztof R. Apt. *Principles of Constraint Programming*. Cambridge University Press, 2003.

16. Krzysztof R. Apt and Andrea Schaerf. The Alma Project, or How First-Order Logic Can Help Us in Imperative Programming. In Ernst-Rüdiger Olderog and Bernhard Steffen, editors, *Correct System Design*, volume 1710 of *Lecture Notes in Computer Science*, pages 89–113. Springer, 1999.

17. Krzysztof R. Apt and Mark G. Wallace. *Constraint Logic Programming using ECL^{i}PS^e*. Cambridge University Press, 2007.

18. Deborah J. Armstrong. The Quarks of Object-Oriented Development. *Communications of the ACM*, 49(2):123–128, 2006.

19. Joe Armstrong. *Programming Erlang. Software for a Concurrent World*. The Pragmatic Bookshelf, 2007.

20. Joe Armstrong, Robert Virding, Claes Wikstrom, and Mike Williams. *Concurrent Programming in Erlang*. Prentice Hall, 2nd edition, 2007.

21. L. Augustsson. *Compiling Lazy Functional Languages, Part II*. PhD thesis, Chalmers University, Sweden, 1987.

22. Franz Baader and Tobias Nipkow. *Term Rewriting and All That*. Cambridge University Press, 1998.

23. Banshee. A Toolkit for Building Constraint-Based Analyses. `http://banshee.sourceforge.net`. last visited 2010-11-07.

24. Henk P. Barendregt. Lambda Calculi with Types. In S. Abramsky, Dov M. Gabbay, and T.S.E. Maibaum, editors, *Handbook of Logic in Computer Science*, volume 2, pages 117–309. Oxford University Press, 1993.

25. Nicolas Beldiceanu, Mats Carlsson, Sophie Demassey, and Thierry Petit. Global Constraint Catalogue: Past, Present and Future. *Constraints*, 12(1):21–62, 2007.

26. Richard Bird. *Introduction to Functional Programming using Haskell*. Prentice Hall, 2nd edition, 1998.

27. James R. Bitner and Edward M. Reingold. Backtrack Programming Techniques. *Communications of the ACM*, 18(11):651–656, November 1975.

28. Alan Borning. The Programming Language Aspects of ThingLab, a Constraint-Oriented Simulation Laboratory. *ACM Transactions on Programming Languages and Systems – TOPLAS*, 3(4):353–387, 1981.

29. Alan Borning, Richard Anderson, and Bjørn Freeman-Benson. The Indigo Algorithm. Technical Report TR 96-05-01, Department of Computer Science and Engineering, University of Washington, July 1996.

30. James Bradley. *Introduction to Discrete Mathematics*. Addison-Wesley, 1988.

31. Johannes Brauer, Christoph Crasemann, and Hartmut Krasemann. Auf dem Weg zu idealen Programmierwerkzeugen – Bestandsaufnahme und Ausblick. *Informatik Spektrum*, 31(6):580–590, 2008.

32. Pascal Brisset and Nicolas Barnier. FaCiLe: A Functional Constraint Library. In Michael Hanus, Petra Hofstedt, Slim Abdennadher, Thom Frühwirth, and Armin Wolf, editors, *Workshop on Multiparadigm Constraint Programming Languages – MultiCPL. Cornell University, Ithaca, NY, USA*, pages 7–22, 2002.

33. Alexander Brodsky. Constraint Databases: Promising Technology or Just Intellectual Exercise? *Constraints*, 2(1):35–44, 1997.

34. Michael Brundage. *XQuery: The XML Query Language*. Addison-Wesley, 2004.

35. Bruno Buchberger. Gröbner Bases: An Algorithmic Method in Polynomial Ideal Theory. In N.K. Bose, editor, *Recent Trends in Multidimensional Systems Theory*, pages 184–232. Reidel Publishing Company, 1985.

36. Timothy A. Budd. Blending Imperative and Relational Programming. *IEEE Software*, 8(1):58–65, 1991.
37. Jordi Cabot, Robert Clarisó, and Daniel Riera. Verification of UML/OCL Class Diagrams using Constraint Programming. In *ICST Workshop on Model Driven Engineering, Verification and Validation: Integrating Verification and Validation – MoDeVVa. Lillehammer, Norway*, pages 73–80, 2008.
38. Stefano Ceri, Georg Gottlob, and Letizia Tanca. What You Always Wanted to Know About Datalog (And Never Dared to Ask). *IEEE Transactions on Knowledge and Data Engineering*, 1(1):146–166, 1989.
39. Manuel M. T. Chakravarty, Yike Guo, Martin Köhler, and Hendrik C. R. Lock. GOF-FIN: Higher-Order Functions Meet Concurrent Constraints. *Science of Computer Programming*, 30(1-2):157–199, 1998.
40. Manuel M.T. Chakravarty, Roman Leshchinskiy, Simon Peyton Jones, Gabriele Keller, and Simon Marlow. Data Parallel Haskell: A Status Report. In Neal Glew and Guy Blelloch, editors, *Workshop on Declarative Aspects of Multicore Programming – DAMP*, pages 10–18. ACM, 2007.
41. Mantis H. M. Cheng, Maarten H. van Emden, and B. E. Richards. On Warren's Method for Functional Programming in Logic. In David H. D. Warren and Peter Szeredi, editors, *Logic Programming, Proceedings of the Seventh International Conference, Jerusalem, Israel, ICLP*, pages 546–560. The MIT Press, 1990.
42. CHIP V5. http://www.cosytec.com/production_scheduling/chip/chip_technology.htm, 2006. last visited 2010-11-07.
43. Kenta Cho and Kazunori Ueda. Diagnosing Non-Well-Moded Concurrent Logic Programs. In Michael J. Maher, editor, *Joint International Conference and Syposium on Logic Programming – JICSLP*, pages 215–229. The MIT Press, 1996.
44. *CHOCO Documentation*. Ecole des Mines de Nantes, 2010. see also http://www.emn.fr/z-info/choco-solver/, last visited 2010-11-07.
45. Marie-Luise Christ-Neumann and Heinz W. Schmidt. ASDL – An Object-Oriented Specification Language for Syntax-Directed Environments. In Howard K. Nichols and Dan Simpson, editors, *1st European Software Engineering Conference – ESEC*, volume 289 of *Lecture Notes in Computer Science*, pages 71–79. Springer, 1987.
46. Philippe Codognet and Daniel Diaz. clp(B): Combining Simplicity and Efficiency in Boolean Constraint Solving. In Manuel V. Hermenegildo and Jaan Penjam, editors, *Programming Language Implementation and Logic Programming – PLILP*, volume 844 of *Lecture Notes in Computer Science*, pages 244–260. Springer, 1994.
47. Alan Colmerauer. Naive Solving of Non-linear Constraints. In Frederic Benhamou and Alan Colmerauer, editors, *Constraint Logic Programming. Selected Research*, pages 89–112. The MIT Press, 1993.
48. Keith D. Cooper and Linda Torczon. *Engineering a Compiler*. Elsevier, 2004.
49. Pascal Costanza. A Short Overview of AspectL. In *European Interactive Workshop on Aspects in Software – EIWAS*, September 2004. Berlin, Germany.
50. Luís Damas and Robin Milner. Principal Type-Schemes for Functional Programs. In *ACM Symposium on Principles of Programming Languages – POPL*, pages 207–212, 1982.
51. Daniel S. Dantas, David Walker, Geoffrey Washburn, and Stephanie Weirich. AspectML: A Polymorphic Aspect-oriented Functional Programming Language. *ACM Transactions on Programming Languages and Systems – TOPLAS*, 30(3), 2008.
52. Richard A. DeMillo and A. Jefferson Offutt. Constraint-Based Automatic Test Data Generation. *IEEE Transactions on Software Engineering*, 17(9):900–910, 1991.
53. Jan Van den Bussche. Constraint Databases, Queries, and Query Languages. In Gabriel M. Kuper, Leonid Libkin, and Jan Paredaens, editors, *Constraint Databases*, pages 20–54. Springer, 2000.
54. Wolfgang Domschke and Andreas Drexl. *Einführung in Operations Research*. Springer, 7th edition, 2007.

55. Hartmut Ehrig, Berd Mahr, Felix Cornelius, Martin Große-Rhode, and Phillipp Zeitz. *Mathematisch-struktuelle Grundlagen der Informatik*. Springer, 2nd edition, 2001.
56. Jonathan Eifrig, Scott F. Smith, and Valery Trifonov. Sound Polymorphic Type Inference for Objects. In *Conference on Object-Oriented Programming Systems, Languages, and Applications – OOPSLA*, volume 30(10) of *SIGPLAN Notices*, pages 169–184, 1995.
57. Sonia Estévez-Martín, Antonio J. Fernández, Teresa Hortalá-González, Mario Rodríguez-Artalejo, Fernando Sáenz-Pérez, and Rafael del Vado Vírseda. Cooperation of Constraint Domains in the TOY System. In Sergio Antoy and Elvira Albert, editors, *10th International ACM SIGPLAN Conference on Principles and Practice of Declarative Programming – PPDP*, pages 258–268. ACM, 2008.
58. Manuel Fähndrich and Alexander Aiken. Program Analysis Using Mixed Term and Set Constraints. In Pascal Van Hentenryck, editor, *Static Analysis Symposium – SAS*, volume 1302 of *Lecture Notes in Computer Science*, pages 114–126. Springer, 1997.
59. Manuel Fähndrich, Jeffrey S. Foster, Zhendong Su, and Alexander Aiken. Partial Online Cycle Elimination in Inclusion Constraint Graphs. In *ACM SIGPLAN Conference on Programming Language Design and Implementation – PLDI*, volume 33(5) of *SIGPLAN Notices*, pages 85–96, 1998.
60. Moreno Falaschi and Michael J. Maher. Introduction to Special Issue on Multiparadigm Languages and Constraint Programming. *Theory and Practice of Logic Programming*, 7(1-2):1–2, 2007.
61. Anthony J. Field and Peter G. Harrison. *Functional Programming*. Addison-Wesley, 1988.
62. Sebastian Fischer and Herbert Kuchen. Systematic Generation of Glass-Box Test Cases for Functional Logic Programs. In Michael Leuschel and Andreas Podelski, editors, *ACM SIGPLAN Conference on Principles and Practice of Declarative Programming – PPDP*, pages 63–74. ACM Press, 2007.
63. Jeffrey S. Foster, Manuel Fähndrich, and Alexander Aiken. Flow-Insensitive Points-to Analysis with Term and Set Constraints. Technical Report CSD-97-964, University of California at Berkeley, 1997.
64. Stephan Frank, Petra Hofstedt, and Pierre R. Mai. A Flexible Meta-solver Framework for Constraint Solver Collaboration. In Andreas Günter, Rudolf Kruse, and Bernd Neumann, editors, *Advances in Artificial Intelligence. 26th Annual German Conference on AI – KI 2003*, volume 2821 of *Lecture Notes in Computer Science*, pages 520–534. Springer, 2003.
65. Stephan Frank, Petra Hofstedt, and Pierre R. Mai. Meta-S: A Strategy-Oriented Meta-Solver Framework. In Ingrid Russell and Susan M. Haller, editors, *16th International Florida Artificial Intelligence Research Society Conference – FLAIRS*, pages 177–181. The AAAI Press, 2003.
66. Stephan Frank, Petra Hofstedt, Peter Pepper, and Dirk Reckmann. Solution Strategies for Multi-domain Constraint Logic Programs. In Irina Virbitskaite and Andrei Voronkov, editors, *Sixth International Andrei Ershov Memorial Conference, Perspectives of System Informatics – PSI 2006*, volume 4378 of *Lecture Notes in Computer Science*, pages 209–222. Springer, 2007.
67. Stephan Frank, Petra Hofstedt, and Dirk Reckmann. Strategies for the Efficient Solution of Hybrid Constraint Logic Programs. In Susana Muñoz-Hernández, José Manuel Gómez-Pérez, and Petra Hofstedt, editors, *Third Workshop on Multiparadigm Constraint Programming Languages – MultiCPL*, pages 103–117, 2004.
68. Stephan Frank, Petra Hofstedt, and Dirk Reckmann. System Description: Meta-S – Combining Solver Cooperation and Programming Languages. In *19th International Workshop on (Constraint) Logic Programming – W(C)LP*, pages 159–162, 2005. Ulmer Informatik-Berichte, No. 2005-01.

69. Stephan Frank and Pierre R. Mai. Strategies for Cooperating Constraint Solvers. Diplomarbeit, Technische Universität Berlin, July 2002.
70. Bjørn N. Freeman-Benson. *Constraint Imperative Programming.* PhD thesis, University of Washington, Department of Computer Science and Engineering, 1991.
71. Thom Frühwirth and Slim Abdennadher. *Essentials of Constraint Programming.* Springer, 2003.
72. Thom Frühwirth, Alexander Herold, Volker Küchenhoff, Thierry Le Provost, Pierre Lim, Eric Monfroy, and Mark Wallace. Constraint Logic Programming. An Informal Introduction. Technical Report ECRC-93-5, European Computer-Industry Research Centre, München, 1993.
73. Gecode – Generic Constraint Development Environment. `http://www.gecode.org`, 2010. last visited 2010-11-07.
74. The GNU Prolog web site. `http://www.gprolog.org`, 2010. last visited 2010-09-07.
75. Arnaud Gotlieb, Bernard Botella, and Michel Rueher. Automatic Test Data Generation Using Constraint Solving Techniques. In *ACM SIGSOFT International Symposium on Software Testing and Analysis – ISSTA*, pages 53–62. ACM Press, 1998.
76. Martin Grabmüller. Constraint Imperative Programming. Diplomarbeit, Technische Universität Berlin, 2003.
77. Martin Grabmüller and Petra Hofstedt. Turtle: A Constraint Imperative Programming Language. In Frans Coenen, Alun Preece, and Ann Macintosh, editors, *Twenty-third SGAI International Conference on Innovative Techniques and Applications of Artificial Intelligence*, number XX in Research and Development in Intelligent Systems. Springer, 2003.
78. Steve Gregory. *Parallel Logic Programming in Parlog: The Language and its Implementation.* Addison-Wesley, 1987.
79. Jurriaan Hage and Bastiaan Heeren. Heuristics for Type Error Discovery and Recovery. In Zoltán Horváth, Viktória Zsók, and Andrew Butterfield, editors, *Implementation and Application of Functional Languages – IFL 2006*, volume 4449 of *Lecture Notes in Computer Science*, pages 199–216. Springer, 2007.
80. Michael Hanus. The Integration of Functions into Logic Programming: From Theory to Practice. *Journal of Logic Programming*, 19/20:583–628, 1994.
81. Michael Hanus. Multi-paradigm Declarative Languages. In Verónica Dahl and Ilkka Niemelä, editors, *International Conference on Logic Programming – ICLP*, volume 4670 of *Lecture Notes in Computer Science*, pages 45–75. Springer, 2007.
82. Michael Hanus, Sergio Antoy, Bernd Braßel, Herbert Kuchen, Francisco J. López-Fraguas, Wolfgang Lux, Juan José Moreno-Navarro, and Frank Steiner. Curry. An Integrated Functional Logic Language. Version 0.8.2, March 2006.
83. Michael Hanus, Petra Hofstedt, Slim Abdennadher, Thom Frühwirth, and Armin Wolf, editors. *Workshop on Multiparadigm Constraint Programming Languages – MultiCPL*, 2002. Cornell University, Ithaca, NY, USA.
84. Michael Hanus, Petra Hofstedt, Armin Wolf, Slim Abdennadher, Thom Frühwirth, and Arnaud Lallouet, editors. *Second International Workshop on Multiparadigm Constraint Programming Languages – MultiCPL*, 2003. Kinsale, Ireland.
85. Seif Haridi, Sverker Janson, Johan Montelius, Torkel Franzén, Per Brand, Kent Boortz, Björn Danielsson, Björn Carlson, Torbjörn Keisu, Dan Sahlin, and Thomas Sjöland. Concurrent Constraint Programming at SICS with the Andorra Kernel Language (Extended Abstract). In *First Workshop on Principles and Practice of Constraint Programming – PPCP*, pages 107–116, 1993.
86. Bastiaan Heeren, Johan Jeuring, Doaitse Swierstra, and Pablo Azero Alcocer. Improving Type-Error Messages in Functional Languages. Technical Report UU-CS-2002-009, Department of Information and Computing Sciences, Utrecht University, 2002.
87. Nevin Heintze. *Set Based Program Analysis.* PhD thesis, Carnegie Mellon University, 1992.

88. Nevin Heintze. Set Based Analysis of Arithmetic. Technical Report CMU-CS-93-221, Carnegie Mellon University, December 1993.

89. Nevin Heintze. Set-Based Analysis of ML Programs. In *ACM Conference on LISP and Functional Programming*, pages 306–317. ACM Press, 1994.

90. Nevin Heintze and Joxan Jaffar. A Decision Procedure for a Class of Set Constraints (Extended Abstract). In *IEEE Symposium on Logic in Computer Science – LICS*, pages 42–51. IEEE Computer Society, 1990.

91. Nevin Heintze and Joxan Jaffar. A Finite Presentation Theorem for Approximating Logic Programs. In *ACM Symposium on Principles of Programming Languages – POPL*, pages 197–209, 1990.

92. Nevin Heintze and Joxan Jaffar. An Engine for Logic Program Analysis. In *IEEE Symposium on Logic in Computer Science – LICS*, pages 318–328. IEEE Computer Society, 1992.

93. Fritz Henglein. Global Tagging Optimization by Type Inference. In *ACM Conference on LISP and Functional Programming*, pages 205–215. ACM Press, 1992.

94. Pascal Van Hentenryck. *The OPL Optimization Programming Language*. The MIT Press, 1999.

95. Ralf G. Herrtwich and Günter Hommel. *Nebenläufige Programme*. Springer, 2nd edition, 2007.

96. Timothy J. Hickey, Qun Ju, and Maarten H. van Emden. Interval Arithmetic: From Principles to Implementation. *Journal of the ACM*, 48(5):1038–1068, 2001.

97. Petra Hofstedt. Better Communication for Tighter Cooperation. In John W. Lloyd, editor, *First International Conference on Computational Logic – CL*, volume 1861 of *Lecture Notes in Computer Science*, pages 342–358. Springer, 2000.

98. Petra Hofstedt. *Cooperation and Coordination of Constraint Solvers*. PhD thesis, Technische Universität Dresden, 2001.

99. Petra Hofstedt. A general Approach for Building Constraint Languages. In Bob McKay and John K. Slaney, editors, *Advances in Artificial Intelligence. 15th Australian Joint Conference on Artificial Intelligence – AI'02*, volume 2557 of *Lecture Notes in Computer Science*, pages 431–442. Springer, 2002.

100. Petra Hofstedt. CCFL – A Concurrent Constraint Functional Language. Technical Report 2008–08, Technische Universität Berlin, 2008.

101. Petra Hofstedt. Realizing Evaluation Strategies by Hierarchical Graph Rewriting. In Germán Vidal and Neng-Fa Zhou, editors, *Implementation of Constraint Logic Programming Systems – CICLOPS*, 2010.

102. Petra Hofstedt and Olaf Krzikalla. TURTLE++ – A CIP-Library for C++. In Masanobu Umeda, Armin Wolf, Oskar Bartenstein, Ulrich Geske, Dietmar Seipel, and Osamu Takata, editors, *International Conference on Applications of Declarative Programming and Knowledge Management – INAP 2005*, volume 4369 of *Lecture Notes in Computer Science*, pages 12–24. Springer, 2006.

103. Petra Hofstedt and Florian Lorenzen. Constraint Functional Multicore Programming. In Stefan Fischer, Erik Maehle, and Rüdiger Reischuk, editors, *Informatik 2009. Proceedings*, volume 154 of *LNI – Lecture Notes in Informatics*, pages 367, 2901–2915. Bonner Köllen Verlag, 2009.

104. Petra Hofstedt and Andre Metzner. Multiple Evaluation Strategies for the Multi-paradigm Programming Language Brooks. In Germán Vidal, editor, *12th International Workshop on Functional and (Constraint) Logic Programming – WFLP*, 2003. Technical Report DSIC-II/13/03, Departamento de Sistemas Informáticos y Computación, Universidad Politécnica de Valencia.

105. Petra Hofstedt and Peter Pepper. Integration of Declarative and Constraint Programming. *Theory and Practice of Logic Programming (TPLP). Special Issue on Multiparadigm Languages and Constraint Programming*, 7(1&2):93–121, 2007.

106. Petra Hofstedt and Armin Wolf. *Einführung in die Constraint-Programmierung. Grundlagen, Methoden, Sprachen, Anwendungen*. Springer, 2007.

107. Hoon Hong. Confluency of Cooperative Constraint Solving. Technical Report 94–08, Research Institute for Symbolic Computation. RISC Report Series, University of Linz, Austria, 1994.

108. John E. Hopcroft and Richard M. Karp. An $n^{5/2}$ Algorithm for Maximum Matchings in Bipartite Graphs. *SIAM Journal on Computing*, 2(4):225–231, 1973.

109. Paul Hudak. *The Haskell School of Expression. Learning Functional Programming Through Multimedia.* Cambridge University Press, 2007.

110. Hyper/J^{TM}: Multi-Dimensional Separation of Concerns for Java^{TM}. http://www.research.ibm.com/hyperspace/HyperJ/HyperJ.htm. last visited 2010-11-07.

111. Walter Hürsch and Cristina Lopes. Separation of Concerns. Technical Report NU-CCS-95-03, College of Computer Science, Northeastern University Boston, USA, 1995.

112. IBM ILOG Optimization. http://www.ilog.com/products/optimization/. last visited 2010-11-07.

113. ILOG Solver 6.0. User's Manual. ILOG, 10/2003.

114. Jean-Louis Imbert and Pascal Van Hentenryck. Efficient Handling of Disequations in CLP over Linear Rational Arithmetic. Technical Report CS-91-23, Brown University, 1991.

115. Joxan Jaffar and Jean-Louis Lassez. Constraint Logic Programming. Technical Report 74, Monash University, Melbourne, Australia, 1986.

116. Joxan Jaffar and Jean-Louis Lassez. Constraint Logic Programming. In *ACM Symposium on Principles of Programming Languages – POPL*, pages 111–119, 1987.

117. Joxan Jaffar, Jean-Louis Lassez, and John W. Lloyd. Completeness of the Negation as Failure Rule. In Alan Bundy, editor, *International Joint Conference on Artificial Intelligence – IJCAI*, pages 500–506. William Kaufmann, 1983.

118. Joxan Jaffar, Michael J. Maher, Kim Marriott, and Peter J. Stuckey. The Semantics of Constraint Logic Programs. *Journal of Logic Programming*, 37(1-3):1–46, 1998.

119. Joxan Jaffar and Micheal J. Maher. Constraint Logic Programming: A Survey. *Journal of Logic Programming*, 19&20:503–581, 1994.

120. Sverker Janson. *AKL: A Multiparadigm Programming Language Based on a Concurrent Constraint Framework.* PhD thesis, Uppsala University, Computing Science Department, 1994.

121. Jang-Wu Jo, Byeong-Mo Chang, Kwangkeun Yi, and Kwang-Moo Choe. An Uncaught Exception Analysis for Java. *Journal of Systems and Software*, 72(1):59–69, 2004.

122. T. Johnsson. *Compiling Lazy Functional Languages.* PhD thesis, Chalmers University, Sweden, 1987.

123. Neil D. Jones and Steven S. Muchnick. Flow Analysis and Optimization of LISP-like Structures. In *ACM Symposium on Principles of Programming Languages – POPL*, pages 244–256. ACM, 1979.

124. Narendra Jussien. e-constraints: explanation-based Constraint Programming. In *CP'01 Workshop on User-Interaction in Constraint Satisfaction*, 2001.

125. Narendra Jussien and Vincent Barichard. The PaLM System: explanation-based Constraint Programming. In *TRICS: Techniques foR Implementing Constraint programming Systems, a post-conference workshop of CP 2000*, pages 118–133, 2000.

126. Paris C. Kanellakis, Gabriel M. Kuper, and Peter Z. Revesz. Constraint Query Languages. *Journal of Computer and System Sciences*, 51(1):26–52, 1995.

127. Sonja E. Keene. *Object-oriented Programming in Common Lisp.* Addison-Wesley, 1989.

128. Gregor Kiczales, Erik Hilsdale, Jim Hugunin, Mik Kersten, Jeffrey Palm, and William G. Griswold. An Overview of AspectJ. In Jørgen Lindskov Knudsen, editor, *European Conference on Object-Oriented Programming – ECOOP*, volume 2072 of *Lecture Notes in Computer Science*, pages 327–353. Springer, 2001.

129. Gregor Kiczales, John Lamping, Anurag Mendhekar, Chris Maeda, Cristina Videira Lopes, Jean-Marc Loingtier, and John Irwin. Aspect-Oriented Programming. In Mehmet Aksit and Satoshi Matsuoka, editors, *European Conference on Object-Oriented Programming – ECOOP*, volume 1241 of *Lecture Notes in Computer Science*, pages 220–242. Springer, 1997.

130. Donald E. Knuth. Literate Programming. *The Computer Journal*, 27(2):97–111, 1984.

131. Norio Kobayashi, Mircea Marin, and Tetsuo Ida. Collaborative Constraint Functional Logic Programming System in an Open Environment. *IEICE Transactions on Information and Systems*, E86-D(1):63–70, 2003.

132. John Kodumal and Alexander Aiken. Banshee: A Scalable Constraint-Based Analysis Toolkit. In Chris Hankin and Igor Siveroni, editors, *Static Analysis Symposium – SAS*, volume 3672 of *Lecture Notes in Computer Science*, pages 218–234. Springer, 2005.

133. Olaf Krzikalla. Constraint Solver für lineare Constraints über reellen Zahlen. Großer Beleg. Technische Universität Dresden, 1997.

134. Vipin Kumar. Algorithms for Constraint Satisfaction Problems: A Survey. *The AI Magazine*, 13(1):32–44, 1992.

135. Vipin Kumar, Ananth Grama, Anshul Gupta, and George Karypis. *Introduction to Parallel Computing: Design and Analysis of Algorithms*. Benjamin Cummings, 1994.

136. Sébastien Lapierre, Ettore Merlo, Gilles Savard, Giuliano Antoniol, Roberto Fiutem, and Paolo Tonella. Automatic Unit Test Data Generation Using Mixed-Integer Linear Programming and Execution Trees. In *International Conference on Software Maintenance – ICSM*, pages 189–198. IEEE Computer Society, 1999.

137. Daan Leijen. Parsec, a free monadic parser combinator library for Haskell. `http://legacy.cs.uu.nl/daan/parsec.html`, 2003. last visited 2010-11-07.

138. John W. Lloyd. Programming in an Integrated Functional and Logic Language. *Journal of Functional and Logic Programming*, 1999(3), 1999.

139. LMNtal PukiWiki. `http://www.ueda.info.waseda.ac.jp/lmntal/`, 2010. last visited 2010-11-07.

140. Hans-Wolfgang Loidl, Fernando Rubio, Norman Scaife, Kevin Hammond, Susumu Horiguchi, Ulrike Klusik, Rita Loogen, Greg Michaelson, Ricardo Peña, Steffen Priebe, Álvaro J. Rebón Portillo, and Philip W. Trinder. Comparing Parallel Functional Languages: Programming and Performance. *Higher-Order and Symbolic Computation*, 16(3):203–251, September 2003.

141. Rita Loogen, Yolanda Ortega-Mallén, and Ricardo Peña-Marí. Parallel Functional Programming in Eden. *Journal of Functional Programming*, 15(3):431–475, 2005.

142. Gus Lopez, Bjørn Freeman-Benson, and Alan Borning. Kaleidoscope: A Constraint Imperative Programming Language. In B. Mayoh, E. Tyugu, and J. Penjam, editors, *Constraint Programming*, volume 131 of *NATO ASI Series F: Computer and System Sciences*. Springer, 1994.

143. Gustavo Eduardo Lopez. *The Design and Implementation of Kaleidoscope, a Constraint Imperative Programming Language*. PhD thesis, University of Washington, 1997.

144. Francisco Javier López-Fraguas. A General Scheme for Constraint Functional Logic Programming. In Hélène Kirchner and Giorgio Levi, editors, *International Conference on Algebraic and Logic Programming – ALP*, volume 632 of *Lecture Notes in Computer Science*, pages 213–227. Springer, 1992.

145. Alejandro López-Ortiz, Claude-Guy Quimper, John Tromp, and Peter van Beek. A Fast and Simple Algorithm for Bounds Consistency of the Alldifferent Constraint. In Georg Gottlob and Toby Walsh, editors, *18th International Joint Conference on Artificial Intelligence – IJCAI*, pages 245–250. Morgan Kaufmann, 2003.

146. Kenneth C. Louden. *Compiler Construction. Principles and Practice*. PWS Publishing Company, 1997.

147. Wolfgang Lux. Adding Linear Constraints over Real Numbers to Curry. In María Alpuente, editor, *International Workshop on Functional and Logic Programming – WFLP*, pages 427–439, 2000.
148. Wolfgang Lux. Adding Linear Constraints over Real Numbers to Curry. In Herbert Kuchen and Kazunori Ueda, editors, *International Symposium on Functional and Logic Programming – FLOPS*, volume 2024 of *Lecture Notes in Computer Science*, pages 185–200. Springer, 2001.
149. Michael J. Maher. Logic Semantics for a Class of Committed-Choice Programs. In Jean-Louis Lassez, editor, *International Conference on Logic Programming – ICLP*, pages 858–876. The MIT Press, 1987.
150. Zohar Manna. *Mathematical Theory of Computation*. McGraw-Hill, 1975.
151. Simon Marlow and Philip Wadler. A Practical Subtyping System for Erlang. In *ACM SIGPLAN International Conference on Functional Programming – ICFP*, volume 32(8) of *SIGPLAN Notices*, pages 136–149. ACM Press, 1997.
152. István Maros. *Computational Techniques of the Simplex Method*. Kluwer Academic Publishers, 2003.
153. Kim Marriott and Peter J. Stuckey. *Programming with Constraints: An Introduction*. The MIT Press, 1998.
154. Ursula Martin and Tobias Nipkow. Boolean Unification – The Story so far. *Journal of Symbolic Computation*, 7(3–4):275–293, 1989.
155. Jean-Luc Massat. Using Local Consistency Techniques to Solve Boolean Constraints. In Frederic Benhamou and Alan Colmerauer, editors, *Constraint Logic Programming. Selected Research*, pages 223–235. The MIT Press, 1993.
156. Robin Milner. A Theory of Type Polymorphism in Programming. *Journal of Computer and System Sciences*, 17(3):348–375, 1978.
157. MINERVA, IF Computer Japan. http://www.ifcomputer.com/MINERVA/home_en.html, 2010. last visited 2010-11-07.
158. Prateek Mishra. Towards a Theory of Types in PROLOG. In *IEEE International Symposium on Logic Programming – SLP*, pages 289–298, 1984.
159. Prateek Mishra and Uday S. Reddy. Declaration-Free Type Checking. In *ACM Symposium on the Principles of Programming Language – POPL*, pages 7–21, 1985.
160. Eric Monfroy. Gröbner Bases: Strategies and Applications. In Jacques Calmet and John A. Campbell, editors, *International Conference Artificial Intelligence and Symbolic Mathematical Computation – AISMC*, volume 737 of *Lecture Notes in Computer Science*, pages 133–151. Springer, 1992.
161. Eric Monfroy. *Solver Collaboration for Constraint Logic Programming*. PhD thesis, Centre de Recherche en Informatique de Nancy. INRIA-Lorraine, 1996.
162. Juan José Moreno-Navarro and Mario Rodríguez-Artalejo. Logic Programming with Functions and Predicates: The Language BABEL. *Journal of Logic Programming*, 12(3&4):191–223, 1992.
163. Roger A. Müller, Christoph Lembeck, and Herbert Kuchen. A Symbolic Java Virtual Machine for Test Case Generation. In M. H. Hamza, editor, *International Conference on Software Engineering – IASTED*, pages 365–371. IASTED/ACTA Press, 2004.
164. Susana Muñoz-Hernández, José Manuel Gómez-Pérez, and Petra Hofstedt. Third Workshop on Multiparadigm Constraint Programming Languages – MultiCPL, 2004. Saint-Malo, France.
165. Martin Müller, Tobias Müller, and Peter Van Roy. Multiparadigm Programming in Oz. In Donald Smith, Olivier Ridoux, and Peter Van Roy, editors, *ILPS'95 Workshop on Visions for the Future of Logic Programming*, Portland, Oregon, USA, 1995.
166. Lee Naish. Adding equations to NU-Prolog. In Jan Maluszynski and Martin Wirsing, editors, *Programming Language Implementation and Logic Programming, 3rd International Symposium, PLILP*, volume 528 of *Lecture Notes in Computer Science*, pages 15–26. Springer, 1991.

167. Lee Naish. Higher-order Logic Programming in Prolog. Technical Report 96/2, Department of Computer Science, University of Melbourne, 1996.

168. Ulrich Neumerkel and Frédéric Mesnard. Localizing and Explaining Reasons for Non-terminating Logic Programs with Failure-Slices. In Gopalan Nadathur, editor, *Principles and Practice of Declarative Programming – PPDP*, volume 1702 of *Lecture Notes in Computer Science*, pages 328–342. Springer, 1999.

169. Ulf Nilsson and Jan Maluszynski. *Logic, Programming and Prolog*. John Wiley & Sons Ltd., 2nd edition, 1995.

170. OCL 2.2 Specification. via http://www.omg.org, 2010. last visited 2010-11-07.

171. Martin Odersky, Lex Spoon, and Bill Venners. *Programming in Scala*. Artima, 2007.

172. The Opal Project. http://projects.uebb.tu-berlin.de/opal/, 2010. last visited 2010-11-07.

173. David Overton, Zoltan Somogyi, and Peter J. Stuckey. Constraint-Based Mode Analysis of Mercury. In *ACM SIGPLAN Conference on Principles and Practice of Declarative Programming – PPDP*, pages 109–120. ACM Press, 2002.

174. Leszek Pacholski and Andreas Podelski. Set Constraints: A Pearl in Research on Constraints. In Gert Smolka, editor, *Principles and Practice of Constraint Programming – CP*, volume 1330 of *Lecture Notes in Computer Science*, pages 549–562. Springer, 1997.

175. Catuscia Palamidessi. Algebraic Properties of Idempotent Substitutions. In Mike S. Paterson, editor, *International Colloquium on Automata, Languages and Programming - ICALP*, volume 443 of *Lecture Notes in Computer Science*, pages 386–399. Springer, 1990.

176. Christos H. Papadimitriou and Kenneth Steiglitz. *Combinatorial Optimization: Algorithms and Complexity*. Prentice Hall, 1982.

177. Peter Pepper. *Funktionale Programmierung in OPAL, ML, HASKELL und GOFER*. Springer, 2nd edition, 2003.

178. Peter Pepper and Petra Hofstedt. *Funktionale Programmierung: Sprachdesign und Programmiertechnik*. Springer, 2006.

179. Simon Peyton Jones, Andrew Gordon, and Sigbjorn Finne. Concurrent Haskell. In *23rd ACM Symposium on Principles of Programming Languages – POPL*, pages 295–308, 1996.

180. Joachim Piehler. *Einführung in die lineare Optimierung*. Verlag Harri Deutsch, 1964.

181. Kent M. Pitman, editor. *American National Standard for Programming Language Common Lisp (ANSI INCITS 226-1994)*. ANSI X3/NCITS TC J13, 1994. via http://www.lispworks.com/documentation/common-lisp.html. last visited 2010-11-07.

182. Andreas Podelski, Witold Charatonik, and Martin Müller. Set-Based Failure Analysis for Logic Programs and Concurrent Constraint Programs. In Doaitse Swierstra, editor, *European Symposium on Programming Languages and Systems – ESOP*, volume 1576 of *Lecture Notes in Computer Science*, pages 177–192. Springer, 1999.

183. Robert F. Pointon, Philip W. Trinder, and Hans-Wolfgang Loidl. The Design and Implementation of Glasgow Distributed Haskell. In Markus Mohnen and Pieter W. M. Koopman, editors, *12th International Workshop on Implementation of Functional Languages (IFL)*, volume 2011 of *Lecture Notes in Computer Science*, pages 53–70. Springer, 2000.

184. Jean-François Puget. Applications of Constraint Programming. In Ugo Montanari and Francesca Rossi, editors, *Principles and Practice of Constraint Programming – CP*, volume 976 of *Lecture Notes in Computer Science*, pages 647–650. Springer, 1995.

185. Jean-François Puget. A Fast Algorithm for the Bound Consistency of alldiff Constraints. In *Fifteenth National Conference on Artificial Intelligence and Tenth Innovative Applications of Artificial Intelligence Conference – AAAI/IAAI*, pages 359–366. AAAI Press / The MIT Press, 1998.

186. C. V. Ramamoorthy, Siu-Bun F. Ho, and W. T. Chen. On the Automated Generation of Program Test Data. *IEEE Transactions on Software Engineering*, 2(4):293–300, 1976.

187. Chris Reade. *Elements of Functional Programming*. Addison-Wesley, 1989.

188. Dirk Reckmann. Integration of Language Evaluation and Constraint Solving. Diplomarbeit, Technische Universität Berlin, 2004.

189. Jean-Charles Régin. A Filtering Algorithm for Constraints of Difference in CSPs. In *12th National Conference on Artificial Intelligence*, volume 1, pages 362–367. AAAI Press, 1994.

190. Didier Rémy and Jerome Vouillon. Objective ML: An Effective Object-Oriented Extension to ML. *TAPOS - Theory and Practice of Objects Systems*, 4(1):27–50, 1998.

191. Peter Z. Revesz. *Introduction to Constraint Databases*. Springer, 2002.

192. John C. Reynolds. Automatic Computation of Data Set Definitions. In A.J.H. Morrell, editor, *Information Processing, IFIP Congress, Vol. 1 - Mathematics, Software*, pages 456–461. North Holland, 1968.

193. Harvey Richardson. High Performance Fortran: History, Overview and Current Developments. Technical Report TMC-261, Thinking Machines Corporation, 1996.

194. John Alan Robinson. A Machine-Oriented Logic Based on the Resolution Principle. *Journal of the ACM*, 12(1):23–41, 1965.

195. Francesca Rossi, Peter van Beek, and Toby Walsh, editors. *Handbook of Constraint Programming*. Elsevier Science, 2006.

196. Michel Rueher. An Architecture for Cooperating Constraint Solvers on Reals. In Andreas Podelski, editor, *Constraint Programming: Basics and Trends. Châtillon Spring School 1994. Selected Papers*, volume 910 of *Lecture Notes in Computer Science*, pages 231–250. Springer, 1995.

197. Michel Rueher and Christine Solnon. Concurrent Cooperating Solvers over Reals. *Reliable Computing*, 3(3):325–333, 1997.

198. Norman M. Sadeh and Mark S. Fox. Variable and Value Ordering Heuristics for the Job Shop Scheduling Constraint Satisfaction Problem. *Artificial Intelligence*, 86(1):1–41, 1996.

199. Vijay A. Saraswat. *Concurrent Constraint Programming*. The MIT Press, 1993.

200. Vijay A. Saraswat and Martin C. Rinard. Concurrent Constraint Programming. In *17th ACM Symposium on Principles of Programming Languages – POPL*, pages 232–245, 1990.

201. Michael L. Scott. *Programming Language Pragmatics*. Morgan Kaufmann, 2000.

202. Ehud Y. Shapiro. Concurrent Prolog: A Progress Report. *IEEE Computer*, 19(8):44–58, August 1986.

203. Ehud Y. Shapiro. The Family of Concurrent Logic Programming Languages. *ACM Computing Surveys*, 21(3):413–510, 1989.

204. Ehud Y. Shapiro and Leon Sterling. *The Art of Prolog. Advanced Programming Techniques*. The MIT Press, 2nd edition, 1994.

205. SICStus Prolog User's Manual. Release 4.0.4, June 2008. Swedish Institute of Computer Science. Kista, Sweden.

206. Helmut Simonis. Building Industrial Applications with Constraint Programming. In Hubert Comon, Claude Marché, and Ralf Treinen, editors, *Constraints in Computational Logics: Theory and Applications, International Summer School, CCL'99 Gif-sur-Yvette, France, September 5-8, 1999, Revised Lectures*, volume 2002 of *Lecture Notes in Computer Science*, pages 271–309. Springer, 2001.

207. Helmut Simonis. Sudoku as a Constraint Problem. In Brahim Hnich, Patrick Prosser, and Barbara Smith, editors, *4th International Workshop on Modelling and Reformulating Constraint Satisfaction Problems (held in conjunction with CP 2005)*, pages 13–27, 2005.

208. F.-R. Sinot. Call-by-Name and Call-by-Value as Token-Passing Interaction Nets. In P. Urzyczyn, editor, *Typed Lambda Calculi and Applications – TLCA*, volume 3461 of *Lecture Notes in Computer Science*, pages 386–400. Springer, 2005.

209. Stephen Slade. *Object-oriented Common Lisp*. Prentice Hall, 1998.

210. Gert Smolka. Residuation and Guarded Rules for Constraint Logic Programming. In Frédéric Benhamou and Alain Colmerauer, editors, *Constraint Logic Programming, Selected Research*, pages 405–419. The MIT Press, 1993.

211. Gert Smolka. The Oz Programming Model. In Jan van Leeuwen, editor, *Computer Science Today: Recent Trends and Developments*, volume 1000 of *Lecture Notes in Computer Science*, pages 324–343. Springer, 1995.

212. Gert Smolka, Martin Henz, and Jörg Würtz. Object-Oriented Concurrent Constraint Programming in Oz. In Vijay Saraswat and Pascal Van Hentenryck, editors, *Principles and Practice of Constraint Programming*, chapter 2. The MIT Press, 1995.

213. Michael Sperber, R. Kent Dybvig, Matthew Flatt, Anton van Straaten, Richard Kelsey, William Clinger, Jonathan Rees, Robert Bruce Findler, and Jacob Matthews. Revised[6] Report on the Algorithmic Language Scheme, 2007. http://www.r6rs.org, last visited 2010-11-07.

214. Bjarne Steensgaard. Points-to Analysis in Almost Linear Time. In *ACM SIGPLAN-SIGACT Symposium on Principles of Programming Languages – POPL*, pages 32–41. ACM Press, 1996.

215. Robert E. Tarjan. Depth-First Search and Linear Graph Algorithms. *SIAM Journal on Computing*, 1:146–160, 1972.

216. Simon Thompson. *The Craft of Functional Programming*. Addison-Wesley, 1999.

217. TOY: A Constraint Functional Logic System. http://toy.sourceforge.net, 2010. last visited 2010-11-07.

218. Kazunori Ueda. Guarded Horn Clauses. In Ehud Y. Shapiro, editor, *Concurrent Prolog: Collected Papers*, pages 140–156. The MIT Press, 1987.

219. Kazunori Ueda and Norio Kato. LMNtal: A Language Model with Links and Membranes. In Giancarlo Mauri, Gheorghe Paun, Mario J. Pérez-Jiménez, Grzegorz Rozenberg, and Arto Salomaa, editors, *Proceedings of the Fifth International Workshop on Membrane Computing (WMC 2004)*, volume 3365 of *Lecture Notes in Computer Science*, pages 110–125. Springer, 2005.

220. Kazunori Ueda, Norio Kato, Koji Hara, and Ken Mizuno. LMNtal as a Unifying Declarative Language. In Tom Schrijvers and Thom Frühwirth, editors, *Proceedings of the Third Workshop on Constraint Handling Rules*, Technical Report CW 452, pages 1–15. Katholieke Universiteit Leuven, 2006.

221. OMG Unified Modeling Language (OMG UML), Version 2.3. via http://www.omg.org, 2010. last visited 2010-11-07.

222. Peter van Beek. A 'C' library of routines for solving binary constraint satisfaction problems. http://www.cs.uwaterloo.ca/~vanbeek/software.html, 1994. last visited 2010-11-07.

223. Arie van Deursen, Paul Klint, and Joost M.W. Visser. Domain-Specific Languages. Technical Report CWI. Software Engineering (SEN) R 0032. ISSN: 1386-369X, Centrum Wiskunde & Informatica (CWI). Amsterdam, Netherlands, 2000.

224. Peter van Roy and Seif Haridi. *Concepts, Techniques, and Models of Computer Programming*. The MIT Press, 2004.

225. Mark Wallace. Practical Applications of Constraint Programming. *Constraints*, 1(1–2):139–168, September 1996.

226. Mark Wallace, Michael Freeston, and Gabriel M. Kuper. Constraint Databases. In *Conference on Information Technology and its use in Environmental Monitoring and Protection*, Holloway College, 1995.

227. Jos Warmer and Anneke G. Kleppe. *The Object Constraint Language: Precise Modeling with UML.* Addison-Wesley, 1998.

228. David H.D. Warren. Higher-order extensions to PROLOG: Are they needed? *Machine Intelligence*, 10:441–454, 1982.

229. David H.D. Warren. The Andorra Principle. Presented at the Gigalips Workshop, Swedish Institute of Computer Science (SICS), Stockholm, Sweden, 1988.

230. Reinhard Wilhelm and Dieter Maurer. *Übersetzerbau. Theorie, Konstruktion, Generierung.* Springer, 1997.

231. Glynn Winskel. *The Formal Semantics of Programming Languages: An Introduction.* The MIT Press, 1993.

232. Pamela Zave. A Compositional Approach to Multiparadigm Programming. *IEEE Software*, 6(5):15–25, 1989.

Index